INVINCIBLE

Viktoriia Pokatis

INVINCIBLE

*a book about the resistance of Ukrainian women
in the war against Russian invaders*

Для Світлани!
Дякую за те, що
приймаєте інформацію
дорогу!
Від авторки
19.04.2023 р.

yakaboo publishing

Kyiv · 2023

UDC 355.01–055.2(477)
P48

Pokatis, Viktoriia
P48   Invincible. A book about the resistance of Ukrainian women in the war against Russian invaders / Viktoriia Pokatis. — Kyiv: Yakaboo Publishing, 2023. — 336 p.

ISBN 978-617-8107-93-2 (paperback edition)
ISBN 978-617-8107-94-9 (electronic edition)

Invincible is a book about Ukrainian women, about stout Ukrainian spirit, about women's unity and the courage they found to leave home and save their families and their country, about the unexpected qualities of Ukrainian women revealed by the war, about how they help the army and dream to rebuild their country.

The book includes 30 stories of female soldiers, paramedics, volunteers, founders of foundations and shelters, lawyers representing the rights of Ukrainians in different countries, and women organizing campaigns so that Ukraine's voice is heard all around the world.

This publication is to draw the world's attention to the all-embracing activities of Ukrainian women, who joined the Armed Forces or the Territorial Defense Forces, gather humanitarian aid and deliver it in a hail of bullets, pull the wounded out of the rubble, provide medical care, evacuate children, the elderly, and animals in peril of their own life. Ukrainian women discovered the qualities they would never have thought they had. The book is about the wisdom and indestructibility of Ukrainian women.

The characters gave interviews in February–September 2022 during the full-scale invasion of Russia. Information about events is presented as of the time of the interview.

UDC 355.01–055.2(477)

Published at the request of Mediamania LLC With the support of:

IT.Integrator

All rights reserved.
No part of this book may be used, reproduced,
or published without written permission from the publisher.

© Viktoriia Pokatis, text, 2023
ISBN 978-617-8107-93-2 (paperback edition)   © Tetiana Kravchenko, cover design, 2023
ISBN 978-617-8107-94-9 (electronic edition)   © Yakaboo Publishing, 2023

Contents

Introduction — 7

Julia Pankova — 11
Regina Kosheva — 19
Julia Mykytenko — 27
Alisa Kovalenko — 35
Uliana Pcholkina — 47
Olga Rudneva — 55
Olha Kudinenko — 63
Anastasia Leonova — 77
Viktoriya Tigipko — 85
Ola Rondiak — 93
Anastasia Tihaia — 101
Vitalia Pankul — 107
Inga Kordynovska — 115
Olena Shevchenko — 133
Olena Shevtsova — 143
Inna Skarzhynska — 153
Inna Popereshniuk — 161
Olena Stryzhak — 171
Iryna Ivanchyk — 185

Kateryna Zirka	195
Nataliya Moseichuk	205
Oksana Misiura	219
Iryna Sampan	231
Nataliia Yemelina	243
Kseniia Drahaniuk	255
Nadiia Omelchenko	267
Oksana Lebedeva	277
Marta Levchenko	293
Olha Belytska	307
Leila Tuvakliieva	321
Acknowledgements	329

Introduction

None of us will ever forget the cold and scary morning of February 24 that woke us to give us fright. Regardless of gender, age, status, or combat training, we could not regain our senses at first. Panic was reigning supreme all around. Enemy tanks approaching the capital, soldiers rushing into action, women and children fleeing their homes and the country, long lines at the border: events we experienced during the first week. But as soon as we realized that we, Ukrainians, were being exterminated, a fierce determination to resist the enemy at all costs emerged in our hearts.

I felt it at the beginning of March when I saw women engaged in creativity, business, and parenting a day ago, now offering support on the home front and helping the army. That's when The *Invincible* project was born—the collection of stories about women's resistance, which later transformed into a book.

Each story of our heroines shows us the qualities accumulated in Ukrainian women: fortitude, determination, endurance, sociability, and creativity. Some use their connections, money, or popularity, while others becjme social activists, although they used to take care of their families only.

Thanks to these Ukrainian women, our battalions receive equipment—from body armor to thermal imaging cameras—women around the world lead marches of mothers and gather medicine and food to send to the Ukrainian military. Once our soldiers announce a need, women on the home front organize fundraisers, buying and delivering everything they need.

Four months of war equipped us with unheard-of experience in resistance. Each of our indestructible heroines has her own recipe for moral courage and has shared this experience with the whole world.

The war is not over, but we want to use these stories to show the world the real face of the war so that it remains in history not just as numbers of casualties but as real lives of real Ukrainian women in this setting.

Viktoriia Pokatis,
Journalist, Editor-in-Chief
of the women's portal WoMo

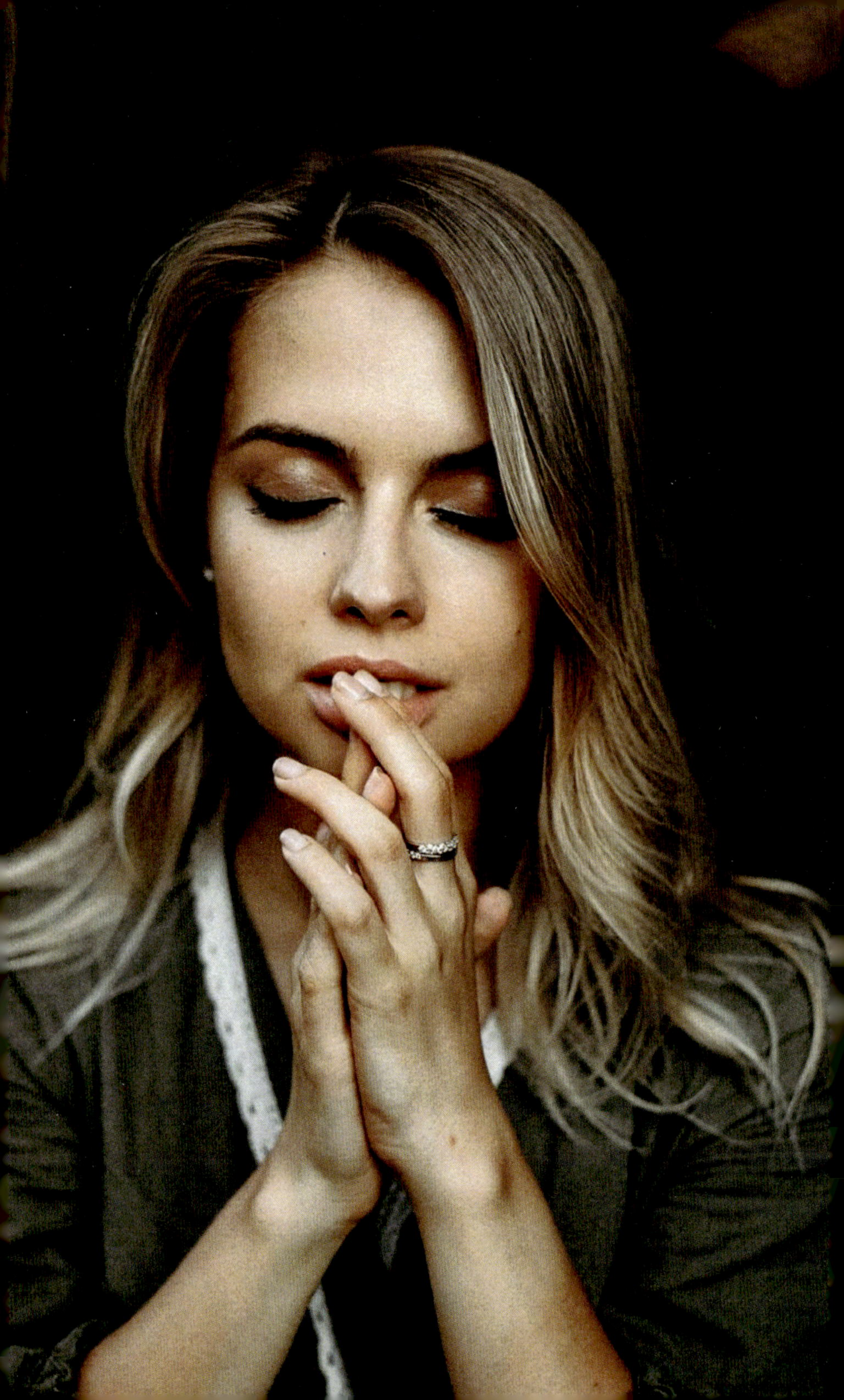

Julia Pankova

Journalist, Host of the Revizor TV show, Public Figure

At the beginning of the full-scale inwasion, Julia survived the occupation in a village near Bucha, having no food, communications, gas, or electricity. Afterwards, Julia and her mother managed to go to Europe, where she started gathering funds to help Ukrainians and sending food packages to people in Kharkiv Region.

Fund-raising dinners in Europe: Helping people in Kharkiv Region

Three dreadful moments — the start of the war, a "visit" by the Kadyrovites, and us leaving the village

Before the war, I planned to promote Ukrainian culture and traditions in different regions of Ukraine by holding gastronomic tours. My mother called me a week before the invasion and told me we had to leave. I thought at the time, "What war are you talking about?" I had master classes, tasting events, and gastronomic tours to hold. I was planning a gastronomic tour through Bukovyna with 900 representatives of the Ukrainian diaspora from Australia.

    I lived in Kyiv on the left bank of Dnipro. On the morning of February 24, being only half awake, I heard the explosions but just rolled over on my side and went back to sleep. Then my mother phoned me, "Julia, the war started, get ready." Ten minutes later, I was in the parking lot. I remember two fighter jets flying over me in the sky. That's when I realized that something really serious had begun. For two weeks I stayed near Hostomel airport with my father, mother, and three dogs. A huge shell fragment fell in our backyard since the Russians had deployed MRLS' *Grad* behind our house. Our neighbor's house was destroyed to the ground. My friends' mother died on the second day of our stay there, but we couldn't bury her. She was lying in a sack in a Hostomel shelter for two months.

We managed to bury her only after our troops liberated those territories.

We stayed there for two weeks. The most terrifying thing happened on March 9, when 13 armed Kadyrovites came to our house. They broke down the gate and took all my father's weapons and our telephones. At first, the thought flitted across my mind that they were going to kill us. But after taking our belongings, they left. That was one of the most frightening moments. Finally, on March 10, our neighbors suggested we leave. I understood that we wouldn't have another chance to leave because the Russians had already started shooting people and cars that tried to leave the village. I figured that if we drove in a convoy of cars, we would have a better chance of staying alive. So, I put my mom, dad, and three dogs into my small car and fastened white flags to it. Then we fixed white armbands and set off.

As we were driving, we saw many bodies along the roads: frozen bodies were our civilians and burned bodies lying near military equipment were enemies.

We passed three checkpoints. My mother held a white flag and prayed because we were afraid that Russian soldiers would shoot us. A lot of enemy equipment on the roads made me truly realize that there — was a full-scale war going on in Ukraine.

I had three most scary moments during that period — the commencement of the war, the "visit" by the Kadyrovites, and us leaving the village. On our way out of the village, I tried to stamp the entire journey in my memory as a journalist, and now I can't get rid of those memories. I haven't gotten over it yet, but I'm glad we got out. I even visited a therapist to get over that traumatic experience. In fact, the more traumatic it is, the tougher you become, so I think Ukrainians will become even stronger after the war.

Food crisis: Helping Ukrainians with food packages

I did not start helping right away. I gave myself time to recharge first. I did some hiking, walked around the city, ate, and tried to sleep. But when I saw what Russians did in Bucha, I was overwhelmed, because I realized that it could have been us. Being in a temporarily occupied village or under shelling, you are forced to adapt to these horrors, your psyche works to survive. Watching these horrors from a safe place, you perceive them differently, more sensitively, because you can see the full scale.

My great-grandmother and grandmother were cooks. My family had been through famine, so my grandmother used to tell me all the time: "Don't play with your food," "You shouldn't leave food on your plate," and "There should always be bread on the table." She always stocked up on some foods; for example, we always had flour so she could bake bread. Now I understand what it means — normally we don't care much buying food, taking a lot of unnecessary stuff.

I asked myself what I could do to help my country. I knew it would definitely have to do with food. Sometime in May, information about a food crisis appeared, although there were no burned fields yet back then. I managed to put volunteers from Kamianets-Podilskyi in touch with representatives of *World Central Kitchen*, a company that helps Ukrainian displaced people. Together we managed to send a truck with humanitarian aid to my village.

I knew I needed a platform to report where and how much money was spent. I decided to contact the dobro.ua team, a platform where you can choose who you want to help. They cooperate with proven charitable foundations. The PR director of dobro.ua is my friend, so I knew I could trust this organization. We contacted the *Alliance* charity organization that buys food and delivers it to persons with reduced mobility in Kharkiv Region. In addition, it buys Ukraine-produced food to support our economy.

We decided to help people from Kharkiv Region because they have been suffering from shelling since day one. Many of them still are not willing to leave, even despite food shortages.

One 800-hryvnia food package is enough for two weeks for one person. We are not stopping this fundraising because people will need this kind of aid for a long time to come.

After launching this project, I decided to involve Yevhen Klopotenko. I was invited to Paris to hold a so-called borscht party. We wanted to bring people together — professors, diplomats, journalists, activists, etc. The owner of the most popular Paris bakery provided us with premises and bread to make bruschettas; some brought wine, others brought vodka to make fruit liqueurs. We didn't spend much money. We had an incredible team that understood why they were doing it.

The admission fee was 100 euros, which allowed us to raise a total of 10,000 euros that night.

That's how the *Borsch Theatre* dinner party by Yevhen Klopotenko was born, which we have held in Geneva and Zurich. Initially, all the money collected from ticket sales was spent on food for persons with reduced mobility in Kharkiv and Kharkiv Region. The money was also spent on food packages for people affected by the full-scale war in Odesa Region. The money is transferred in two equal parts to two Ukrainian humanitarian organizations — the *Institute of Culture of Ukraine* and the dobro.ua charity platform in partnership with the *Ukrainian Charity Alliance* — to purchase food for the affected population of Ukraine. Many Europeans believe that they can help once and forget. Such events acquaint people with Ukrainian culture so that they continue helping, as they are interested in Ukraine and don't forget about it.

2022.07.25.

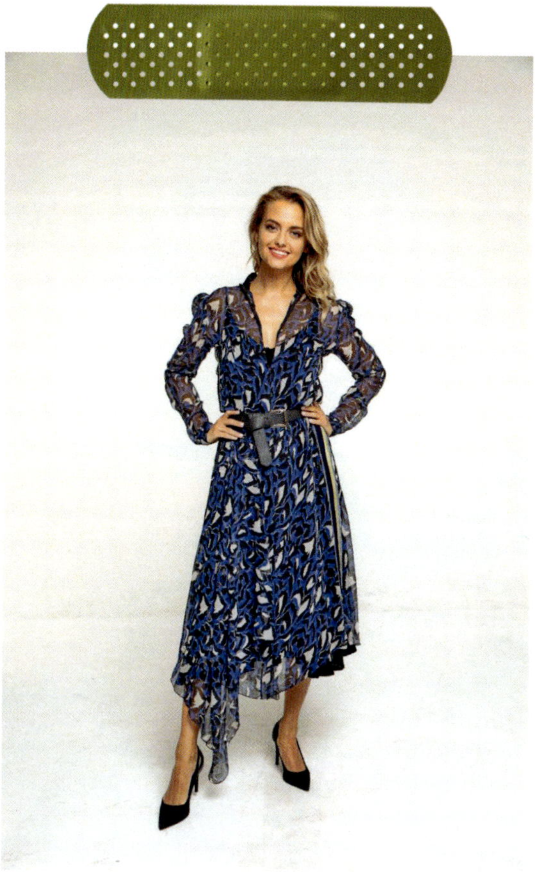

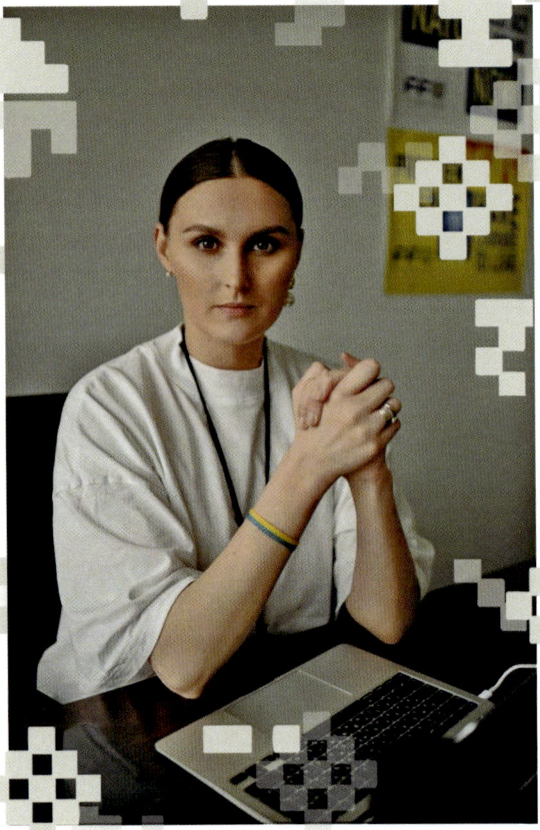

Regina Kosheva

*Former Communications Director
of the Future for Ukraine Foundation*

Before the war, Regina Kosheva headed the Communications Department of *BADOEV ID A*gency. When the full-scale war started, her husband joined the Defense Forces, and Regina began working as Communications Director for the *Future for Ukraine Foundation* in Poland.

Working with international foundations to receive humanitarian aid for civilians and the military

How we established the Foundation

Going to Poland and staying there was not an immediate decision. On our way from Kyiv, my family, a few colleagues, and I decided to stay in Bukovel first, as our agency had a corporate party scheduled for February 25. Obviously, we did not have time for fun, but we had accommodation for a few days on the way to the border. In Bukovel, we created supportive content for the agency, as support was crucial for all of us back then. It means we were determined to take an active stance from the very beginning. Then, we went to different parts of Europe. I went to Hungary at first and stayed there for a few days, all alone. Then Ania Kovalova, CEO at *BADOEV ID*, called me with an offer to organize a relief fund based in Warsaw. Initially, there were six of us, and later, our trusted friends joined us to form a team of ten people. It took us a month and a half to register the foundation in Poland. We understood that they would not take us seriously without it. We also registered the foundation in Ukraine and created a website. It is much easier to work in Europe if you are an official organization with a transparent structure. But at first, we did not have any large cases to show our future partners, including major Polish foundations that help children. We were lucky enough to deserve credit, so we were able to get started. Our foundation's Vice President Olena Sotnyk, who worked as a secretary of the Parliamentary Committee on European Integration, was the most effective communicator with Polish state institutions and European partners thanks to her contacts in literally every country and every city. Her competence and experience opened all doors, so we quickly established a dialogue with European administrations.

Assistance with medicines and medical equipment

The next task was to decide whom and how we would help. When choosing focus areas for our help, we were guided by the following principle: "don't take on more than you can do."

Medical assistance was the first area we chose at once. Olena Nikolaienko, the strategist of our foundation, has a medical degree and managerial experience in clinics and pharmaceutical companies. We understood how we would build ways to help war victims both in Ukraine and abroad and how to supply medicines to Ukrainian hospitals.

We initiated cooperation with *Medical Help Ukraine*, the Irish foundation established by Ukrainian doctors working in Ireland. They deliver ambulances to Ukraine. We started our cooperation by delivering 400 *IFAK* first-aid kits to the front line. After that, our girls drove a large ambulance (even with a right-hand drive) to Lviv, wherefrom our driver later took it to its destination — Katerynopil. Shortly after, we transferred medicines from the *American Rochester Foundation* to Ukraine. The medicines were delivered to Kharkiv hospital. We also cooperate with Ukraine's largest national rehabilitation center, *Unbroken*, in Lviv. We take part in a prosthetics program, and our partners from Japan have already provided the Center with special wheelchair traction devices that offer maximum mobility. In August, we will be able to provide the Center with more wheelchairs and more of these devices.

Our partners and friends helped us open a humanitarian headquarters in Kyiv. At first, we provided food and humanitarian kits to displaced people and those who found themselves in difficult circumstances due to the war. But later, we changed the format and launched humanitarian missions to liberated and frontline cities.

Children Hub — supporting mothers and their children in evacuation

We chose the third area of our activity based on our own experience of being refugees. For instance, I am a mother of a five-year-old girl. When I came to another country, I didn't have a place to leave her and go settle some organizational matters or find a job. Back then, people had to wait in huge lines at different administrative offices to get the Polish equivalent of our taxation ID code. We faced a problem: there were no specialized hubs to leave your child for a few hours. So we organized child centers for Ukrainian children where they could be in an environment they understood. We also opened a second hub in downtown Warsaw. It is much bigger and can hold 250 children a day. Unfortunately, children can't stay there all day because we can't feed them like in a daycare center. The first hub in Warsaw that works in two shifts of 25 children each was opened due to support of the local administration. Children can communicate with a psychologist, draw, and play educational and active games there.

The problem is that children from the territories of active hostilities are pretty traumatized and need psychological support. Over time, we plan to open such centers in other Polish cities that host the largest number of Ukrainian refugees and in other European countries.

Standing with war-affected children

Our cooperation and communication with representatives of Ukrainian orphanages made it clear that the problem of war-affected children was huge. For instance, several orphanages in Lviv Region alone house over 160 children who lost their parents in the past three months. All of them had families and normal life, and some didn't even know what an "orphanage" was, much less they could think of getting into one of them. We have established cooperation with partners to help war-affected children and orphans as much as possible.

It seems that people are somewhat tired of war. We started fundraising in April and addressed people with a specific focus of our help: treatment of war victims, creating a network of child hubs, and supporting war-affected children. Everybody worries about children, regardless of the level of fatigue with the war. When people understand what the problem is, they donate willingly. We always have fair donations without much of a downturn.

On July 8, we organized an exhibition of children's drawings, "Children.War.Future", at the *Golden Gate* subway station in Kyiv. It lasted ten days, after which we created a page with children's artwork on our website so that everyone could buy a drawing and join the initiative to help establish Ukrainian child centers in Europe. I am sure we need to help children now as it means we help our future.

How to hold on and keep your spirits up

My husband is at the front line while my daughter and I stay in Poland. My husband and I got married in 2013, and in 2014, he went to participate in the ATO (anti-terrorist operation) for over a year without rotation. I realized that he experienced restrictions, both in terms of general comfort and food. It was when I decided that I should support him, and that meant I have to get out of my comfort zone time to time as well. I took part in a training program with great physical exertion and food restrictions. That was my personal way of being in full solidarity with him. I improve myself for him — to please both him and myself more… and to divide our life into 'before' and 'after'. We both changed a lot during that time.

What keeps me going now is that I am a mother and have to hold on for my daughter's sake. I also have an important job. When my colleagues and I finally manage to launch a new project, we exhale a sigh of relief — and much inspired we are. It wasn't that long ago that we realized it's OK to have weekends. But we still spend our weekends together and speak mostly about our work and Ukraine. Neither of us is planning to settle abroad. Coming back is one of the reasons we work. Our victory doesn't mean that all the problems caused by the war will disappear at once. That's why our foundation will exist for as long as it is needed.

2022.06.20

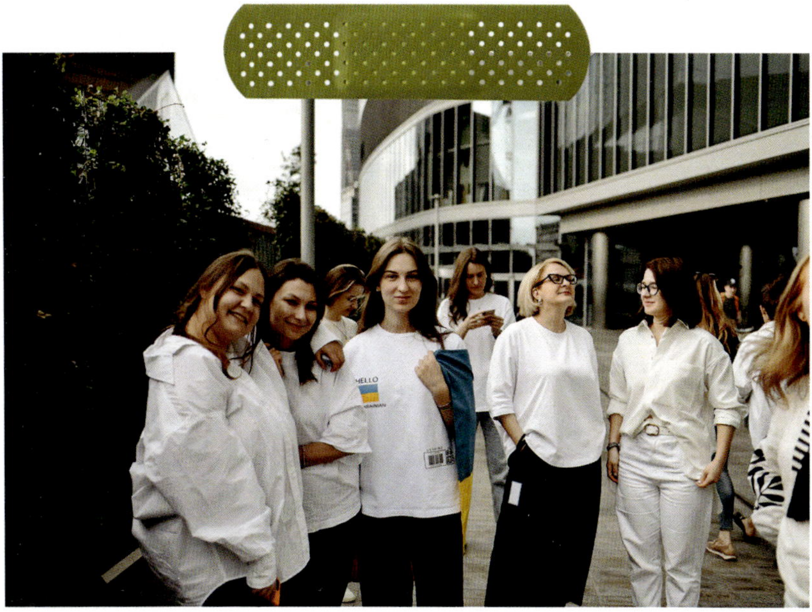
HELLO

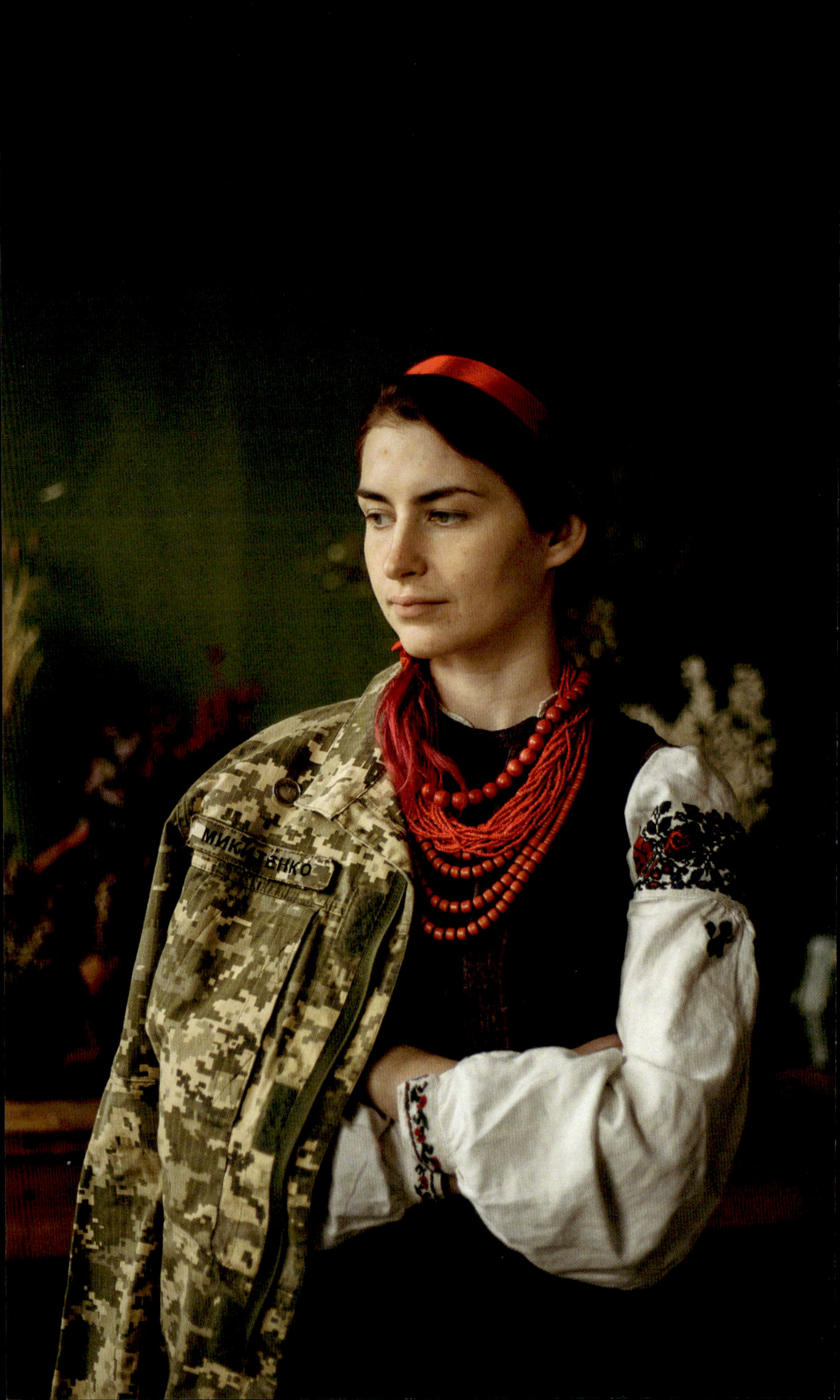

Julia Mykytenko

Senior Sergeant of the Armed Forces of Ukraine

Julia and her husband enlisted in the Armed Forces of Ukraine (AFU) in 2016. After working at the staff headquarters, she entered the Hetman Petro Sahaidachnyi National Army Academy and returned to the front line as a combat officer. After her husband's death in February 2018, Julia started working at the Kyiv Military High School. The day after our interview, the indestructible Julia Mykytenko had a combat mission in the East of Ukraine.

A woman's psychological adaptation to war

Six months of peaceful life

I resigned from the AFU six months before the full-scale invasion. Before that, I worked as a platoon commander at the Kyiv Military High School. I did resign because I thought that it made sense to be in the army only as long as you were at war. As a matter of fact, I never planned to devote my life to the army for good. It just happened that way. Going to war in 2016 was my husband's and my joint decision. At the time of my resignation, I thought I had completed my mission, and it was time to return to civilian life.

I have a degree in philology and graduated from Kyiv-Mohyla Academy. During six months of my civilian life, I worked as a project manager for an IT project for veterans and the *Invisible Battalion* that studies gender equality and sexual harassment in the military. In other words, I didn't move to away from military life. The first month after leaving the service was unusual for me: no need to put on a uniform and run to the formation, no need to ask for leave and write reports. I felt more freedom. I really liked that job. I would have still worked there but for the invasion.

Getting back in service

Just like everyone else, I was shocked to hear about a full-scale invasion. The military understood that this armed conflict could not continue as it had for eight years in the East and that escalation had to happen sooner or later. Many of my Western colleagues talked about this, too. Meanwhile, no one had anticipated that it would start like this. On the morning of February 24, I awoke to a loud sound. I didn't even realize it was an explosion, although I, of all people, should have known. When I heard the sounds for a second time, I jumped out of bed, understanding that the explosions were heard from the town of Vasylkiv.

When I left the army, I made a promise to myself: in the case of a full-scale war, I would return to military service.

I also knew that I had been trained psychologically and professionally, so I would definitely be useful. War is more difficult now because the enemy uses missiles you can't hear flying out. In the case of artillery in the East, you hear shells flying out, so you can time it and hide. Now you can't even tell that a missile is coming at you. The fear of uncertainty feels worse than continuous artillery fire. As veterans, we are better prepared for that. I think that's why so many of us returned to the army. The desire to protect our families is also a strong motivation, as all regions of Ukraine are at risk now.

When Kyiv was under threat, it was important for me to stay there to protect the city and my loved ones, which was exactly what I did. I had never seen so many civilian casualties on the front line in the East. My relatives living in Bucha and Irpin survived the occupation, and some of them were injured. And I defended the capital next to them. It had been easier for me to fight in the East because I knew my relatives were safe in Kyiv.

Women in the army

I feel that the attitude towards women in the army has changed compared to 2016. Commanders used to be surprised at my desire to get into a combat unit instead of sitting somewhere in the staff headquarters dealing with documents. They wouldn't let me into a combat unit and loaded me with all that paperwork, saying that that's where a woman belonged. Now, commanders want me in a combat unit and do not ask questions about my readiness to perform tasks. I think the media deserves credit for this change because we do hear now not only about servicemen but servicewomen, too. Here's the real state of affairs: the percentage of women in the army is enormous. There are 37,000 of us! That's one-fourth of the whole army! Not all women perform combat operations, but everyone does her work to ensure the functioning of the army.

I also see a change in volunteers' attitudes towards women in the service. For instance, even though they do not know for sure if there are women in the unit, they do bring feminine sanitary products and female underwear. In 2016, there was no such thing. No one was thinking about pads when meeting the needs of the military at the front.

Men's attitude has also changed. In 2017, I was appointed unit commander. I faced strong resentment from men, who even told me, "You are a woman, so I refuse to be in your unit." Now I am commander again because I am an officer. I received a pretty reserved welcome from my subordinates, who kept poker-faced until they found out what kind of commander I was. Things have improved over time, and now I am treated as a professional getting the respect I deserve. I have a lot of people in my unit that I served with in the past, but no traces of former disrespect left.

Support from the home front

People on the home front must not forget that the war is not over yet. Personally, I have nothing against Instagram stories with coffee and cute cats. If you go to a coffee house, you help the place to operate and pay taxes, which means the army gets supplies, and people get their salaries. Not everyone can be a soldier. Just don't forget to post important things about the war, inform your foreign friends, and add important hashtags like #ArmUkraineNow. We really need weapons right now. This is a war of artillery, a war of missiles. We can't fight just burning down human resources like the Russian Federation, so we need weapons. If you know languages, that's great! Join in creating and translating important material.

How to hold on during the war

I have grown tremendously as a professional during my service. I came into the army having no particular skills. Now, I carefully treat my training as a military officer: it's critical to survive the first two minutes of combat, which means you have to train your body and emotions. I've also grown as an officer. A college helped me a lot with that. I have matured psychologically. I understand that, unlike hostilities in 2017, now I have a much higher chance of dying, just like everyone else. But I rely on fate and am prepared for death. I know I haven't done that much in my life, but I've put maximum effort into it.

When my husband died in the East in 2018, I was terribly stressed and depressed for a long time. The only thing that kept me going was my work. Work really helps suppress bad thoughts. Also, I wouldn't ignore psychological support. A lot of therapists, both domestic and international, are available for consultations in Ukraine now. You should visit them, or you can quickly burn out. Believe in the Armed Forces of Ukraine and our victory!

2022.06.30.

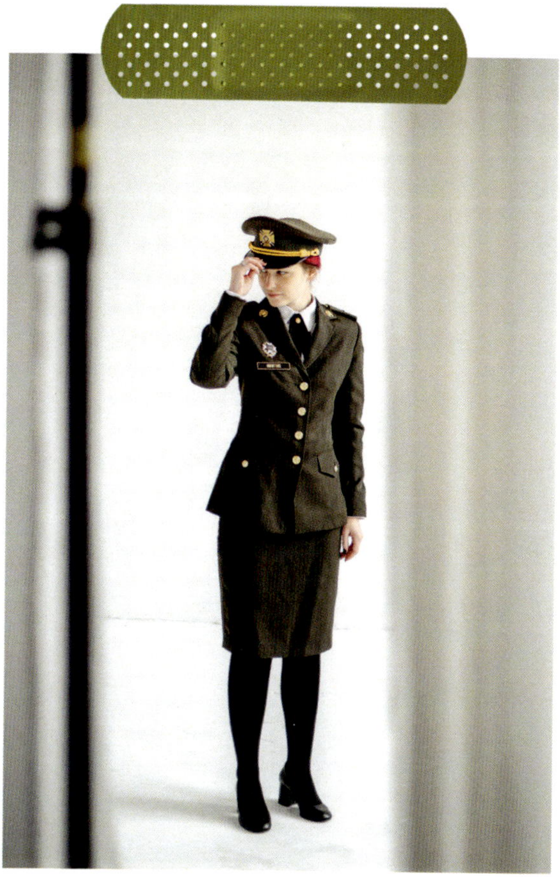

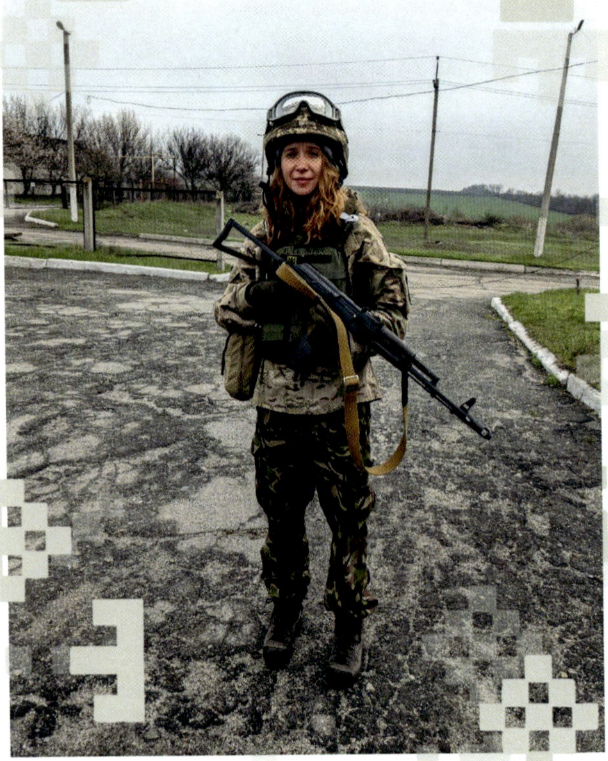

Alisa Kovalenko

Ukrainian Documentary Director

Alisa Kovalenko, a member of the European Film Academy, is a Ukrainian documentary director whose films have won numerous awards at international film festivals. Her first feature, "Alice in Warland", released in 2015, tells about the war in the Donbas and her experience as a captive. The documentary took part in over 50 festivals and won three awards. Then, she made a promise to herself: in the case of a full-scale war, she would take up arms. She put her money where her mouth was.

Why is it sometimes harder to be at home than in a trench?

Film "Expedition 49" and the trip to Donbas

Before the invasion, I worked on the film "Expedition 49". It is a story about five teenagers living on the front line and dreaming of traveling. Three years ago, they took part in a rehabilitation adventure project—an expedition to the Himalayas. I filmed their lives during those three years, and last May, I filmed their trip to the Himalayas.

Before the invasion, we edited a rough cut and were planning a trip to Donbas with a sound director to film some more footage about our characters and the atmosphere.

About a week before the full-scale invasion, military escalation started near towns of Shchastia and Stanytsia Luhanska. Some tried to dissuade us from going, but we didn't postpone our trip. The reason was that three of my characters were from Stanytsia Luhanska, and I thought I might help evacuate their families. On February 24, I was on a train headed for Donbas. At five in the morning, my mother called to tell me about the explosions in Kyiv. She and my little son were at my home in Kyiv. A young border guard from Chernihiv was traveling with me in the compartment. He had to report for duty at a checkpoint on the front line near the village of Zolote-4, which is where the two documentary characters lived. His parents called him, too, saying that Russian tanks had entered Chernihiv Region. The two of us sat there in shock, taking turns answering calls from family and friends and reading the news and information about what was happening. All passengers started smoking in the car's platform upon hearing the news from their families and friends. I remember thinking, "Where are these people going? They have kids with them, they should get back immediately!"

We arrived in Rubizhne around 9 a.m. One of my character's father picked me up there and took me to Zolote-4. We drove through the empty streets of the town of Lysychansk. We saw huge lines at gas stations and heard the announcement of evacuation from Luhansk Region on the radio.

It had hardly ever been quiet in Zolote-4: you could always smell the war there. When we got there, it felt just like some intensification of the shelling. Maybe that's why I didn't have such a keen realization of the war entering new level. The hostilities persistently intensified for all five days that I stayed in Zolote-4. My husband Stefan called me asking to get out of there as soon as possible. It was difficult to tell what was going to happen next, but Zolote-4 was on the front line, which made my husband worry that Russian tanks would enter the village and occupy it and that I would be taken captive again. And it would end up worse than the first time.

I lived with my character's family in Zolote-4. We've been shooting the film for three years now and have become good friends. I had stayed there before, so I knew almost everyone in the village.

We were working on the film in the first days of the invasion and discussed with the characters what to do next. I tried to persuade their families to leave but to no avail. They did not want to go even after the terrible multiple-day shelling by the enemy. It was no longer possible to get to the characters living in Stanytsia Luhanska, as the town was occupied on the fifth day of the war. The situation worsened very quickly.

My colleague, a director from Belgium, who also filmed in Donbas, and I managed to take one of my film characters out of Kharkiv. Her name was Liza, and she lived in a dormitory. The girl was in a bomb shelter all the time, with nowhere else to go back to. She studied design at Kharkiv university, and her hometown was occupied by Russians. We evacuated the girl, her friend, and a guy in a wheelchair, one of the characters in a Belgian director's film. I also managed to convince my friends from Irpin to evacuate. We took them all to the Polish border, where our friends helped them get to Belgium and Poland.

My son and mother left Kyiv and stayed at my friends' place in Uzhhorod for a month. My father was in Zaporizhzhia. Then my husband took my mother and our son

Teo to the Polish border, whence our relatives took them further to France. They are now back in Ukraine.

"I had to stand by my promise made in 2015": the decision to become a soldier

After Donbas and the evacuation of people, I spent two days with my son and then went to Kyiv, resolute to join the army. In fact, as early as the seventh day of the invasion, I realized that I wouldn't be able to make documentaries like I used to. I still think it's important, but at that moment, I was confused and felt as if I had lost myself as a director. At the beginning of the war (2014) I managed to concentrate on journalism and news. This is because a documentary needs some temporal perspective, a story you delve into for a long time, and characters you travel a certain path with.

To be honest, while making my films, I always wanted to really participate those events, while the camera created distance and made me just an observer, not a participant. I was constantly torn between these desires. Back in 2015, I wanted to join the army, but most of my friends and their fellow soldiers went back to civilian life at some point, so I didn't do it then. But as for this surge of war, it was obvious to me that I would now keep that promise and pick up a gun instead of a camera.

I wanted to join the Armed Forces of Ukraine. I went to several military enlistment offices, but they told me I couldn't enlist without a military ID and that I had to wait for the second wave of mobilization. Then I called my friend nicknamed Hawk from the Ukrainian Volunteer Army. At first, I was supposed to go to Dnipro, but there was a curfew in Kyiv for several days in a row, and I couldn't leave. I learned that my friend and commander, whom I had known since 2015, was at the front in Kyiv Region. Their unit was deployed between Kyiv and

Chernihiv Regions. I texted him right away that I would come to fight. After a pause, he answered, "We'll see." So I joined the ranks of the second assault company of the 5th Battalion of the Ukrainian Volunteer Army (UVA).

When I was in Pisky village in 2014–2015, soldiers often taught me how to shoot. When you are at the front line, you learn a lot, even by watching the military. I already knew what the front was like, I could shoot a little bit, and I was versed in artillery, so I wasn't utterly useless. I still had a lot to learn, but you learn much faster at the front line than at the training facilities.

At first, we were in Kyiv Region, then in Kharkiv Region. We performed different functions as infantry. We served together with the 92nd brigade in one of the front positions of our sector in Kharkiv Region. For the last two months, we controlled the greenery* between settlements almost at the Russian border. First, the greenery was conducive to our possible offensive, and second, it masked an important road. Everyone was waiting for the Russians to counterattack because they had already captured several settlements near us. Had they tried to strike at us, we would have had to destroy their tanks on the road. We controlled the sector for 24 hours and then had a rest for two days. I called this greenery "the greenery of death" because there were a lot of killed in action and wounded in action. Russian sabotage and reconnaissance groups sneaked there. It was hard as we suffered from an intensive mixed fire. We used to joke that the Donbas in 2014–2015 was like kindergarten stuff compared to what was happening then.

One night, when I was in a trench, the Russians shelled us with everything they had: planes, tanks, mor-

---

* The "greenery" is Ukrainian military slang for "forest terrain," or "dense bushes". — Ed.

tars, helicopters, cluster shells, and phosphorus bombs. I was not afraid of shelling much, because my experience in Donbas made me a tough old bird. I didn't have jitters, especially when I understood how far away the incoming strike was. But that night I had thoughts that if I died, my son would grow up without me and forget his mother after a while. I was so sad at these thoughts and felt sorry for myself. But I quickly pulled myself together and thought, "Why am I even thinking about this? I can't change anything; there's nowhere to go from the trench. Your life at war is a toss-up. And in any case, we are small, the universe is big." I joked like that and let it go. It was the only time I had such thoughts.

Actually, humor really helps during the service. It helps take things easy. You can't fight the enemy if you have hard thoughts because you can go crazy. You should take hard reality lightly.

We had a lot of funny stories. Once, we were sitting in a trench in heavy rain. It was cold, and we got soaked to the skin. Just then, one soldier went to the commander, who was at the position a bit further away and came back... with ice cream. We were taken aback: we were sitting in the planting, in the rain, and our comrade brought us ice cream! We asked, "Where did you get it?" "The platoon leader from the 92nd brigade brought it," he said. I still don't get where the platoon leader got the ice cream from. I don't really like ice cream, but at that moment, such a treating in the rain was absolute bliss.

After being in action, we had two days to rest at a base a little farther from the positions. But sometimes, Russians shelled the base even more intensively than the trenches because they knew where it was. First of all you have a good sleep, and then you communicate with comrades, and cook food. When we had *Starlink* Internet, I talked with my family and always tried to call my son

Teo to keep our emotional contact. I knew that 5-year-old children need as little as four months to forget their mother. They can quickly lose that emotional connection, which I wanted to keep. I even made blogs for Teo, telling him what was going on. Some days were monotonous, so it was hard for me to think of things to tell him.

I was not feared when I decided to go to the front line. I even felt relieved that I was following my heart. When something explodes near you, you feel a healthy fear that protects you. It's your safe mechanism that helps you stay alive. Losing this fear means losing the sense of reality. The bar of my fear was somewhat lifted when I survived captivity. It was such an extreme experience that afterwards, anything less extreme seemed normal.

I saw some soldiers experiencing panic that paralyzed them, and they couldn't do anything. I didn't have that kind of fear.

Many factors affected my future. Russian occupiers destroyed our base, our comrade and my friend Mykhailo Shtyk was killed, and the commander left the Volunteer Army to sign a contract with the regular army. I also wanted to sign a contract and be in his unit. I even passed a check. But after all, I decided to finish *Expedition 49* because I have obligations to my partners and to the film characters.

Things are harder at home than at the front line

I get more tired at home than at the frontline. Things are easier there. You have some tasks to do. Everything is clear. There is so much to do at home: so many household and work problems, so much work, and all. The good thing is all this work keeps me off sad thoughts; it's like I try to replace stress with work. Some things may trigger thoughts now and again, but that goes away too. I think about seeing a therapist, but it hasn't worked out so far. I put it off because of work and busyness. I think psychotherapy is important. There will be a lot of hurt people who can't overcome their traumas on their own. And we're going to live together in society, so we need to get back to normal.

The mobilization contract stipulates that I will be in the unit until the end of the special rule, and no one knows how long it will last. It could be a year, or two, or three. I hope to sign a flexible contract that allows me to leave from time to time due to work or to visit my family, but now I need to finish the film so that I can return to the front with a light heart.

Right now, I'm taking a break. I spend time with my child, who I haven't seen for four months, and then I'll go to Poland with my team to edit the film.

At first, I didn't want to shoot anything at all at the front; I didn't feel like a director for a while. But it was important for me to keep the art space, the people, and the atmosphere, so I forced myself to shoot sometimes. It was mostly small things like cherry blossoms, landscapes, smoke from explosions, ants in trenches, and people around. Nothing dramaturgical or coherent to make a film. I just wanted to keep all these moments.

But when I came back and watched the material, I realized I had managed to capture the waiting state and the frontline routine. War movies are usually about action, explosions, people with machine guns and so on. In fact, 70 percent of war is a tense expectation when you gaze into the same landscapes and listen to the sounds of silence and explosions.

I have seen a few documentaries that show this routine, so I thought it might be worth making something out of this material.

Shtyk's death also made me realize that I wasn't filming in vain. I have a lot of footage of Shtyk standing pensively, riding the bus, etc. At first, it was hard for me to watch this footage because I would immediately start crying. Eventually, it got easier.

At first, I was angry about the camera I took with me to the front. It got in the way and distracted me from the service because I thought I had to use it once I had taken it. And after everything that had happened, I realized it wasn't all for nothing. There's a reason I spent so much energy dragging it around and forcing myself to shoot because, hopefully, something worthwhile could come out of this material. I don't know yet, just thinking about...

2022.07.27.

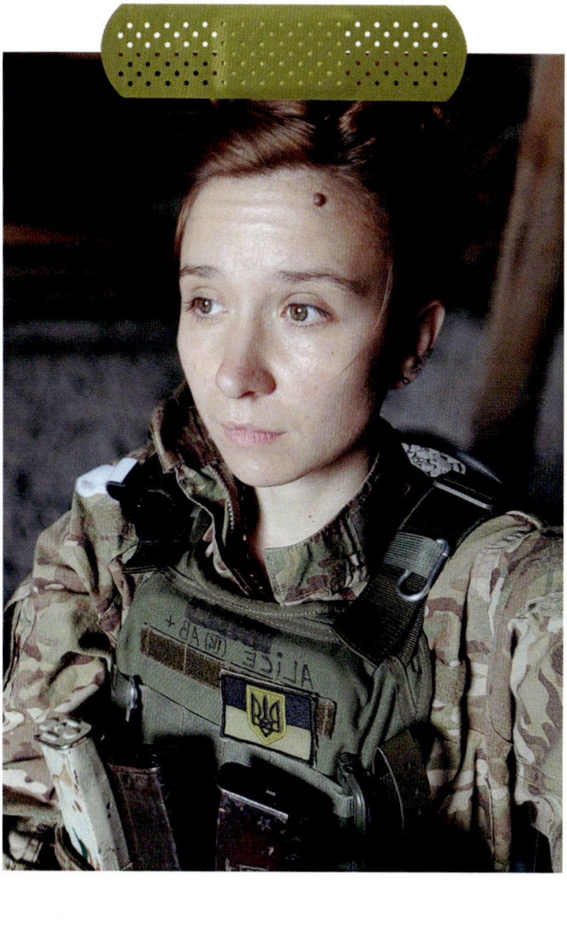
ALiCE

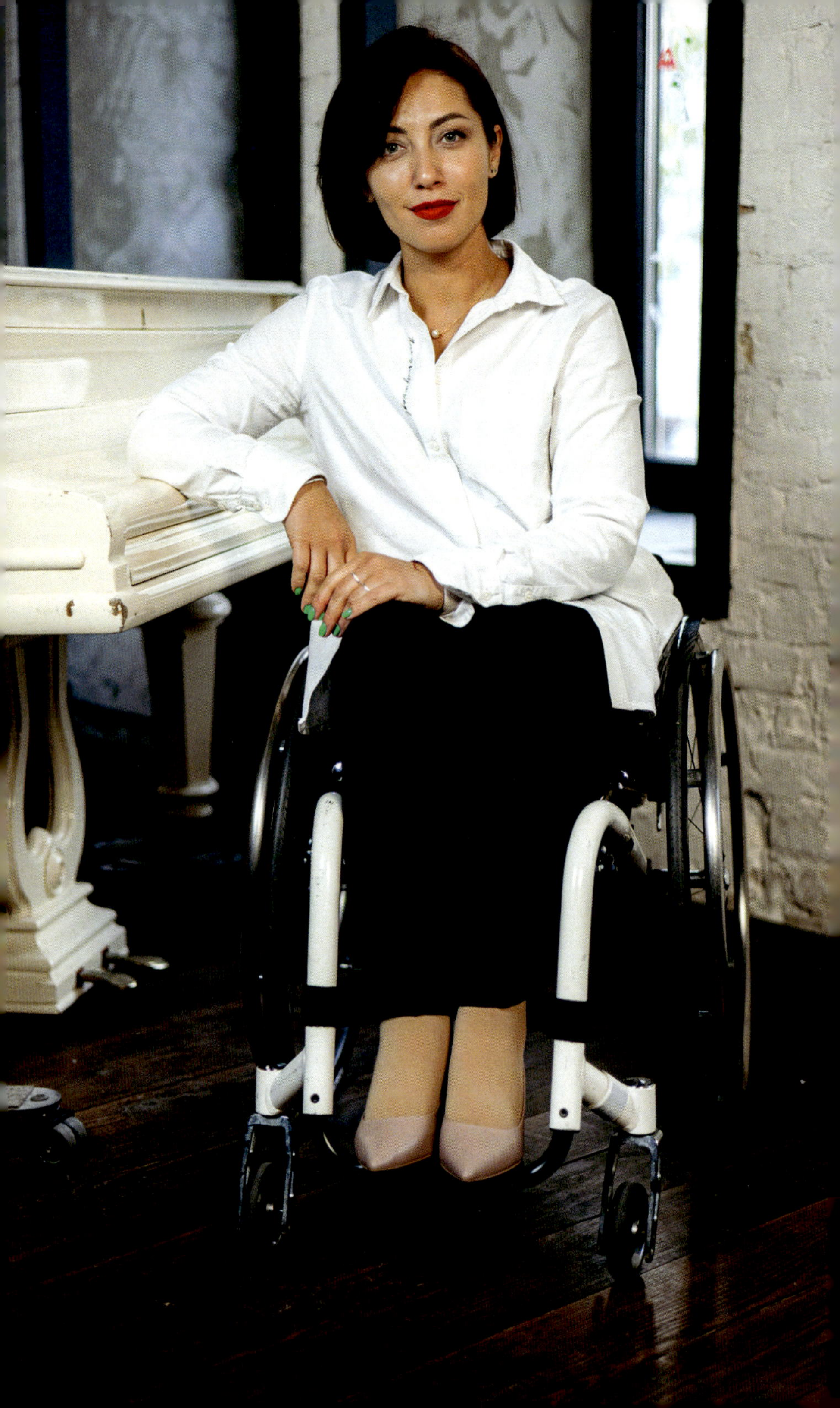

Uliana Pcholkina

Member of the Board of the Group of Active Rehabilitation NGO, world champion in female wheelchair karate

Uliana Pcholkina, member of the Board of the Group of Active Rehabilitation NGO, world champion in para-karate, and a public figure, escaped by the skin of her teeth from occupied Bucha. After moving to safer Lviv, she and other NGO members help Ukrainians with spinal cord injuries receive the necessary medicines and hygiene products and evacuate.

Helping persons with disabilities during the war

Particularly vulnerable people

A spinal cord injury is almost untreatable. It usually causes a severe disability. What's most important is that people have mobility problems. Such people will not be able to fall to the ground during shelling or walk downstairs to shelter. Most people with a spinal cord injury also have impaired pelvic organ function. It means they need special incontinence hygiene products not available in regular stores or pharmacies. You have to order them, but relevant state programs do not cover all regions. Imagine the quality of life when a person is unable to properly void the bladder or bowels.

The war has made it difficult to buy these specific products, as many manufacturing companies are at a standstill and warehouses are empty. While we had communications in Bucha, Vitalii established a coordination center. Our team ensures its functioning and has managed to engage foreign organizations and activists.

My husband and I lived in Bucha. Unfortunately, the war came suddenly, and we didn't have time to leave in the first few days. Bucha residents supported each other, actively shared information in the local chat room until mobile services were lost, and then just communicated with neighbors. But things were getting worse dramatically. One morning, our neighbor came to tell us there would be a humanitarian corridor to leave. It was March 9. We figured this was our chance. We evacuated with our neighbors in our car and a van with a lifting device that we had rented for the needs of our NGO and that we had to buy out. While leaving, we didn't realize this was an uncoordinated "green corridor". But against all the odds, we got through. We made it to Lviv and joined our humanitarian hub.

Our work during the war

Since December, we are getting back to our regular programs. We have already conducted training for future First Contact instructors, who will work (and some already do) in medical facilities with newly injured people. It has been made possible thanks to *ISAR Ednannia* organization and the European Union. We plan to organize camps of active rehabilitation.

Since February 24, our team has managed to help several thousand people with disabilities. As part of the humanitarian hub, we provided incontinence products, housed people in temporary shelters in Ukraine, and evacuated over 200 people with disabilities and their families abroad.

For me, the war is in its ninth year. I know well what it's like to live under occupation, what it's like to evacuate. We helped people in the East of Ukraine many times. We continue to do so, but the geography has expanded due to Russia's full-scale invasion.

Standing together with those who have it hardest

The active rehabilitation movement has existed in Ukraine since 1992, and the *Group of Active Rehabilitation* NGO was founded in 2008. Relying on the peer-to-peer principle, the NGO works to ensure that people with spinal cord injuries (SCI) can return to living as independently and as soon as possible, enjoying their rights and freedoms on an equal footing with everyone else.

With the outbreak of war, many Ukrainians who use wheelchairs found themselves without the necessary hygiene supplies, medicines, medical care, and the opportunity to move to a safer place.

We used to have an ongoing program of rehabilitation camps and separate projects, such as the program for women with disabilities, *I Can*, implemented together with Olena Pinchuk Foundation, special online formats adapted to the pandemic situation. In March, we planned to hold a meeting as we were awaiting responses to our grant applications, including for *Fashion Inclusia 2.0*, a project designed to help people with disabilities to realize their dreams in fashion and design. We planned a series of training sessions with journalists as part of my work as inclusion coordinator at *Starlight Media* company. We now slowly get back to all our plans.

Not putting life on hold

The shock of a full-scale invasion now reminds me of the trauma shock I've seen in many people. You start putting off normal life for later. I'll look after myself (work, fall in love etc.) "when I get better." But a spinal cord injury is permanent in the vast majority of cases. You have to live now and get back to the daily grind. It's the same with war: not washing your hair will not make the war go away.

The war is a massive catastrophe, but your refusal to do ordinary things will not bring our victory any closer. That's why I advise you not to put life on hold. If you want to meet your girlfriends, go ahead; if you feel better with a manicure or a new haircut, get them done. To take care of others, you must first take care of yourself.

You should also find something for yourself, your own front, and give it some time. It doesn't have to be something huge like a big volunteer project. Even your pre-war work you managed to keep is a contribution to victory. Distributing information is also a front. For instance, you can report to a special telegram channel about enemy accounts. That's just as important. Devoting at least an hour to your front is a big deal, believe me. Don't blame yourself for not doing enough because that's not true.

If you feel awful, seek for psychological help. A lot of specialists now work for free. Our peace, confidence in victory, and common sense should support those who defend us with weapons in their hands.

2022.04.21.

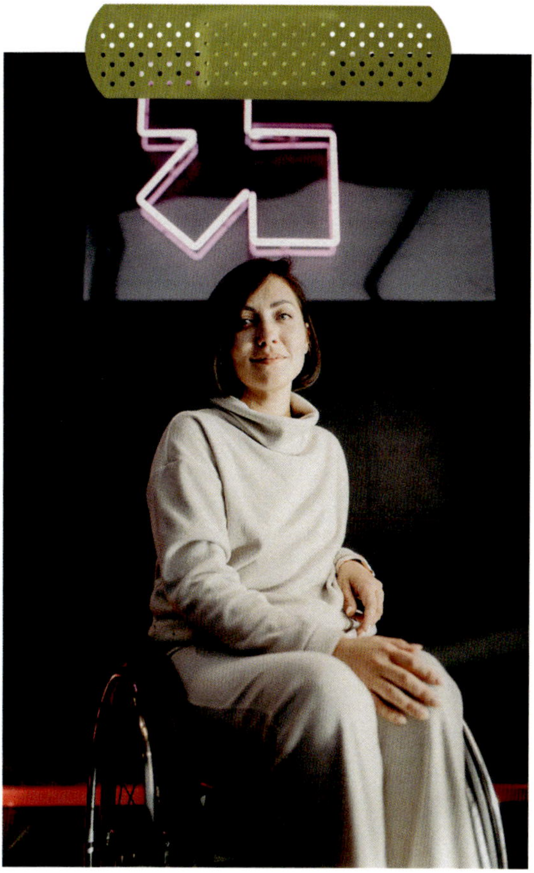

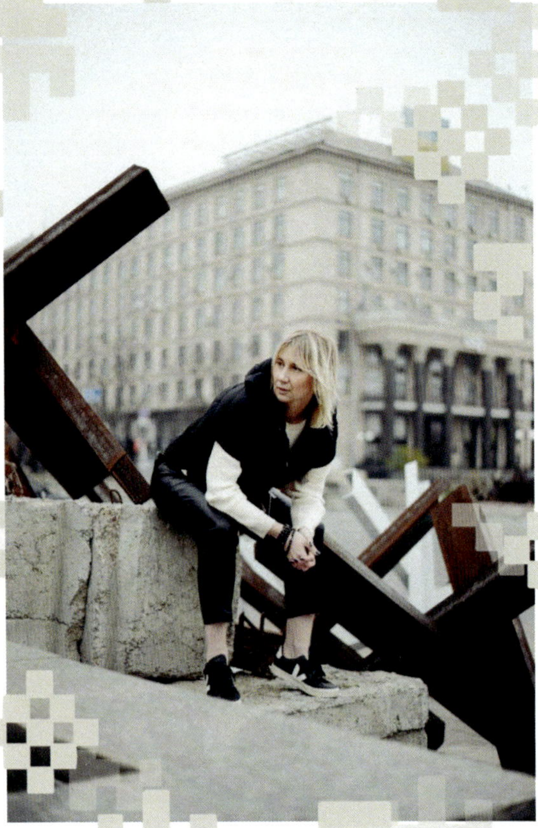

Olga Rudneva

CEO at Superhumans

Olga Rudneva, former Director of the *Olena Pinchuk Foundation*, is now CEO of *Superhumans*, a prosthetics, reconstructive surgery, and rehabilitation clinic for war-affected people.

How to organize over three thousand tons of humanitarian aid every month and the work of 760 volunteers

Being as helpful as possible

The war caught me abroad: on February 23, I went there to bring my mother to Ukraine, and in the morning, I learned about the Russian invasion. I started looking for opportunities to return, but as our Foundation has been working with the ATO veterans since 2014, I knew how civilians could hamper the work of the military. I asked myself if I would be helpful in Ukraine. My husband also urged me to think over whether I knew exactly what I would do in Ukraine and how I would be able to help. I didn't know it, so I decided I would be more helpful to my country abroad. Now that so many Kyiv residents are returning to their homes, I am asking myself again whether I want to be at home as one of the people who need help rather than as one who can help as much as possible. Should I return home only to put on my clothes? I could do with two pairs of jeans here. That's why I'm staying in Poland, where I can be of maximum help to my country.

As the Director of the *Olena Pinchuk Foundation*, I managed our activities remotely while the rest of the team were in Ukraine. They decided to stay there despite the calls to evacuate. It did not prevent us from providing psychological aid to teenagers and women. At the end of March, the *Foundation* opened an HIV testing room. We purchase medicines for hospitals that apply to us, provide food parcels to HIV-positive people, and help evacuate HIV-positive teenagers. The *Olena Pinchuk Foundation* also supports Polish volunteer organizations working with Ukrainian refugees. That's good enough, given the short period since the beginning of the war, but it is hardly the colossal work we did in peacetime.

Working at the *Help Ukraine Center*

Some time ago, I saw a post about an initiative of Ukrainian business people to create a *Help Ukraine Center* to gather, sort, and deliver humanitarian aid from Europe to Ukraine. That involved launching a logistics hub in Lublin. *Nova Poshta, Rozetka,* and other Ukrainian companies joined the initiative. I wrote to Andrii Stavnitser (the founder of the *Center*) that I was ready to come if needed, and I started working at the Lublin hub from the first week of the war. Except for me, 23 other people are engaged in management non-stop. A total of 760 volunteers responsible for unloading, sorting, and loading are involved. The number of people we need every day varies, and we announce it in advance on our social network page.

Anyone can bring targeted aid here. Let's say you gathered in Europe something necessary and need to transfer it to Ukraine — we'll deliver it by *Nova Poshta*. Brands, embassies, and humanitarian organizations send us trucks of humanitarian aid from different European countries. At first, aid in Europe came from ordinary people, and now mostly from large companies.

We transferred over three thousand tons of cargo to Ukraine during the first month. It's about 10–15 trucks daily of sorted and labeled humanitarian aid. It seems like a lot, but it's a mere droplet of what our country needs.

We are accredited by the Ukrainian government, which is why non-targeted aid is distributed in coordination with state authorities. We send all medical cargo to Lviv, where a commission from the Ministry of Health sorts them out and distribute as needed. Everything relating to tactical medicine is forwarded to the medical department of the Ministry of Defense. Food, water, hygiene products, and clothes are sent to *SpivDia*, a volunteer association coordinated by the Office of the President of Ukraine in conjunction with the Ministry for Communities and Territories Development. They pack everything in boxes and give them out to people who need this aid.

Stories about people and the war
We were all really touched by the story of the five cabs (taxis) from Great Britain that took food and diapers across Europe to us. The drivers said they wanted to demonstrate solidarity with Ukraine, not just to transfer cargo.

There was also a guy who brought a really expensive and modern mobile hospital. It turned out that he was a Belarusian political prisoner who managed to flee abroad. Now he is doing everything to help Ukraine win this war.

The story of a six-year-old boy from Kyiv moved us all to tears. His mother was in Greece, and there was no one to take him to Poland. So, the adults passed him on to each other as he made his way to Poland. We met the boy, fed him, took good care of him, and brought him to his mother two days later.

Many European families donate toys specifically for "children born in basements" and children from particular cities who personally wrote letters. Recently, we forwarded one such large cargo for infants in Kyiv. Many Europeans who send aid are British and French, but most are from Poland.

Is the world getting used to war and refugees?

The volume of humanitarian aid has decreased compared to the beginning of the full-fledged invasion, but not because everyone is sick of us. It's just that many ordinary people did the best they could in the first few months. Everyone was shocked and rushed to help. We understand that an average family can't give part of their budget for help all the time. But still, in Ukraine, we are just now entering the peak of the humanitarian crisis. We need humanitarian aid even more than we did at the beginning of the invasion, which is why we address to large companies. Now, we know exactly what Ukraine needs, so we make lists and ask big companies for specific help.

Speaking of fatigue with refugees in Poland, I do not feel it. Like most of my colleagues, I decided not to apply for refugee status but chose a volunteer status. We are not looking for an opportunity to stay here or get any additional preferences. Except for my job, I have no other opportunities to interact with the Polish people. I behave correctly, don't ask anything of anyone, and always thank everybody. I am not saying that there are no cases of bias, but the attitude of local people towards us depends a lot on our expectations and behavior. Support and help are great, but no one owes us anything.

How to stay sane under stress

I am not doing anything specifically to relieve stress yet. I go to bed at about 1 a.m. and wake up at 5:30 in the morning. According to my friends, after a few weeks of this daily routine, I "got somewhat erratic." So I took a little break during the week when it was my birthday.

That day was very active. I asked for money for Ukrainian hospitals as a gift. We collected more than I expected — nearly one million hryvnias. After that, I visited my mother, who had been staying at Madeira since the war began. A change of scene helped a lot.

And then, I went back to that same crazy rhythm of work. I believe the precepts of Viktor Frankl, a psychiatrist and psychotherapist who survived a concentration camp; *help a lot not to get lost in stress*. According to him, the main thing is to find a reason to wake up every day. I also advise you to look for your superpower: what you can do and love to do. Find it and do a little more of it.

2022.04.27.

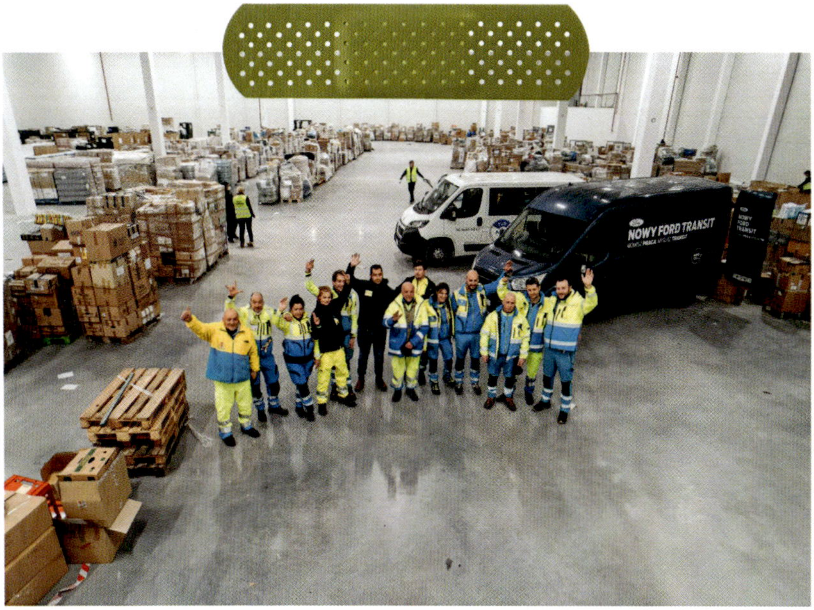
NOWY FORD TRANSIT

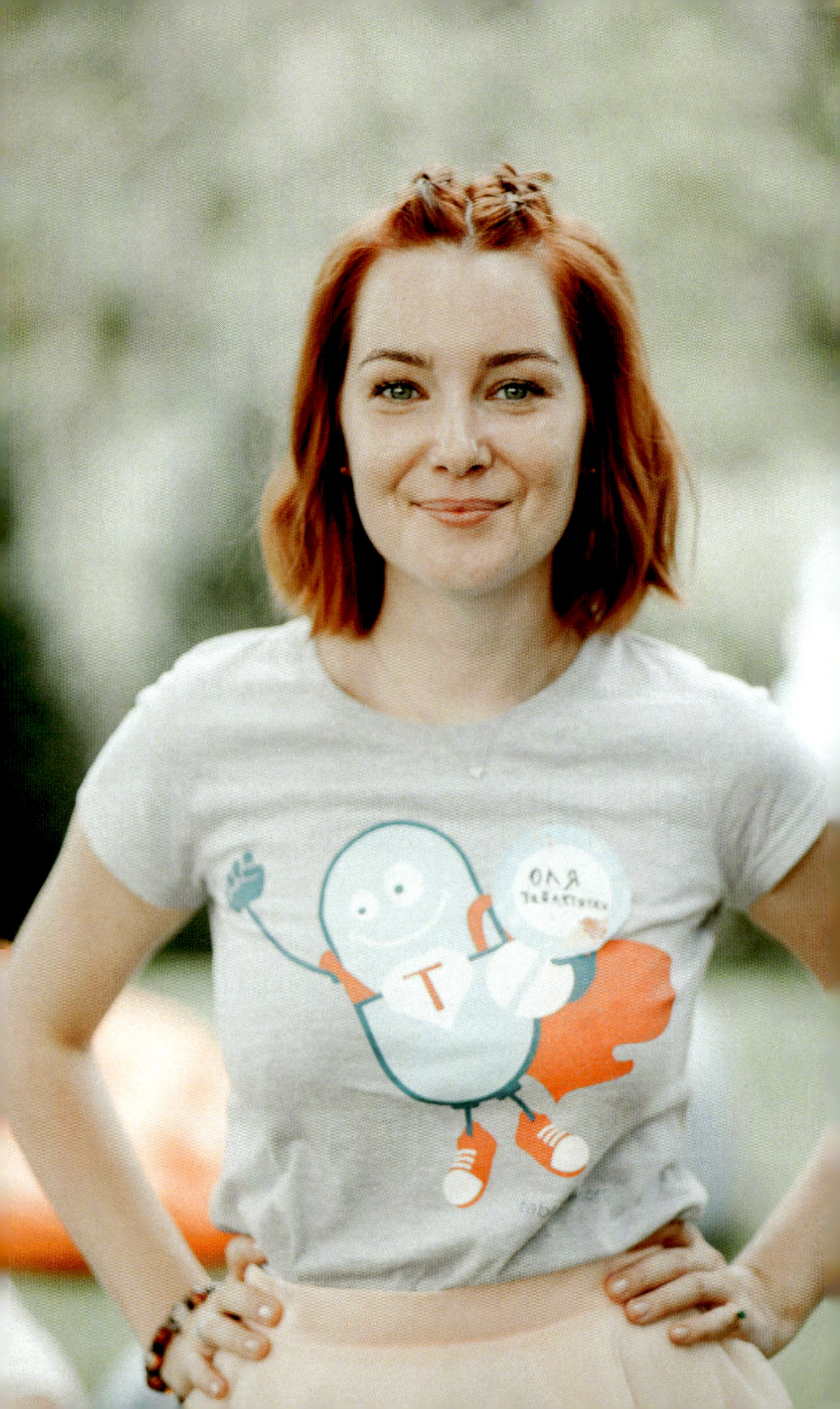

Olha Kudinenko

Founder of Tabletochki, the Ukrainian charity foundation for children with cancer

Olha Kudinenko, a founder of the *Tabletochki Charity Foundation*, a fundraiser, and a member of the Board of Trustees of the Specialized Children's Hospital "*Ohmatdyt*", had gone abroad with her mother and daughter before the invasion. She planned to return to Ukraine, but the war put an end to those plans.

Helping children with cancer during the war

Heading into 2022, we were hopeful for the development of the Foundation

I have been engaged in charitable activities at the *Tabletochki Foundation* for almost 11 years. My job is to work with our strategic partners and develop the *Foundation*. During the past two years, I worked on one major project. A month before the war, we met with the project's advisory board to talk about plans for the year. And a week before the Russian invasion, we met with a potential partner. The negotiations resulted in the first agreements on a donation. We are talking about tens of millions of dollars. We received confirmation on February 15, which was a special day as it was International Childhood Cancer Day. It was fitting to receive confirmation of a large donation for the children on that day. Everything was shaping up perfectly, and we started planning our annual fundraising dinner and developments for the *Foundation*. This year was full of hopes for the development and more effective treatment of childhood cancer in Ukraine.

I didn't believe at all that a war could start. Even influential and wealthy people from the project's advisory board were quite positive: they said that the rumors of the Russian invasion were exaggerated. No one could even imagine what was going to happen. Everyone was planning to stay in Ukraine, and so it happened, but our work responsibilities changed. In the middle of December last year, I bought an apartment in Kyiv and started to make repairs.

On February 15, a rumor went around that the sky in Ukraine might be closed, and we had a weekly vacation planned in Thailand. Then it occurred to me that maybe we should leave earlier. But we couldn't do it because I had several work meetings scheduled. I only checked whether we would get a refund for the hotel if the flight was canceled. On February 18, my daughter's school holidays officially started. She, my mother, and I set off on our longed-for trip. At Boryspil airport, I even recorded a funny story about my mother mistakenly taking the wrong passport.

We were supposed to return to Ukraine on March 1, but the terrible news of February 24 changed our plans. We learned about the war at 10 a.m. because of the time difference with Kyiv. Our first reaction was to return home immediately. On reflection, I realized there was nothing I could do to help my country. I would not even be able to drive cargos around, as I had not been driving for five years. My brother has three children — 12, 6, and 3 years old — and has a private house near Makarov. So in the first days of the war, he went there with his wife, children, and my dad. They stayed there for five days. With the hostilities getting more active, he and his family decided to go to Germany. And my father stayed there. We did not have stable communication because of power and internet problems. Every few days, my dad would go out to a certain place that had mobile communication to call us. We barely talked him into leaving there. After two weeks there, my father finally decided to leave. He also took my puppy my assistant had earlier brought him, for which I am very grateful. During the first days of the invasion, it was at the canine center located between Irpin and Bucha.

Helping hospitals
and evacuating children with cancer

As soon as I heard about the Russian invasion, I texted the directors of the *Tabletochki Foundation* in a work chat, asking if the intense military action had really started because I couldn't believe it despite all the *Facebook* posts and news reports.

We immediately paid salaries in advance, as it was the end of the month, and no one knew how the banking system would work. We started taking daily roll calls to check if everyone was safe. We started making phone calls to the hospitals where children under our care were treated, asking about their needs. No stores were open back then, so we contacted the *Epicenter* (a big network of hardware stores) team and asked for adapters and extension cords for doctors to use in the basements. They gave us the phone number of the warehouse manager and told us to go to him and get everything we needed... but he warned us about shelling. We found a volunteer who went to the warehouse, took the things ordered, and delivered everything to the hospitals.

We provided hospitals with food and anything else they might need because it was impossible to foresee how things would unfold. All of our partners responded exceptionally well — they provided help for free and very quickly.

On the first day of the full-scale invasion, we called our US partners from St. Jude Children's Research Hospital, one of the best childhood cancer clinics in the world. We have been partners since 2018. It was during the invasion that we could appreciate this partnership to the full. In 24 hours, they deployed an office to help children with cancer in Ukraine. We developed an evacuation route for children with cancer. Depending on the hospital location, we brought them to *Ohmatdyt* in Kyiv, then to the Western Ukrainian Specialized Children's Medical Center in Lviv, and then to Poland. UNiCORN triage clinic operated in Poland, where children underwent a primary medical examination, had their condition corrected, and were transported to clinics in other countries for treatment. Overall, children with cancer are now treated in 16 countries. This *SAFER Ukraine* initiative helped evacuate more than a thousand children. I also helped evacuate orphans.

I remember that everyone was on call almost around the clock. People slept from three to six in the morning if no one called. And then it would start all over again.

**Fundraising and registering
a foundation in the U.S.**

After March 20, I decided that I had to go to the USA to raise funds to support sick children so that we could fulfill our promises. On March 26, my colleague Svitlana Puhach and I set off to the USA. We planned to stay there for six weeks but had to extend for another one.

We met various partners and looked for money and support. We tried to understand how things worked in the United States because, after all the news about the devastation in Ukraine, I realized that the need for help was incredibly great. I used to think that we could do everything on our own in Ukraine, but now it turned out that the involvement of international partners was badly needed. The needs are very significant, and help is extremely important.

I went to the United States and registered a foundation there. I am waiting for the approvals now. I know that it takes at least two or three, if not five, years to build a foundation in the USA. The US foundation will raise funds to help Ukrainian children, and aid programs will be implemented in Ukraine by the *Tabletochki Foundation*, as before.

"I will live between two countries"

We were going to Thailand with my mother and daughter only for a week, so I had no valuables to pawn in case of need. I had a bunch of swimsuits, dresses, and some cash in my suitcase. I didn't even take my laptop with me. It was delivered to me later from Kyiv. When the mass invasion started, I hoped it would end very quickly. I really believed that we would return home on March 1. So I canceled the tickets just a day before the departure date. I decided to stay abroad, mainly because of my child. As it happened, she hadn't seen the horrors of war, and I wanted it to stay that way.

I paid to stay in a hotel for another five days because I hoped it would all be over in two weeks. Then I realized that it wouldn't happen so soon and started thinking about what we would do next, where we would live with my child. I love her very much. She is the most precious gift life has given me. But there were moments I envied people who either did not have children or had grown-ups or teenagers. In the first case, you have no responsibility for the child; in the second, you have more freedom because your child can go to school alone. My situation is different. My daughter is six years old, and I should be there for her. Besides, I have a lot of children under my care, and I have to help them, too. That's why I thought I had to choose the country whose language I know to raise funds for help. Almost all European countries were off the menu because I had neither the resources nor the time to learn a new language. When choosing, I settled on Canada, the USA, and Britain. Ultimately, I chose the USA because I studied the whole culture of philanthropy in the States, a big country with many opportunities. I thought I would build a foundation there, as I did with the *Tabletochki Foundation*, to support Ukrainian children from abroad. I thought I would live between two countries.

Right now, my daughter is in Germany with her father. She is supposed to join me in New York when I'm done fitting out our rental apartment. Then I will be able to go to Ukraine and work between the two countries. I have a lot of experience living between two countries, so I know how it will go and what possible results to expect.

Right now, I'm spending a lot of time settling in because the service in the USA leaves much to be desired. I spend several hours every day on the phone dealing with delivery services. It's no joke: I have to explain everything long and hard, and it doesn't help that we get disconnected all the time. For example, I ordered chairs, and when they arrived, they turned out to be wobbly. I booked a service call. They first promised that the repairman would come on Monday and then assured me he would come on Wednesday... But he never showed up. In the end, they told me to send the chairs back and order new ones along with the repair service. And it happens all the time. For example, instead of five curtains, they sent me four; instead of a closet, they sent me a bed because they mixed up the address. Frankly, these conversations with the delivery service are very draining. But I am not complaining and try to have a sense of humor about it. I am just very grateful that we are safe.

Apart from setting up the apartment, I'm working on establishing a foundation by developing relationships and getting to know people. We decide which projects to keep in Ukraine and which to add. We need to adapt because not all projects will work, and some will be transformed.

So far, we have finished the website for fundraising in the USA, and I hope to start gathering money in September.

"I admire the Ukrainian strength and resilience"

Thanks to my work, I did not feel lonely abroad. I had no time to reflect. I think that most Ukrainians haven't reflected yet because it's too difficult to comprehend all that has happened and all those horrors this war has brought. I can't come to grips with what is happening to me and my friends — successful and self-fulfilled people.

Yesterday, a Ukrainian who left our country during the invasion came to me. I called him to help me assemble the furniture. It turned out that this man and his wife left their hometown Lysychansk on March 15. He is over

60 years old. He worked as a miner and has two apartments—in Lysychansk and in Crimea. He says that he worked hard all his life so that he could live his life in retirement. So did my parents. They put in great effort to prepare some descent environment to spend their late years. Now his house in Lysychansk is partially destroyed by enemy shells and has no roof. And this man himself has to make living assembling furniture.

I admire the Ukrainian strength and resilience and how we behave as refugees. I am amazed at this man's resilience and proud of many of my fellow compatriots. Everyone just pulled themselves together and started working. It makes me get my hopes up. Our resilience and strength will definitely help us win!

People concentrate on what is closest to them. It was clear even at the beginning of the invasion. Foreigners sympathize with us and support us, but they will never understand what the Ukrainians are going through now. Only those who survived the war can understand us, but everyone else can't. And that's okay. I don't want these people to live through the horrors of war and really get this experience. It's like we won't truly understand parents who have lost a child to cancer. Do we want to have that experience? By no means! And that's okay.

The invasion has changed values

I realized that our skills and knowledge are the most valuable things we have. That and human relations are the only things you can take with you.

I have lost the ability to enjoy material things. I used to adore shopping and always thought through my purchases, but now I know I need to buy the cheapest chairs because I don't know how long I'll be here. Things like that have become minor. It seems you can no longer feel the joy of the things you used to like. And that's how a lot of people I know feel.

Last year, I bought a dinner set for the New Year holidays at an American store. I thought this tableware would last for many years. I had a sense of the future. And now I don't.

What I want to do most is to return to Kyiv, which I left on February 18. I want to go into my apartment as I left it and live as I did before. But at the same time, I know it is impossible. I don't have that rented apartment anymore, and all people I used to communicate with are no longer in Kyiv.

I work with what I have now. I don't reflect because I know I don't have a time machine to go back. So I just adapt to the situation I have.

What I miss most right now is calling someone and asking to meet in 15 minutes at Yaroslaviv Val street, not far from the house where I used to live. Or going to visit a friend who lived in my neighborhood. I miss being able to walk into any restaurant and meet friends. I miss conversations with friends, making peaceful plans, and a bright vision of the future.

This victory is coming at a very heavy cost. Sometimes I read on social media that people plan to throw a party and celebrate for a few days in a row after the victory... But I think it will be a day of great mourning because we lost so many people —military and civilian. The price of this victory is very high. We, Ukrainians, pay a high price. But we will get through it!

2022.08.11.

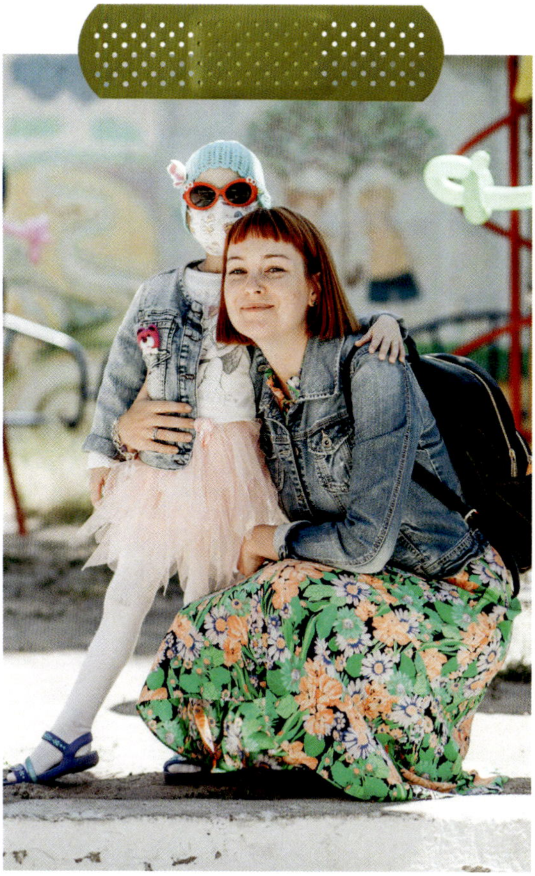

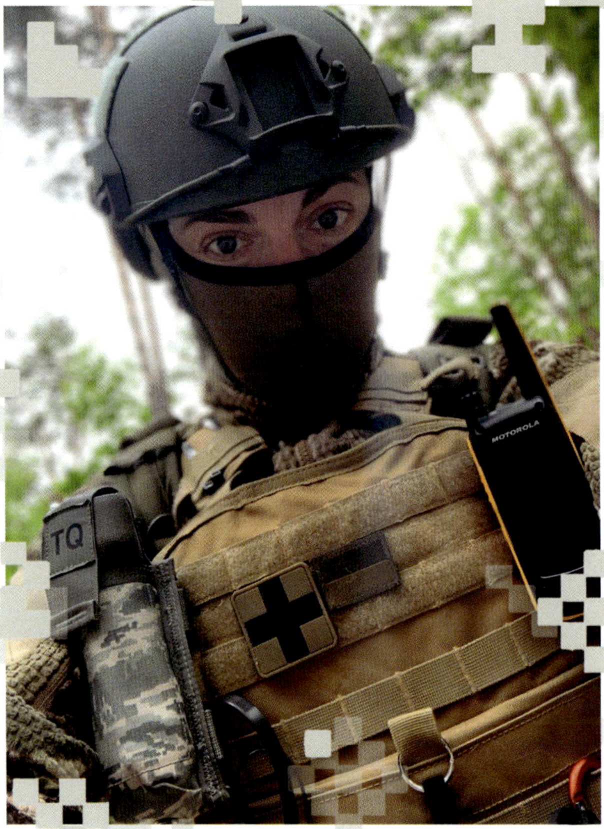
TQ
MOTOROLA

Anastasia Leonova

*Tactical
Medicine Instructor*

Anastasia Leonova says she came to Ukraine in 2015 because she felt part of the collective responsibility for Russia's actions. In civilian life, she is a sommelier. As a tactical medicine instructor, Anastasia has already taught more than three thousand Ukrainian military personnel.

Principles of the paramedic work according to modern NATO tactical medicine manual

Tactical medicine instructor

In civilian life, I'm a sommelier. I had my own wine school and was a wine import manager. I did a lot of tastings and taught people since I like to learn and teach others. I took a course to be a paramedic when we had terrorists blowing up apartment buildings in Russia. My colleagues and I translated a modern NATO tactical medicine manual in 2014–2015 in Moscow. I used to come home from work and get down to the translation, knowing that if someone found it on my computer, I would be in trouble. When I came to Ukraine, I even took that course using my own manual. In 2015, I taught tactical medicine to almost three thousand Ukrainian soldiers at training ranges. I don't have a medical degree, but you don't need one to be a tactical medicine instructor.

Before Russia's full-scale invasion, I knew something would happen because I read analytics and watched the news, including Western ones. I realized that all these predictions were for a reason, but I harbored a tiny hope that they weren't completely insane to bomb Kyiv. On the night of February 24, I woke up early because my cat was sick, and I didn't sleep well. In the morning, I heard the explosions. At some point, I felt animal fear, my hands were shaking, but I managed to pull myself together.

It never even crossed my mind to fly abroad. I knowingly chose Ukraine as my home and had no intention of running away. Of course, it was impossible to enlist in the army having a Russian passport. So at first, I coordinated help: I had a lot of chats and managed to connect those who needed help with those who could provide it.

Then, my friends invited me to teach a course in tactical medicine to one of the volunteer battalions. It started with one evening lecture, after which I was invited to join the battalion as an instructor and combat medic.

I couldn't go home because of the curfew, so I pondered throughout the night, and in the morning, I said I would stay with the battalion and teach volunteers. I returned home only to get the necessary items and have a neighbor take care of my cat. I've been working as an instructor ever since.

Women at the frontline

The army has changed a lot since 2015. The soldiers are better trained now. There has never been any bias towards me. What's important is what kind of person you are. If you behave like a naive, dreamy girl and only say, "Oh, I don't know, please help me," you will be treated accordingly. If you're a responsible person and a professional, no one cares what your chromosome set is. So women in army don't experience any real problems right now. That is why we were deeply hurt by the words of Oleksii Arestovych that women were treated like dirt in the army. Definitely, those were the words of a person having no idea of the actual situation.

Now, women in the army are as respected as male soldiers. After all, during the war, women demonstrated their professional abilities, trying to perform their military duty on an equal footing with men.

Everyday life in the army is, of course, different from civilian one. But every woman tries to be feminine even in field conditions. For example, my daily care includes washing and applying sunscreen with maximum protection. At this point, the beauty routine is done in field conditions. I do not know what the case is in the East, where we are going, but now everything is fine. You can always find at least half a liter of water for hygiene needs. There are also special sponges to wash the whole body without water. We also have a portable shower that lasts seven minutes, which is enough for hygiene needs. The shower is not included in the basic supplies, but you can always buy one.

Front line needs

The soldier's motivation matters. Take our unit, for instance. When it consisted of volunteers, it was one thing because everyone was highly motivated. When we were further staffed with mobilized people, the difference became noticeable. You can get them on the right track with competent work, even though they arrived untrained and unprepared. However, I believe the army should not be a punishment. It is wrong when they hand out call-up papers to some troublemakers on the streets. It's better to send them to community service. The army needs professionals: IT specialists to work with drones and officers.

We need robust people. Some guy who weighs 50 kilograms won't be able to run with an assault rifle. It's the same when they send us civilian nurses. We had one totally unathletic woman who was a lactation consultant in the clinic. Why should she be in the army in the first place? She was much more productive in that clinic and returned there eventually.

We are grateful to everyone who helps us. But some things are of no use. For example, some spend a lot of time and money on homemade tourniquets. They sew some rings, eyelets, and sticks on latex, but unfortunately, it does not work that way. On the other hand, we really need camouflage nets.

How to live in the home front

The military really like to receive letters and drawings from children; we show them to each other. Once, my colleague and I got little drawings at the supermarket checkout, and some drawn kitty still lives in my purse.

Adequate soldiers are pleased when someone in the rear goes to a café or posts flowers and kittens on social networks.

That's what we're fighting for: the possibility of going to a café with peace of mind. We are happy that Kyiv, which we defended, is living a more or less normal life. I even bought myself red lipstick to cheer myself up. Of course, I will not wear it in the operations, but I like to know that I have it. I think people who criticize others for a normal life are not those at the front line but those who are safest or even abroad. I am happy someone has a normal life because of our work.

Health should always be a top priority for women. If you lose it, you can't be useful to those you love. Get routine checkups with the gynecologist and mammologist, visit the dentist, and monitor your psychological state. Unfortunately, there's no other option now but to learn to live with stress. Take a course in tactical medicine or first aid if you can. This will increase your and your children's chances of survival.

After we win

Things are very complicated now. Nobody in our unit has ever been at war or trained to serve. Luckily, I have tunnel vision — when I work with the wounded, I know exactly what to do and don't get distracted. When we rescued our first wounded man, I didn't even notice that there was mortar fire all around. I was among the first to arrive at the liberated territories of Kyiv Region with a humanitarian convoy. I didn't cry at what I saw only because I had a lot of work to do, and while working, I'm concentrated on what is to be done. But what I saw made me literally go gray. I will never forgive anyone for that. I've probably become more of a Ukrainian and a nationalist than some Ukrainians. By the way, I haven't been able to get citizenship for a long time. They say that I will get citizenship under the simplified procedure as soon as I sign a contract with the AFU. It will be a big day! But our victory will be a much bigger day. I already have a bottle of champagne saved for this long-awaited celebration. After we win, I would like to give birth and bring up a new Ukrainian boy or girl. Previously I didn't plan it, but the war changed my mind. I believe the father of my child will be a man defending Ukraine now, just like me.

2022.07.01.

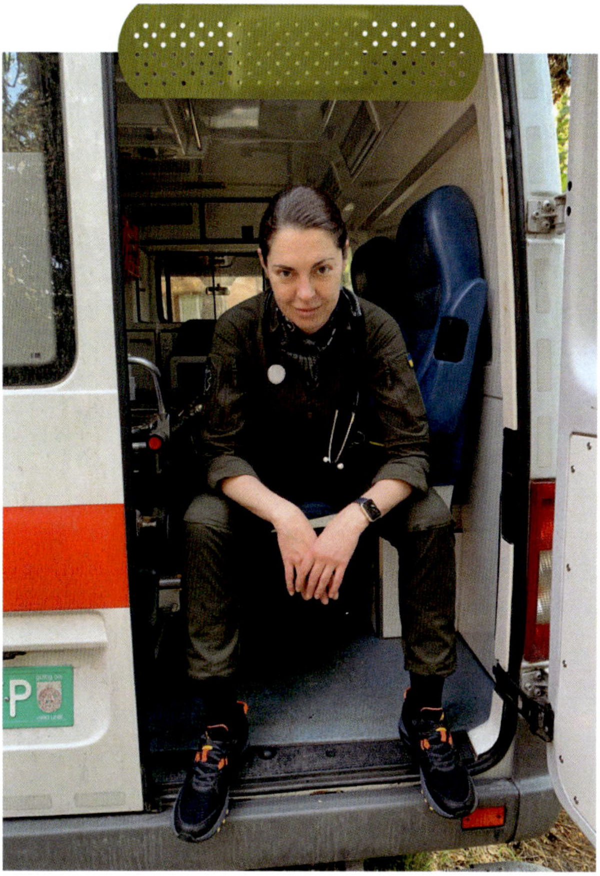

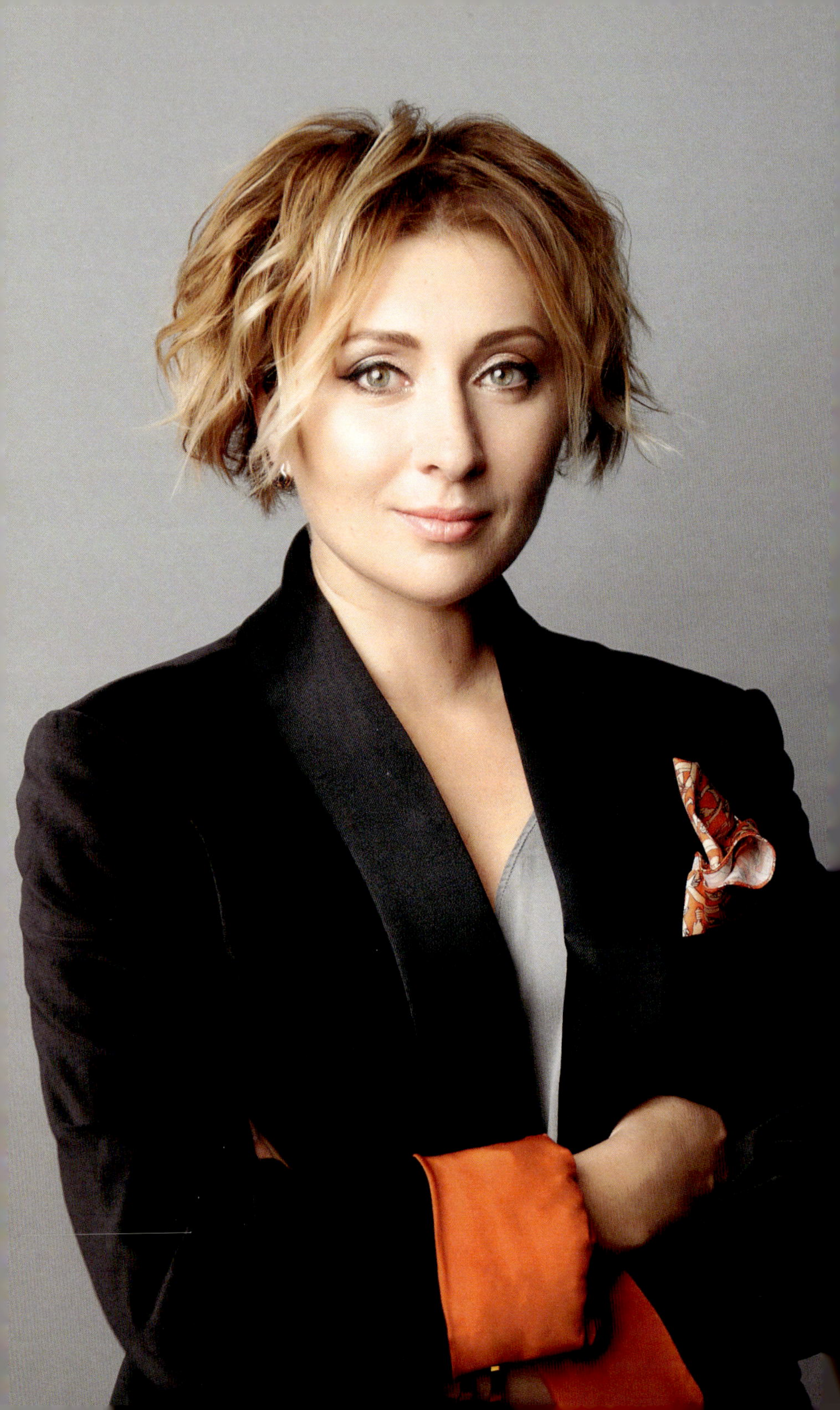

Viktoriya Tigipko

*Founder and managing partner of TA Ventures,
President of Odesa International Film Festival*

Viktoriya Tigipko, a founder and managing partner of *TA Ventures*, President of *ICLUB Global* private investors club, and President of *Odesa International Film Festival*, had an active, multifaceted life before the full-scale invasion, invested in startups, developed film culture in Ukraine, and had many other major projects. When the invasion started, not only did she stay active, but focused her contacts on helping Ukrainian families and evacuating refugees to Australia. She created the *One Ukraine* platform, where international entrepreneurs and investors came together to effectively help Ukraine during the war and reformat the film festival.

War is a time for action

"There was no time for reflection"

Before February 24, I had already been out of Ukraine for several months, attending international conferences in Europe and the USA. When I learned about the full-scale invasion, I realized we had to act immediately. There was no time for reflection, and it was not worth wasting energy. Of course, I was constantly in touch with my family and team. We all started to work to our fullest potential right away.

All our project teams — *TA Ventures, ICLUB Global, WTECH*, and *Odesa International Film Festival* — continued working 24/7. We immediately set up a chat room for quick response. We were in touch with each other and our partners worldwide all the time. We were informing our international community about what was going on in our country, about Russia's attack on Ukraine.

We all understand that it is essential to be as focused as possible. Panic is the enemy of our reality. My team and I immediately had a scenario in place for financial and logistical assistance and support for our employees, colleagues, and their families. Safety is our priority.

In the first weeks of the war, we communicated with the teams in real time for emotional support and to address any emergencies together. Our PR team was constantly in touch with the international media. We all became donors and donated blood for our army.

The format of our work has not changed much. We are used to working in an integrated and coordinated manner, being flexible, and responding quickly. *TA Ventures* fund did not stop its investment activities in 2022. The fund invests in the early stages that are less prone to crises, which makes us well-positioned. Together with *2048.vc* fund, we launched the *1kproject* to help Ukrainian families affected by war. We have already helped more than 8,000 families.

Our *ICLUB Global* private investor club has over 300 members. We operate in Ukraine, the United Kingdom, Switzerland, Monaco, Poland, Kazakhstan, and Cyprus. Plans are underway for Singapore, Austria, Portugal, Saudi Arabia, and Germany. Our *ICLUB Online* platform is up and running, promoting our geographic expanse and making the process of investing even more convenient.

Our *Wtech* community (for women in tech and business) is actively working. We also aim to support and unite those community members who left Ukraine because of the war. We work in the Netherlands, Portugal, Switzerland, Poland, France, Spain, Great Britain, Germany, and Cyprus and already have over 5,000 members. We opened the first American *Wtech* in Washington recently. We unite our networks to help each other because that's what makes us strong.

This year, we held the *Odesa International Film Festival* in different European locations. The industrial part took place at film festivals in Karlovy Vary and Priština. The national competition was held as a part of the *Warsaw International Film Festival*. Our Ukrainian Film Academy also continues its busy international work. We implemented a project with *Netflix* to support Ukrainian filmmakers. We were involved in organizing the *CinemAid Ukraine* international film marathon.

At that point, it was crucial to unite our professional networks with individual ones. That's how the *OneUkraine* project was born. It is a platform where international entrepreneurs and investors come together to help Ukraine effectively during the war. Each of the founders and operating team members has been actively involved in providing help since the early days of the massive invasion. But as an organization, we began operations in May.

OneUkraine and evacuation of the population

At first, we were involved in immediate response: evacuating refugees and delivering humanitarian aid, mainly at the request of the Ministry of Health. We continue to provide this essential aid, but we also focus on laying the foundation for the reconstruction of Ukraine and the lives of Ukrainians.

Within *OneUkraine*, we have partnered with the German company *Gropyus*, which has created a technology enabling us to construct buildings quickly and with high quality. We are also working on a mental health program to combat stigma, provide educational opportunities for Ukrainian professionals, and help domestic organizations develop accessible mental health services for the population.

We evacuated almost 12,000 Ukrainian refugees to Austria during six months of work.

In Austria, we cooperate with a partner organization that provides shelter and everything necessary for Ukrainian women and children. We also continue accumulating resources to ensure further evacuations for our citizens and their return home, when the time comes.

As part of the evacuations, we actively help organizing treatment for children with cancer and other serious illnesses if access to such treatment is limited.

These are mostly children from the East, in particular from Kharkiv Region. Nearly 200 children got access to quality treatment in Austria, Italy, Bulgaria, and Poland thanks to our operating team and the support of international partners.

We deal with complex cases and try to find an individual approach to each of them. Also, women who suffered violence, some of whom have lost children, apply to us. All women now live away from their husbands and relatives and bear the significant burden of war losses. That is why we allocate an operational resource for developing psychological assistance for Ukrainian families. Our goal is to support families now and help them come together after the war is over. To make sure our women have a place to come back to, we are actively working with municipalities and businesses to develop a housing construction platform. We want everyone who has lost their home to reunite with their families and continue living in comfort. We have almost completed a project that allows us to build one 30–40-apartment-house in 4 months, plus the time required to legalize construction and set up utilities.

We are working on building partnerships with local Ukrainian manufacturers to maximize the involvement of domestic businesses in our reconstruction program. Our main goal is to allow foreign investors to easily and transparently channel funds into the reconstruction of Ukraine.

We are sure that together with such strong ally of powers that rallied around helping Ukraine, the process of recovering the country after our victory will be even faster and more efficient.

The war spurs us into action

We need to work and rebuild the country right now, without waiting untill our victory. That is why I focus all my energies, both personal and working, on this thing. Of course, I read the news, keep my finger on the pulse, and know everything that is happening. I tell my international partners a lot about Ukraine, the war, and Russian aggression. I visit many international events and I see that people abroad still know very little about our country, our history, and our statehood. So I fill these gaps by explaining that Ukraine has a really long history and it was not created artificially, as our northern neighbors are trying to present.

We will definitely win. In fact, we are already winning. And we should prepare for the active recovery of our country. I believe that we are getting stronger when we support each other and unite our individual networks. All our project teams are now committed to that.

2022.10.21.

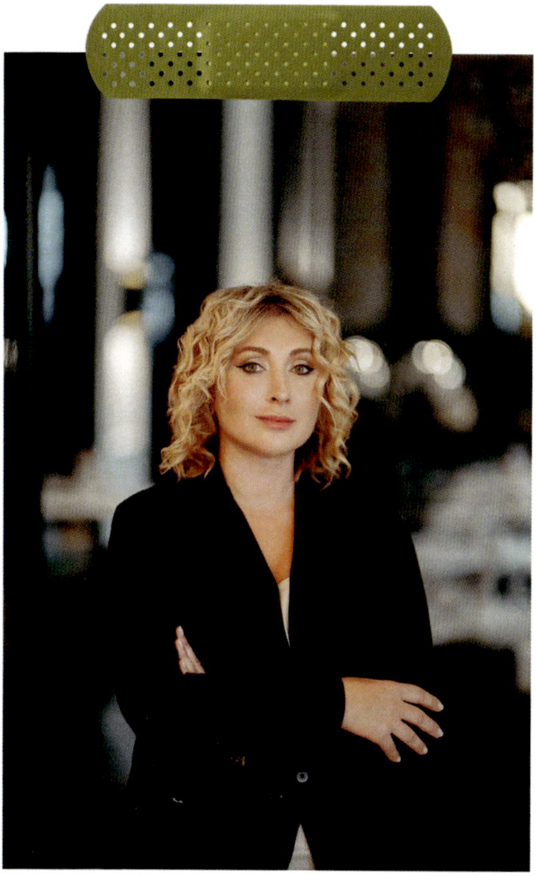

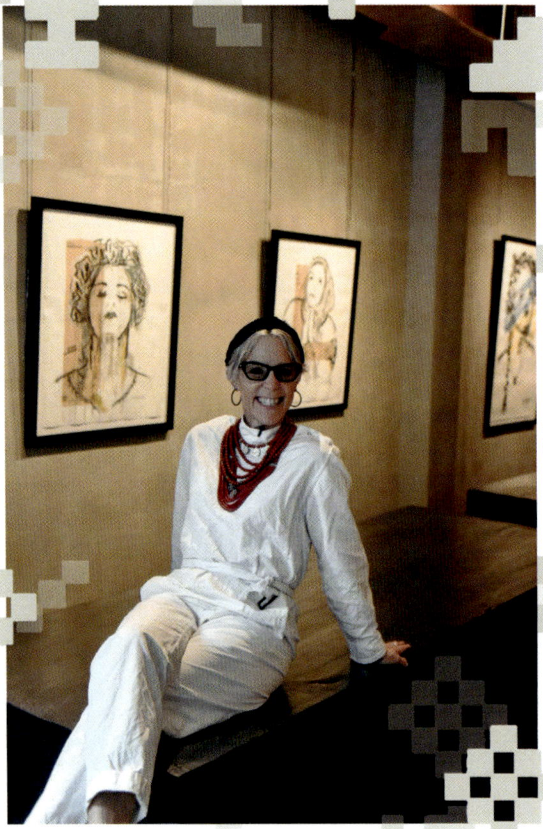

Ola Rondiak

American artist
of Ukrainian heritage

Ola Rondiak was born and raised in exile, but after Ukraine's independence decided to return to her ancestral homeland. Living abroad since the end of World War II, Olha's family has maintained a Ukrainian identity. The artist sees that Ukrainians feel this identity and fight for it again. It is what she reproduces in her paintings.

The story of preserving Ukrainian identity

I am Ukrainian. And I'm proud of it!

After WWII, my parents had to emigrate: my mom and grandfather ended up as refugees in Austria, and the Soviet communist regime exiled my grandmother to a labor camp in Mordovia. It is a tragic chapter of our family's history. So my parents were eager to pass on the Ukrainian culture to their children. They feared Ukraine would lose its culture as the totalitarian authorities conducted widespread russification in the Soviet Union. It is unbelievable how history is repeating itself. As a child, I always said I was Ukrainian and was proud of it. Every Saturday, I went to a Ukrainian school, which was my life, my inspiration, and my identity.

When Ukraine became independent, my husband and I decided to move to Ukraine to understand our roots.

I knew Ukraine through my mother's stories, as she left it when she was 11. But when I came to Kyiv, very few people understood me because everyone spoke Russian. It was like a thorn in my flash. Why does nobody understand me? What is going on? The reality surprised me. Of course, 60 years of being a part of the Soviet Union had done its worst: Ukraine didn't develop as it was supposed to.

Then the Orange Revolution happened, and afterwards, the Revolution of Dignity. That was what unbreakable Ukrainians chose.

My parents were forced to leave Ukraine. They lived in Western Ukraine. My grandfather was a Ukrainian philologist and a professor. He really believed in his homeland and didn't want Ukraine to be subjugated to the Soviet Union, for he understood that Ukrainian schools and churches would be destroyed. He wanted Ukrainian to be the language of instruction at school, which is why he was arrested.

My mother told me that when my grandfather came back from under arrest, they barely recognized him. He was all skin and bones because of terrible tortures. They knew that he would not withstand that again. So the family decided to send him (and my mother) west to Austria. My grandmother could not go with them. She stayed in Kolomyia town because her 19-year-old sister Olha (I was named after her) was very sick and could not walk. Unfortunately, she died in my grandmother's arms after a while. When my mother and grandfather were in Austria, my grandmother was arrested and evicted to a Soviet concentration camp in Mordovia — for helping Ukrainians, who was against Soviet rules. She was sentenced to 25 years of labor in that camp. Luckily, ten years later, in 1956*, she was released like many other political prisoners. While in the labor camp, my grandmother stealthily embroidered icons (the Soviet regime forbade it). She took her embroideries with her when she was released, sewing them into her underwear. She managed to keep them and then gave them to a priest who immigrated to Chicago. In 1980, a local newspaper

---

*   When Nikita Khrushchev came to power in the USSR. — *Ed.*

published an article about my grandmother and her embroidery. The diaspora helped find my family in Ohio and send them these embroideries.

After the Revolution of Dignity, I made a collage of articles about the events in Ukraine from the magazine. It is also emblematic. Ukraine is once again proving that it is a free state.

My grandmother and grandfather never saw each other again… But they exchanged letters. I make copies of these letters and put them in collages. Unfortunately, my mother hasn't seen my grandmother since she was 11. My mother is now 89.

My mom saw the trip as an adventure

My mom told me she had a good life because her dad was always around, even though he was 55 at the time. He didn't know English, so he experienced communication difficulties. When they came to the United States, my mother was 16. That growing-up period without her mother around was not easy. But my mother was still glad that they had started this journey. She saw it as an adventure, as most children would do. Children adapt more easily and quickly to new circumstances than adults. It is too hard for me to think about the women who are now with young children.

Ukrainians have an unbreakable spirit. It is not the first time they have experienced genocide. They should be resilient and strong and have enduring faith. I try to participate in every US charity event that transfers money to help Ukrainians.

Ukrainian women are indestructible!

In 2013, I started to fulfill myself as an artist. My grandmother's example made me realize that Ukrainian women are determined, indestructible, and strong. These are exactly the kind of portraits I create.

When my children had gone to school, I decided to turn my hobby into a job. I left my car outside to set up a workshop in my garage and started working every day. I believe it's not just my job, it's my destiny.

As early as in March, I started a new series called *Women of War*. I didn't have a clear idea of what to do, but I knew that crying wouldn't help, so I had to find the strength to do something to help people during the war. Although I had never worked with it, I took charcoal and asked a friend to be a model. As soon as I started a series of paintings, a gallery in Miami started selling them. I didn't even have time to think of names for all the paintings, and there were over 50 of them. Subsequently, they started selling them at an online auction. Recently, one of the paintings in this series was sold for $20,000. All the money was donated to Ukraine.

Once, I read about a woman on a social network. Her name was Nastia. I was incredibly impressed. Even without reading her story about the dogs, I just looked at her face, got inspired by her emotions, and immediately created a painting.

I believe that art is an effective way to get through difficult times.

2022.05.18.

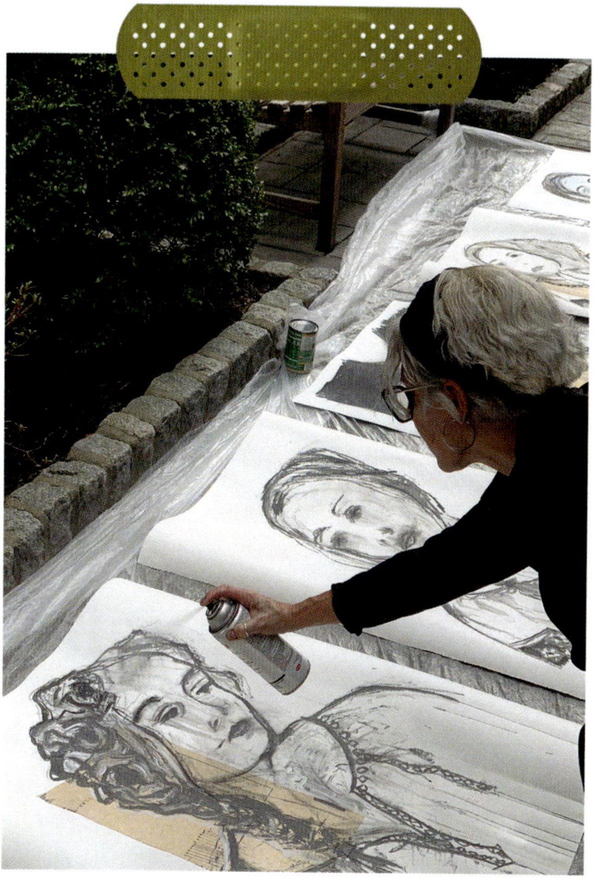

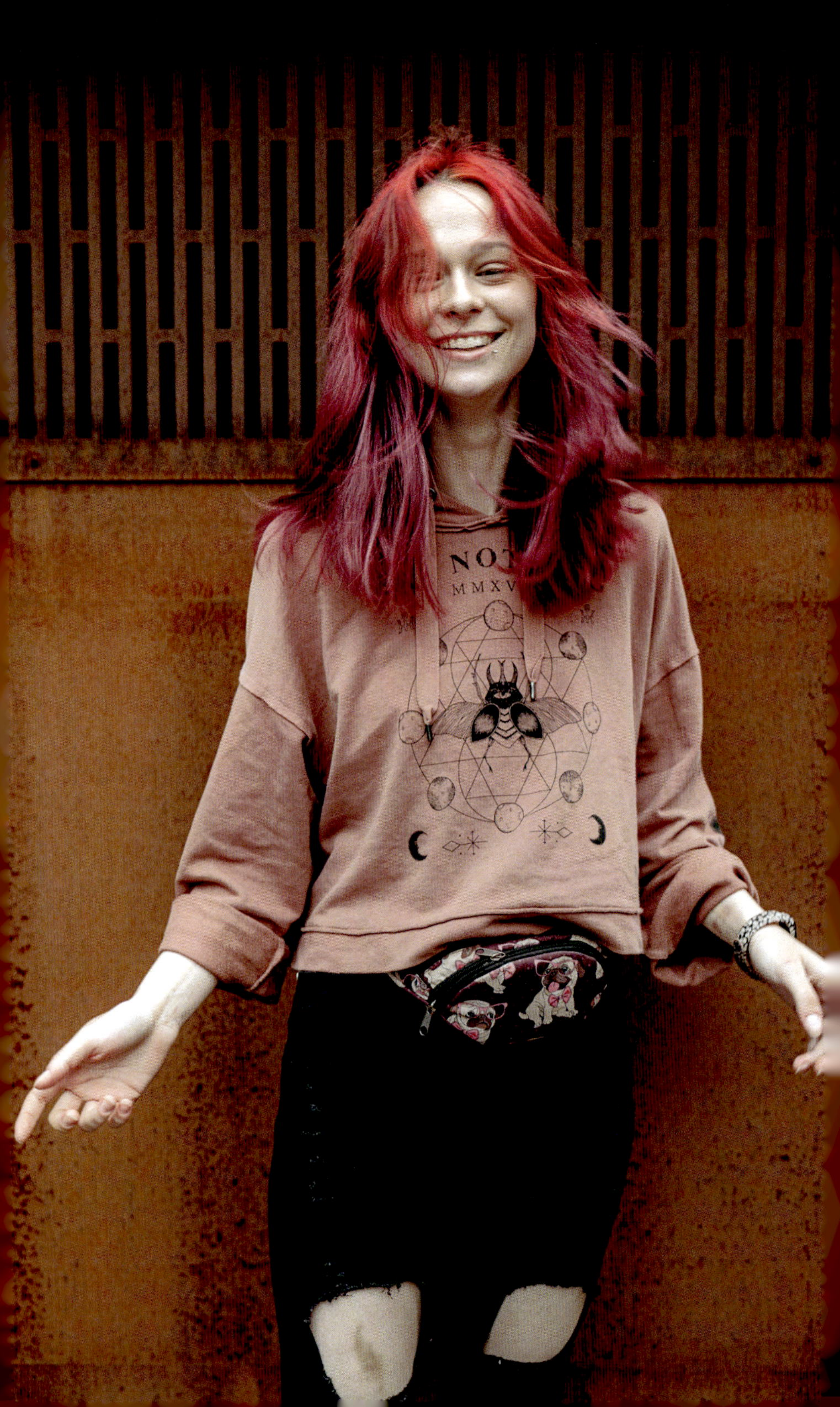

Anastasia Tihaia

Volunteer

Twenty-year-old Anastasia Tihaia and her husband Artur evacuated 19 dogs from Irpin under the shelling. Some dogs were sick and mutilated, and some weighed over 20 kilos! It took them three hours to walk to Romanivka, where their friends were waiting for them in a car. The legendary picture of Anastasia and her dogs pulling her in all directions that spread all over the Internet and media was taken by journalists near the famous bridge in Irpin.

Becoming a symbol of indestructibility, rescuing dogs from Irpin under constant shelling

I am a zoo volunteer, which means I pick up a stray animal, treat it, and then look for a family for it. Until then, the animal lives with me in love, affectpon, and with complete medical care. I decided to be a volunteer, as I have always had animals around me. I got my first dog when I was 6. Shortly after, my parents organized a kennel in our household. My adult life began with looking for a job related to the care of animals.

I am from Kyiv and used to live in the capital, but over four years ago, my husband Artur and I rented a house in Irpin. This house was also home to dogs. Besides our shared passion for animals, my husband has another job.

My relatives approve of my volunteering, and my friends even foster the dogs. The only ones who don't really understand it are my grandparents.

I found out about the invasion at five in the morning on February 24. My friend who lived near Boryspil called me to tell that the military operations had started. My husband and I went to a pharmacy and store to buy medicines and food. The first week passed quietly. And then the light, gas, and water began to disappear. It was really difficult. A shell fell in the neighbor's backyard but, luckily, didn't explode. Artur and I decided to go to Kyiv. Since the beginning of the invasion, we had picked up several more dogs, so we had to evacuate 19 animals, some of which were in carriages.

At first, we thought we would have to walk because we couldn't find a driver who would agree to take them. We had to walk over three hours from our house to Romanivka with 19 animals. At first, the dogs impeded and didn't want to leave, trying to get back into the house. But then they calmed down a bit and became obedient.

I am cursing in that picture of the dogs pulling me in different directions. It is not that easy to take out so many dogs, especially since some weigh over 20 kilograms. But I am pleased that this photo was useful.

In Romanivka, men from the Territorial Defense helped carry some dogs over a makeshift bridge, and our friends picked us up from there. My husband and I rent a house near Kyiv. 12 dogs are living in the living room. We have already given four of them a good home, and we are still looking for the other three that ran away on our way from Irpin.

We didn't feel fear back then because we were thinking only about the dogs. But the animals were nervous. We also evacuated five cats, a hamster, a chameleon, and a bird spider from Irpin.

All my family members are in Ukraine. My parents are now near Borodianka. They have 27 dogs: 20 older dogs and 7 puppies. They are not going to abandon the kennel, although food and water are hard to come by. They survive as best they can.

We only need things that we could not take from Irpin. For example, litter trays and feed for cats, mattresses for dogs, and feed for allergic animals.

We also need financial help since many dogs were left without handlers, people who, among other things, provide them with feed. But many handlers experience even more challenging times. One of them lives in the occupied city near Chernihiv. A girl is trying to evacuate abroad the dog which was under her care.

I cooperate with 20 volunteers from different cities and countries. For example, I had six dogs left from the *Pliushka* volunteer organization, and now only wan is left. Half of them were sent to Germany, and the rest found a home in Ukraine.

Taking care of the dogs is not that difficult: they need regular washing and feeding, some also need physiotherapy, and aggressive ones need training. We deal with complex cases: aggressive dogs, sick dogs, and disabled dogs. My husband is also involved. He helps wash and feed dogs and takes care of the animals in my absence. I taught him everything I knew myself, including medical care.

We have three dogs of our own: a beagle Ziuzia (Zeus), a paralyzed dog Beilis, and a spitz mix Stepan, who was once hit by a car.

Now we are looking for new families for the dogs, both here and abroad. Most of them will go abroad because people usually don't want to take handicapped dogs in Ukraine. I have a dog that has lived with us for four years now. These dogs have a chance of being taken to Germany or Spain, where they will find owners.

2022.03.18.

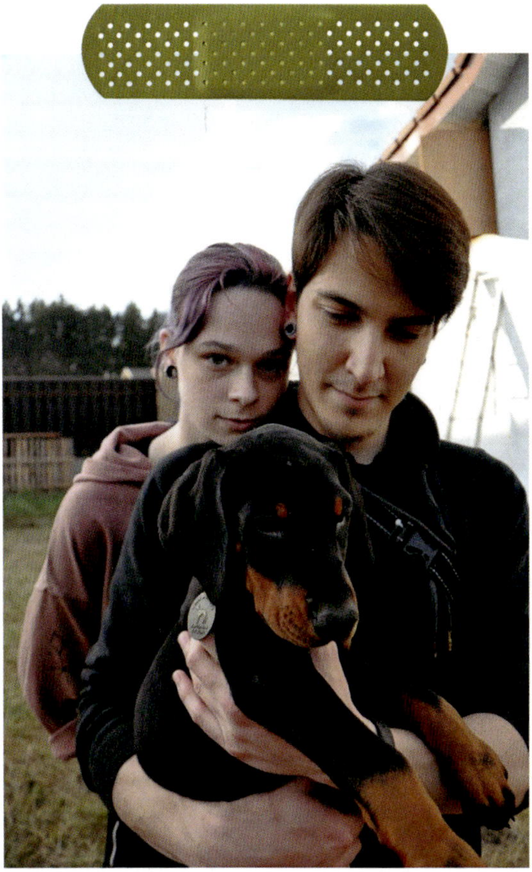

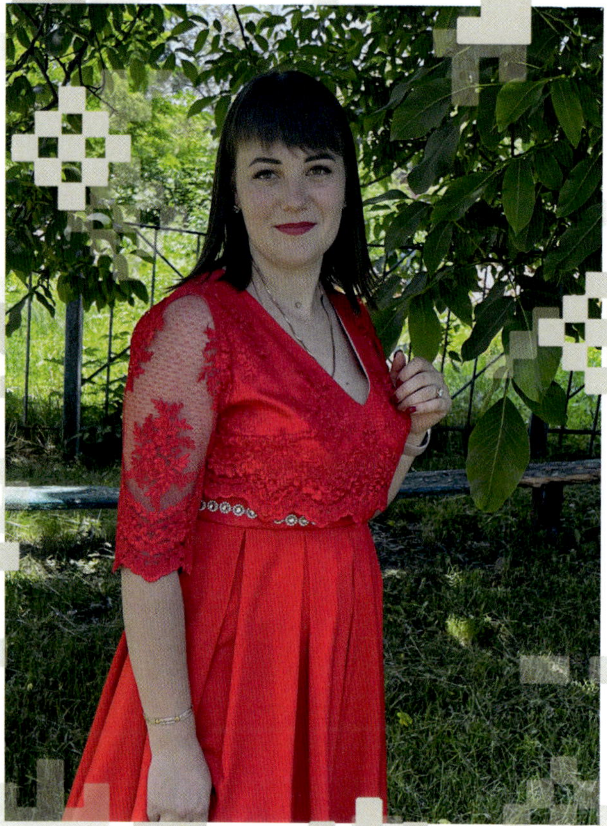

Vitalia Pankul

*Volunteer, co-founder
of the Turnkey House initiative*

Vitalia Pankul is the director of a preschool facility, a mother of two young children, and a woman who has proved that it is possible to set up a shelter for displaced people even without outside help.
Vitalia and her friends Tetiana, Olha, Olena, Karina, Julia, Iryna, and Alla renovated about 50 houses for IDPs in the village of Pancheve in Kirovohrad Region. Serhii Shulha, head of Kirovohrad Region Council, awarded the volunteers with honorary diplomas, "For the significant personal contribution to the organization of charitable assistance, active social and volunteer work and on the occasion of the Day of Ukrainian Statehood."

Giving shelter in the village to people who fled from occupants

I was scared, but I became a patriot

Before the war, I was engaged in everyday stuff like household chores and children. We planned to go on a trip throughout Ukraine with my family this year. But it didn't happen, and we decided not to make post-victory plans.

On the morning of February 24, we woke up to a phone call from our friends in Kyiv, who told us that Russian troops had begun massive invasion. There was a general panic. Air forces were flying up in the sky. I cried all day because I had two children — 8 and 3 years old — and I didn't know what to do. My husband tried to calm me down as best he could. The two of us went to buy food for stock.

I didn't even think of leaving, although my husband urged me to go together with children. I said I wouldn't leave him, so we stayed.

I was scared, but the war made me a patriot, and I was sure I was of use here. It seemed that it would be even harder abroad. Who said someone would need us there? We would be refugees for a few months, and then we'd have to settle and find a job. Many of my friends who left are now returning to their homes.

My friend Tetiana Bosko, director of the *Prykhystok Charity Foundation*, has a two-story house with a basement. We lived there for a week together with my two children and four of hers. Our husbands went to service in the territorial defense.

They were there almost around the clock and came home for just a few hours to eat and sleep. My friend and I kept the house.

In spring, the planting season came. So my husband went to field as he is an agronomist. We often leave our children with my parents, who live near us. They didn't leave the country. Most people from our village stayed in Ukraine.

Turnkey House

At first, I joined the neighborhood volunteers. We cooked food for our soldiers on the front line: our cousins reared pigs, and we made canned meat. We didn't have a single day to rest.

In March, displaced people started arriving, and we did not know where to accommodate them. Then we made an agreement with the village mayor and visited some house owners to get their keys. These houses used to be inhabited by the elderly people, who then moved to live with their children, or were empty altogether. Some houses were originally bought only for the sake of the gardens, so the owners didn't really need the living quarters available. All house owners provided shelter for free and did not charge any rent, and displaced people had to pay only for electricity and gas. People came, took pictures of the meters, and then contacted the owners directly (we got them connected).

These houses were in poor condition, so we started repairing them and giving them to the displaced people — turnkey houses, so to say. Several girls helped us. We have a group on *Viber* where we ask the villagers for help with the repairs. For instance, we asked men for help when we needed to move something heavy. People responded whenever possible. But sometimes, Tania and I had to work alone. My husband usually helped in such cases.

We used our cars to deliver pots, brooms, linens, and all the necessary utensils to the houses. We cleaned houses where no one had lived for years: plaster was crumbling, and mice were running around. We washed, spackled, whitewashed, painted, put up wallpaper, hung curtains, and even carried beds. It was cold back then, so we laid carpets on the floor and hung them on the walls to keep the rooms warmer. If we were out of other quick options, we used an oilcloth and stapler to decorate walls. We also connected the houses to the Internet at the expense of the people who had moved in.

Running water was not available everywhere, so we installed makeshift sinks. Later we bought new electric stoves and shower tanks. Now every displaced person has an outdoor shower.

We get materials from people and one volunteer who has a construction store. We bought everything at our own expense.

When there was a significant influx of people in March, we managed to set up two or three houses in a day.

Since the beginning of the war, we have repaired over 50 houses. About 70 families live there, but it's like a conveyor belt: some come for a few days, and some leave. About 250 displaced people came to the village during the full-scale invasion. Some are planning to stay in our village because they have nowhere to go back to. They've even found a job.

There are grocery and household stores nearby.

We provide everything we can. For example, *Masha Yefrosinina's Foundation* sent us funds, and we bought food packages for 50 displaced families and for some residents of the nursing home also located in our village.

People come to us from the towns of Sievierodonetsk, Lysychansk, mostly from Donetsk and Luhansk Regions. IDPs are mostly city dwellers, so we warn them that life in the village is nothing like they are used to. But people are so grateful to have a roof over their heads and live in a quiet place without constant shelling that firing up the stove and carrying water from the well are no big deal. We bought large 300-liter barrels at our own expense to make it easier for them to use water.

Prykhystok Charity Foundation

In April, we officially registered the *Prykhystok* Charity Foundation in the village of Panchevo. We were advised to do this to make it easier to receive official aid. We received aid from the *Sylny Razom* Charitable Organization (based in Khmelnytsky) and from *Nestle* company. *Velta* company provided equipment and clothes for the military conscripted from the village.

Once a week, an Odesa organization brings food packages for IDPs, and the village mayor goes by car to pick them up at his own expense.

We need more help because there are lots of displaced people. They ask for sweets for the children. Women in the canteen bake cookies every day, pack them in boxes and take them several times a week to Novomyrhorod town (the administrative center of our community). The boxes then go to the front line. IDPs also receive the cookies. Eggs and flour for cookies are either purchased or asked from people through the Viber group, for most people produce food for theselves around here.

Displaced families also step forward to unload something, put things in order, or clean up. Recently, volunteers sent us children's clothes and food. The clothes are all mixed, so we should arrange them by age. We involve everyone who volunteers to help. Then we pack parcels for the displaced children and send them to all regions where *Nova Poshta* or *Ukrposhta* operates.

We can't give it up, even though it can be tough.
We have already gotten used to this pace of work, although it was difficult at first. We were dead on our feet in the evening. For instance, we decided we needed to rest. But then we get a phone call that some displaced people are coming. Can we let down those who have lost their homes? We can sleep in our beds in our houses, and those people are left homeless. We can't abandon them to their fate.

I feel like repairing and volunteering. I get so used to this regimen that I do chores and rush to volunteer work even when I have a day off.

I wake up in the morning, quickly feed the cats, dogs, ducks, and chickens and cook breakfast and lunch for my husband and kids. I leave my three-year-old daughter with my eldest son and go to the warehouse (we set it up in an old abandoned restaurant building) to arrange clothes and pack parcels. Then I go home to my family. We do the chores, have dinner, and go to bed at about 11 p.m.

In fact, we lived at such a frantic pace even before the war. We spent the whole day busy with the household, vegetable garden, children, and work.

Sometimes, we manage to go out into the countryside as a family to relax and fish. The last few days, we had a kind of emotional recreation. There have been a lot of birthdays of our relatives. It was like going back to a past life...

2022.08.03.

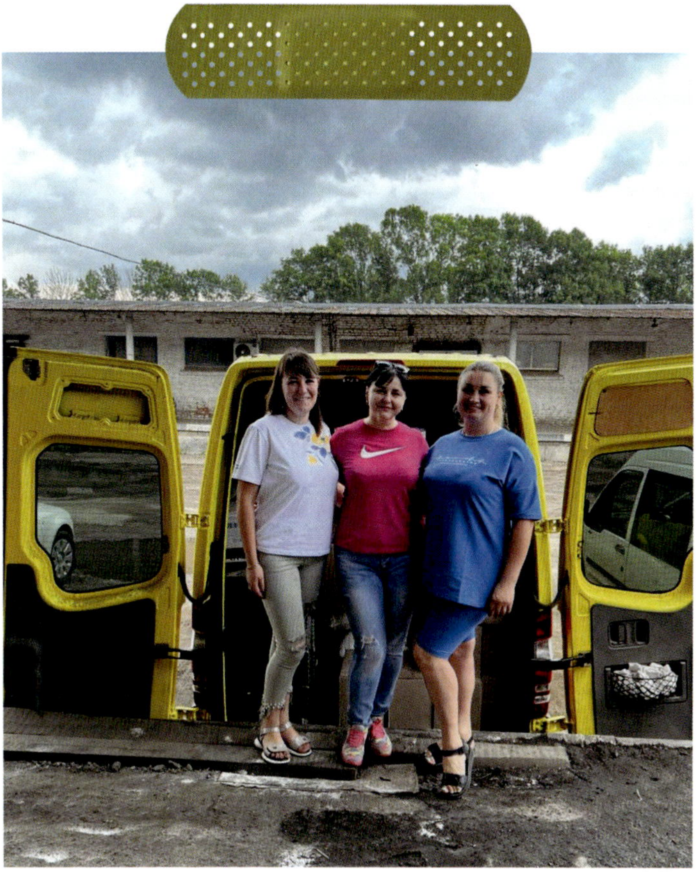

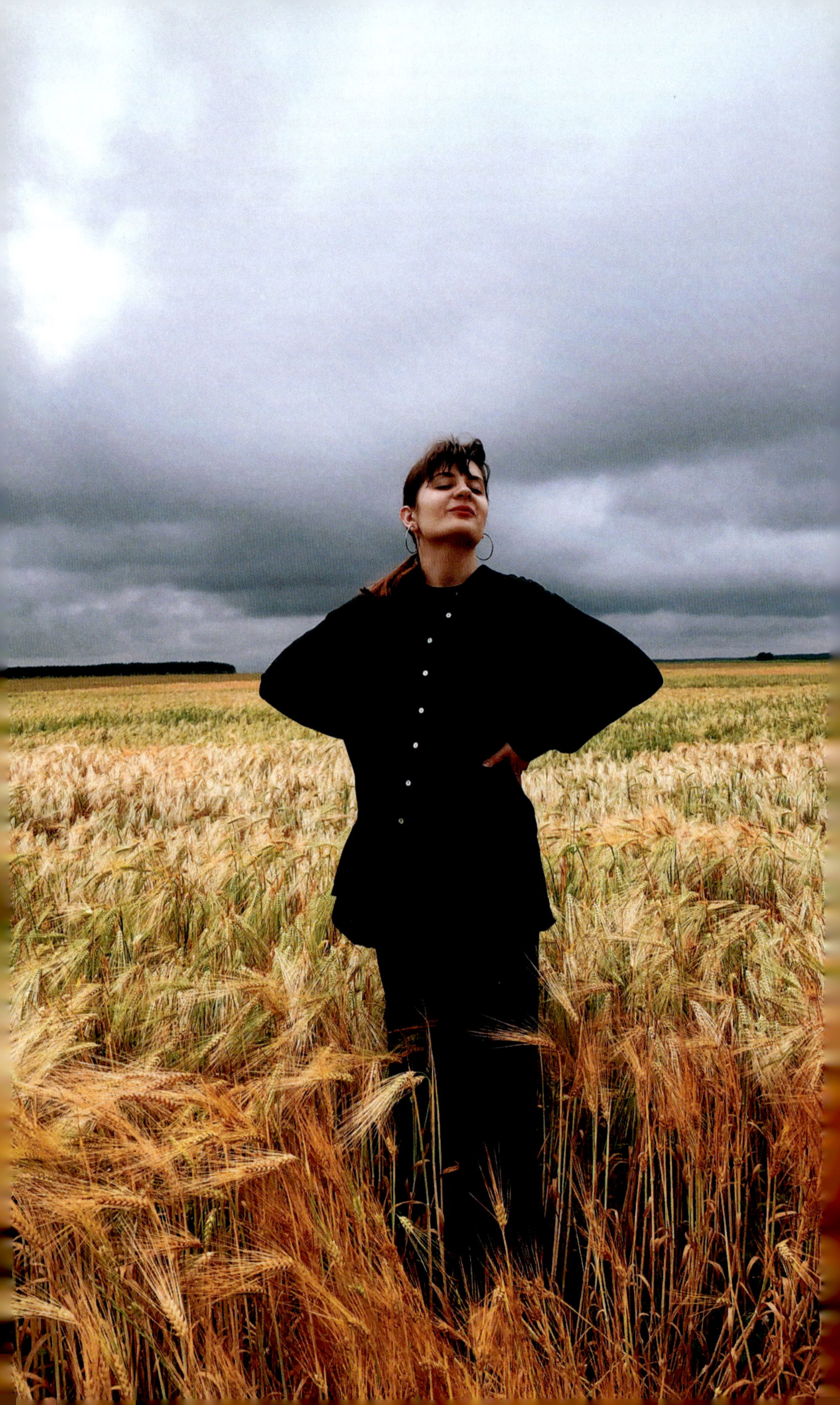

Inga Kordynovska

*Founder
of the humanitarian center in Odesa*

Inga Kordynovska is the *ID Partners Law Firm* owner who, despite the threat of occupation of Odesa, stayed in the city at the beginning of the full-scale invasion and founded the Odesa humanitarian volunteer center and two more projects to help displaced people, particularly mothers.

Taking the war as a new challenge

We haven't dealt with the war yet, but we'll settle it, too

I am the owner of a law company. Our lines of work include legal support for business activities, international trade, family law and heritage, and support for public initiatives. I was in charge of family law and business because I am an entrepreneur and have legal science and management degrees. I understand business needs, and that's why I come up with good legal solutions. I took the beginning of the massive invasion as another challenge. The news came as a shock. But it's a challenge to deal with. At first, it was COVID-19, and now Russian troops.

Our company has a practice of taking on cases that seem impossible to solve. We are talking about those that last for over 20 years or involve state interests or oligarchs. You start unraveling this tangle, learn various details, and gradually get to the bottom of things. After several such cases over the past ten years, I realized that nothing is impossible, so I took the wartime as another challenge, albeit a really crazy one.

On that February morning, I woke up at 7 a.m. Despite the terrible news, I thought it all over and decided to stay in Odesa. I remember that at 9 a.m., clients whom I was to meet that day began to call.

I assured them everything was as scheduled because there were cases that could not be put off, such as those related to the kidnapped child or domestic violence. Even war should not interfere with these urgent cases.

I analyzed my options through the lens of resources, money, and transportation. The first option was to do nothing and leave, but I remembered the advice from Mastering Fear*, a book written by a former U.S. Navy SEAL. I read it a long time ago from the perspective of legal practice: I handled corruption cases and faced threats. At times like this, you start to wonder what fear is, how it works, when it protects, and when it frightens and paralyzes. The authors gave an excellent account of how a person can curb their fear and how to distinguish when fear is rational and conducive to avoiding danger and when it is panic. On the morning of February 24, fear was panic-driven. It is when you grab your suitcase to run somewhere. But, remembering the practices from the book, I began to analyze the situation. And I realized that psychologically, leaving and doing nothing somewhere in a foreign land means a depressed state. You lose your strength that way. So I dismissed this option.

The second option was to go to Western Ukraine to my parents' house. But I have been living in Odesa for 14 years and often engaged in the social processes that have been going on since 2014. So it was a morally unacceptable decision. Besides, the safety situation in the country was very questionable since Russian missiles could hit anywhere. Odesa was at a high risk of occupation in the first days, so my parents were worried about me and panicked. But I decided I would only think of

---

* Webb B., Mann J.D. Mastering Fear: A Navy SEAL's Guide.

leaving if Russian troops landed and took over the city. The city needs me. I have knowledge and experience, and I could do a lot. It's not for me to move somewhere safe and do nothing.

The third option was to go to Europe and organize a humanitarian hub. But I dismissed it too. I divide all people into two categories: war people and peace people. The first category always fights for something. I belong to this category because of my character, childhood experience, and profession, and I constantly fight for someone's rights and interests. Living in Europe would not suit me. This is more about peace people who can organize some kind of help without any real threat to life and crazy pressure.

After analyzing my skills, experience, and ability and curbing my fear, I realized where I could be of use. I stayed where I am now to do what I can do here.

I have a practice that has saved me many times: during a crisis, you have to think about what you would do differently than everyone else. I knew everyone would rush to leave, roads and customs would be crowded, and fuel would be scarce. I realized if I decided to leave Odesa, I should do it in 2–3 days. If everyone is running hysterically in a specific direction, you must do the opposite. When you decide anything in a panic, this decision works against you because it is illogical and irrational. I understand people who started moving out because missiles were flying over their houses, but many people were guided by panic. For example, when I visited my parents (they live near the border) in two months, my mother said, "Everything had been quiet in our town since the beginning of the invasion, but residents rushed to the border in the first days, actually blocking from leaving those who really suffered." It is a vivid example of inadequate fear that does not protect but provokes to do crazy things, which leads to a stalemate.

The idea of creating a humanitarian center in Odesa

Happy people don't come to a lawyer; they come with pain, a problem, suffering, and force majeure. War is like a legal problem, but it is the case of the whole country, not just one client.

In the early days, some volunteers went hysterical, and others were frustrated. Some were buying up food and taking it to the military without asking if they needed it, while others were doing nothing. These are classic human reactions to stress: to run somewhere or freeze. You have to channel such reactions on the right track.

One of the goals of establishing a humanitarian center was to help people who stayed in Odesa cope with stress. Some would work at the center and keep their mind off the news, while others would donate funds and feel involved. It worked. I didn't expect such a scale: 300 people joined as early as the first week.

People's herd mentality also helped: when one zebra stray from the herd, it's more likely to die than when they run together. It's the same with humans: when we're scared, we don't want to be alone but prefer to join a community that will give us a sense of security.

It worked for me, too. The center was a mess during the first week, but afterward, things got well-ordered.

My mother called every day asking me to come to them, but I couldn't do it: the people who came to the center saw me every day, got used to me, and relied on me. I was like a safety island for them, and it would not be good to go away and demoralize them. My mother gradually calmed down and cried less, which made me feel better because the constant pressure from my relatives was depressing.

    The center became a place of my strength. You read the news, shells explode above you, you hear air raid sirens, and to make things worse, Odesa is full of sabotage groups. You feel this danger in the air when you return home at two in the morning. You get stopped at checkpoints (I never managed to complete my work in the center before curfew, and I just didn't have enough time to make a pass), there are mountains of sandbags on the roads, barbed wires, lights out, and depressing darkness. It's so creepy! I've only seen this kind of apocalypse in movies. But working at the center saved me from that.

Organizing the humanitarian center and scaling up the work

At first, one day felt like a month of normal life. Everything was going on at such pace that I still don't understand how we could endure it. Problems came up and changed unbelievably fast. The things we had been doing a week ago were no longer relevant. The first task was to help the army. Odesa was at a high risk of occupation, so we had to be as prepared as possible to fight back. The second task was to give people new sense so that they could overcome new challenges.

In three weeks, Mykolaiv stopped the front line, so we breathed a sigh of relief. We stopped apprehending the occupation all the time. Then we saw the horrors in Bucha and Irpin and decided we had to help civilians, too. We guessed there would be many victims after the liberation of the occupied cities, but no one had imagined the scale of the atrocities.

The city authorities joined us. It was a great challenge because, unfortunately, Odesa authorities had demonstrated a pro-Russian sentiment before the war. Our mayor did not post a single word on social media about the war during the first two weeks of the invasion. That shocked me. So I was skeptical when the city authorities contacted us and offered cooperation. But one of my partners, Mykola Viknianskyi, convinced me to do it because of the war. On March 27, we opened four humanitarian aid centers together with the authorities. We brought aid, which was donated by the twin cities, from large warehouses in Odesa. Our volunteers set up the process. We organized quick service at the centers so that people wouldn't have to wait for hours and created a system for tracking aid delivery.

In mid-April, refugees lined up at the centers, and as soon as in May, the centers already worked without my involvement and with a different set of volunteers.

On June 9, we terminated the memorandum with the local authorities because the mission was accomplished. We are moving on, although the centers still operate. In early May, we moved from our temporary location at the *City Food Market* to a school building because the *Market* would resume its work as a restaurant. One part of the school was a refugee center, while the other was a primary headquarters that focused on helping the army because the centers only helped refugees. Now the school has asked to vacate the premises because they are getting ready for the school year. Our work is on hold as we prepare to sign a contract for new premises and do an audit.

Go-to Room and **Sandbox Kidx**

Back in early May, I noted that humanitarian aid was like a resuscitation for people who had lost everything. We needed to launch projects to help them recover and return to life because a person cannot always be in resuscitation. That's why I launched two new projects.

The *Go-to Room* initiative helps find housing, job, doctors, and everything a person needs to get back to a normal life in a new place.

Shelters are good, but people can't live in gyms for months; they need housing and jobs. Displaced people don't know which realtor to trust or where to look for a job. And we'll tell them everything.

I moved to Odesa many years ago, but I remember how stressful it was. And the war multiplies this stress. So we started looking for ways to become a friendly center to help people adapt, socialize in a new environment, and feel at home. Home is not just the apartment you live in. Feeling at home is knowing where the coffee tastes best, where to buy meat, where the food is cheaper, which medical facility has the best doctor, and so on.

At first, our office was supposed to be based at the Food Market, but something didn't work out for them, so we'll work online for now. We have applied for grants and expect to win at least some of them to continue our work.

The second project is called *Pisochnytsya* ("*Sandbox*"). We are developing it co-authored with the same-name foundation and designer Julia Paskal, a client of mine. The idea for the project came to me when Maryna, the founder of the *Pisochnytsya Charitable Foundation*, which helped supply the military with sandbags, visited me. I told her that every other woman said she wanted to find a job but had no one to leave her children with because kindergartens were closed, and there was no money for a babysitter. So I suggested using the *Sandbox* for its intended purpose and creating a small kindergarten or a room with animators where the child could stay while mom was at work. This same mom could come on her day off to look after other people's children. It would be a kind of mutual assistance and socialization because moms could communicate with each other.

We are looking for premises with a bomb shelter, which complicates the task. We are negotiating with several owners of the premises, and we hope to settle this issue shortly.

We will launch the pilot project in Odesa and then introduce it in other cities because the number of displaced people is increasing, including women with children who have no friends or an opportunity to pay for babysitters. I think this project will operate even after the war because kindergartens work until evening, and mothers often stay at work late into the night. This way, we want to help women be independent. When I put forward these two ideas, not everyone supported me. Many volunteers were offended. They said, "How so? People need food and clothes, and we will offer them a job and babysitter?" But I believe these projects are necessary because the amount of aid is decreasing day by day, and it is expensive to bring it from Europe, which means it makes sense to make our money circulate in our economy.

The war shattered the illusions of people who scolded Ukraine

When I worked as a lawyer, one of our main values was zero corruption. They told me I was an idealist and that one could die of hunger in Ukraine with such an approach. I answered that it was what I believed in no matter what because I could not do otherwise. My clients often wanted to solve an issue by giving a bribe, but I refused, and we would win the case through court. After that, clients said I had returned their faith in the state as institution because they didn't believe in a fair trial.

I had won court cases without bribes for 13 years, even though it was always extremely difficult for me to lean into the wind. Now I'm relieved because the wind has finally turned toward my values, and I feel better because everyone has realized how cool our state is. People who went to Europe and compared life there and here started to appreciate Ukraine more than any other place.

Our company has a great practice of working with foreign courts. I know how long it takes to get the necessary certificate. I never had any illusions about it. Maybe that was one of the reasons why I did not want to go anywhere—I understood nowhere would be better than Ukraine.

I love my country. When people tell me that it's no good here, I say they have no idea how good our country is, compared to other countries. For example, four years ago, I was in The Hague, attending a conference on innovations in justice. I was proud to speak about such innovations to representatives of European countries, who listened to me wide-eyed.

The war shattered the illusions of many people. Everyone realized what a great country we live in. Ukraine has its problems, but so does every country. We should solve these problems instead of moving to another country. Should a problem appear, we deal with it. This is a normal process of development.

I am glad I don't have to prove now that our country is strong because everyone has fully realized it. Many people have changed their attitude toward Ukraine and begun to appreciate what seemed common or imperfect.

They tried to make us believe we were poor and miserable, but the war destroyed this inferiority complex. It all starts in our minds: when we berated the country for everything being wrong, we created a strong energy message. Now we see that we are strong, and Europe has a lot to learn. At the same time, analyzing all the progressive things those countries have and learning from them is crucial. The war revealed all the shortcomings we will have to fight in the years to come to build the country as it deserves to be. I was amazed to find out from a book about Winston Churchill how quickly some European countries surrendered during the Second World War — some in an hour, some in two or four days. We've been holding on for months! And they still tell us about the signing a peace treaty? Many foreign journalists also say they would not fight as we do but would surrender immediately. We faced the attack and showed that we fight and give our lives for European democratic values and freedom, which is a powerful indicator. Russia appropriated the victory in the Second World War, although it essentially took place on the territory of Ukraine. They forced Russia's victory on us for 70 years to make us forget our significance.

It is crucial to understand that this is our land, country, and future victory and that we won't let anyone take this away from us. The inferiority complex must vanish into thin air.

We should switch from "war and struggle" mode to "life" mode

Some part of me resisted when I tried to get back to my pre-war life, like dancing, sewing dresses, or even taking a bath. For instance, when I saw large lines for a few liters of water in Mykolaiv on the TV, I thought, "How the hell can I think of a bath if people don't even have drinking water?!" Although I understood that even if I forbade myself to take a bath, it would not solve the water situation in Mykolaiv. As long as I can permit myself small pleasures in these settings, I should do it. If you have an opportunity to wear dresses, bake pies, or dance, and it gives you at least some positive emotions, do it. Add such pre-war things to your life gradually: ten minutes each day at first, and then more and more. These things will add to your strength. We should switch from "war and struggle" mode to "life" mode when we're not fighting but filling our life with positive energy. Even if it is some little things, they will bring back joy and strength.

Enjoying life, reading books, practicing ballroom dancing, and sunbathing in Odesa backyard help me recharge. Such moments remind me that life goes on. Every day I try to find more time to do things that make me feel alive and give me the strength to move on. Some worry that they might spend this time on work, but there is no cause for worry. It will give them more energy and strength to do everything planned more quickly. The extra energy will make it possible in two days to do things that used to take a week.

I was physically exhausted at the end of April because I worked without days off. And suddenly, I had to go to Lviv to sign a memorandum with two foundations. Leaving Odesa felt much like a betrayal. And then, sitting at my parent's summer house, I felt I shouldn't rush like that. Back in Odesa, I changed my schedule to keep working.

I started looking for energy resources, remembering what made me happy. Of course, you can't do many things because of the war, like going to a concert, but you can take a bath or get a massage. I have the strength and desire to do something again. Now I try to balance things.

Some accuse me of not engaging in the processes as often now. My answer is that I can't work 18 hours a day all the time. I did it when it was absolutely necessary, but now I have to take care of myself at least a little. If I'm gone, everything else will be gone, too.

I remember one teacher at my Lviv school once said, "You have to remember that every entrepreneur is an engine of their project, so they have to take care of their common sense. Nothing will move forward if you lose your resource and stop controlling the process. So one of your biggest challenges is to stay resourceful." The skill of not burning out is your responsibility so that you can always be resourceful to run this marathon. It helped me to have small mercies back.

Women have a harder time with ascesis than men. Little things like coffee, a manicure, and a dress are really important for women. You should get them back into your life, even though it seems absurd when you have a front line 100 kilometers away. It's what gave me my resource back. I managed to run the firm, keep the center, and not feel like an exhausted horse.

Life has changed for good: plans after the war

Life has changed for me; nothing will be like it was before the invasion. I reorganized the work so that we could earn money in new settings because the business has to live, and I have to pay salaries no matter what. My personal accomplishment is that in June, people got salaries at the pre-war level. I have been working on this since March. Many entrepreneurs justify not paying full salaries by the war, but I wanted to set the bar right away. It seemed fantastic in April, but I found a way to achieve the goal. You have to imagine that the environment will always be like that, and you have to adapt to it. Victory will come, but we don't know yet when. It is essential not to wait for victory because waiting can kill you. You have to work in the new reality instead.

No one wants your business now? Do another one. You have to adapt quickly and look for opportunities, accepting reality. That's probably one of the biggest things I've achieved in my 30s: accepting reality. That said, I do a lot to change reality and bring victory closer. It's not an attempt to undo reality but to smooth it. All I can do is respond to reality. You should become like water and streamline all obstacles without trying to move them.

In 2014, an ex-boyfriend of mine who served in the ATO as a sniper said, "When I know I have to go back because someone is waiting for me, I will go back no matter what because I have a future ahead. But when there is no future, there is no point in living here and now." So it is important to set a goal and not cancel your dreams and plans. You may need to adjust the time frame or partially change the goal. It creates a thread from the present to the future, and you follow it even when the hell is breaking loose around you.

Many projects and contacts emerged during the war, and I learned a lot, so the legal sector alone won't be enough for me anymore.

I don't know yet whether I'm going to be involved in social activities or business. Probably, some of the projects I started will transform into a business. I grew up as a person during the last four months.

2022.07.18.

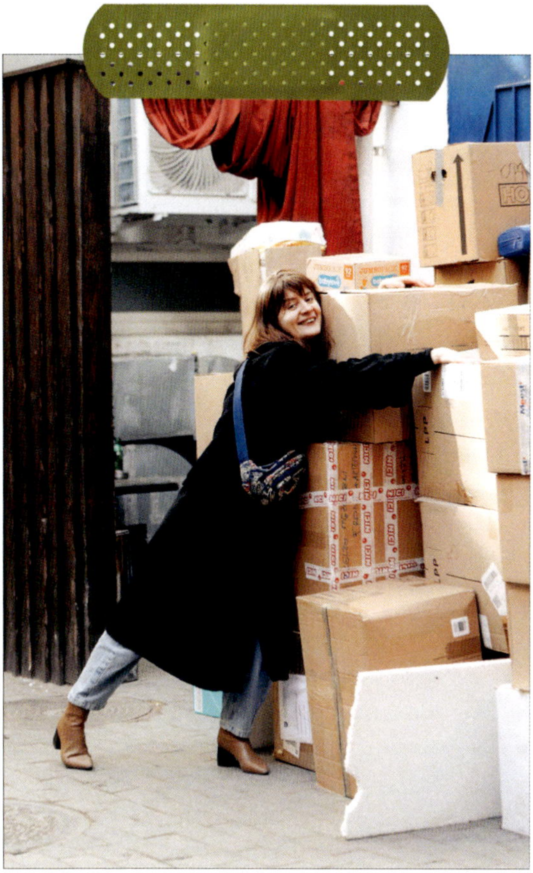

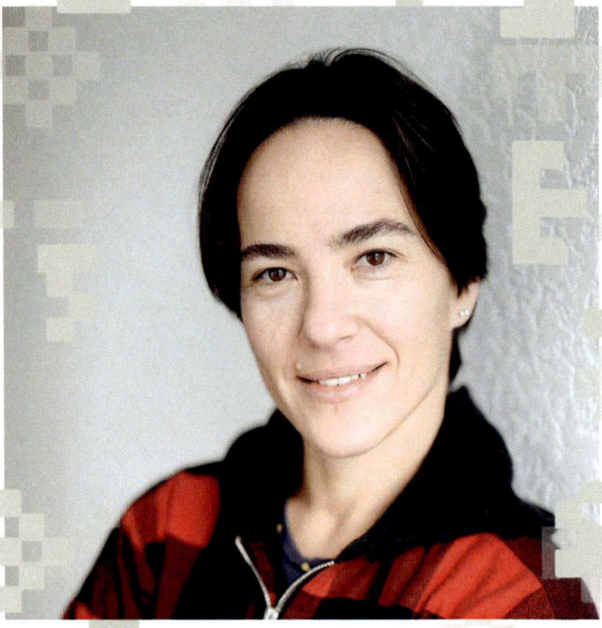

Olena Shevchenko

Head of the Insight Public Organization, founder of the Women's March Organization

Olena Shevchenko is the head of the *Insight* Public Organization and a founder of the *Women's March* Organization. The organizations help and protect the rights of the LGBTQI community.

Supporting the LGBTQI community, providing humanitarian aid to women who went abroad during the first weeks of the full-scale invasion, and helping them to settle down

The first days of the invasion, moving to western Ukraine, and requests for help

Some partners warned us there might be invasion of Russian troops, but we didn't want to believe it. We had a discussion scheduled for February 24 in Kyiv, so it never occurred to us until the last day that this would happen. We were also preparing for the *Women's March* scheduled for March 8. We canceled it a week after the hostilities started.

On February 24, I woke up at 4 a.m. I lived near the Zhytomyr highway, so the explosions were loud and distinct. At first, I didn't plan to go anywhere and stayed in Kyiv for 16 days, but then my family and I decided to leave. We did it for several reasons. First, it was impossible to work as it was hard to get to the office. I had to walk twice over 6 kilometers through checkpoints. And I had to organize efficient work because we started setting up shelters in Chernivtsi and Lviv in the first days of the invasion. We also wanted to create humanitarian aid centers in these cities, which was unreal in Kyiv then.

The second reason was that I had to take my parents to western Ukraine.

It was an immediate decision. There was no time to plan and think about what would happen in a few weeks. Even now, it's impossible to plan what we're going to do in a month. My team and I still work in an immediate mode, responding to people's requests and needs.

We don't have a clear direction for our work. The *Insight's* priority is to help LGBTQI people, but we also have the *Women's March*. Women, particularly those having many children, applied to us asking for specific help with getting to western Ukraine and then abroad. They asked for food and money. That is how we started to help.

Setting up shelters, a helpline, and a humanitarian center and our cooperation with Airbnb

On the first day of the war, we launched a psychological helpline. Now we have two lines, one for LGBTQI people and one for women. We designed the lines from scratch. We engaged several psychotherapists who had worked with us before. We also have over 30 volunteers on call (working for several hours a day each), providing psychological help 24/7. At first, it was a one-time consultation. But later, we created another list of people who needed up to 10 consultations as the number of requests for long-term help increased.

During this time, there were two bursts of appeals: during the second week of the invasion and now. But the subject of requests has changed. At first, people applied to us because of stress, anxiety, and constant nervousness. Now it's about quarrels in the family and domestic violence, as it was during the pandemic when people found themselves alone with a partner. Generally, it's a line for women, but men have called a few times, too.

We partnered with *Airbnb* about ten days after the full-fledged hostilities started. They called me asking what kind of help we provided and how we worked. We did all the work. We made a form, started receiving applications, checking people, and transferring the data into the *Airbnb* form. We had no idea how many requests we would get and how hard this work would be.

Over 5,000 people have already received vouchers for free accommodation, and the number of applications is not getting any smaller.

At first, it was just the two of us: me and my colleague, who is also in Lviv now. But we could not cope with such a flow of applications and other lines of work, so another colleague, who now deals only with *Airbnb*, helped us out.

We also created two shelters in Chernivtsi and Lviv. People also have to apply to get there. We also have forms for humanitarian aid and hormone therapy for transgender people. We collect all these applications, then we call people back and send what we can.

We get requests through Google Forms and social media. For example, it's up to 500 requests daily on *Instagram* and 50–100 requests on *Facebook*. We make 100–150 calls and 70–120 dispatches a day. We have already processed 8,000 requests, 60–70 percent of which are from women with many children, women with children with disabilities, and women who care for elderly relatives. We have 7 employees and 12 volunteers coordinating our work in the regions. Plus, we have created a volunteer group in Chernivtsi.

Humanitarian aid at our own expense and goods lost at the border

At first, we thought we could get humanitarian aid through large organizations. But we have not been able to contact *UNICEF* and the *Red Cross* yet. We use two approaches in our work. The first option is to buy what we need abroad with the help of our friends and partner organizations. They bring the cargo to the Polish border, where we take it and transport to Lviv and then distribute it. The second one is to buy what we need abroad or in Ukraine ourselves, pack boxes in Lviv, and send them.

So far, we have delivered cargo in full using these approaches. There was a case when a friend transported humanitarian aid from the USA in large suitcases. When we sent her a photo report, she said that a lot of shoes, some medical supplies for the military, and many more were missing. Unfortunately, that happened.

The needs have changed, and everything's gotten more complicated because people are filling out requests for the second or third time. Mothers with many children need diapers, child food, hygiene products, and medicines. We deliver crutches and wheelchairs for children with disabilities. These are very expensive. We also brought L-thyroxine and insulin for those who needed it since we were short of it in Ukraine.

We helped both the military and the paramedics because many LGBTI people are in the army. We sent them targeted help. Another priority is to help female soldiers with women's armor vests, underwear, and hygiene products because their needs are ignored. We also had a chance to get tactical first-aid kits from abroad and sent them to everyone we knew.

We buy almost everything at our own expense, spending about 2 thousand euros a day, and that's just for humanitarian aid. We don't have enough resources, which is, unfortunately, a common problem. Attention to Ukraine is decreasing, and much fewer people are donating. The greatest flow of funds was from ordinary people, who sent $20–30. A month ago, it was almost enough.

Also, we have repurposed all of our foundation aid, which used to go to other work, to support people. We decided that we would deal with the donors in time. It is not that important now.

Legalization, registration, language barrier: problems Ukrainians faced abroad

Our organization advises people who went abroad on registration, residence, etc. Although countries have created conditions for refugees, many programs are imperfect. For example, under the British *Homes for Ukraine* program, refugees cannot enter the country without finding a sponsor who will accept them. But not everyone speaks English and knows how to find a sponsor. Besides, even if a sponsor is found, refugees are still dependent. The person who shelters them receives remuneration from the state, and no one controls the living conditions and whether Ukrainians will get a job, for example.

Almost all countries have different situations but the same problems. Besides, countries are tired of accepting refugees, especially in overpopulated regions such as Poland and Germany. Everything is not as rosy there as they describe it to us.

Here's a vivid example: some time ago, there were many volunteers who took pictures with Ukrainians and offered tea on the Polish border. Now there are no such volunteers, and on top of that, the toilets on the border are now paid for. We can expect increased discontent in these countries about the situation as they reach their psychological and financial limits. Right now, Romania is more or less acceptable in terms of conditions, but no one wants to go there because it is not the best choice for LGBTI people.

As for the LGBTI community, especially couples with children and parents, it is difficult for them to find a place to live. At first, people were willing to accept 2-3 adults with children and animals, but it's been a few months now, and people can't provide these services all the time.

Legalization is not that easy, too. One example is a couple of girls who cannot find a place to live together in Germany because there is no way they can prove that they are a couple. To prove it, they must collect a bunch of notarized certificates in Ukraine.

The world does not realize the scale of the humanitarian crisis and war

Recently, I attended the *ILGA* World conference as a board member of this international organization. I had meetings with representatives of the United Nations and donor organizations for ten days. People have quite different information about the events in Ukraine. And we should ask the Ukrainian media covering the events why it is like that. People there don't have enough reliable information.

Some foreigners still believe this is some "special operation", so they can't imagine the scale of the humanitarian disaster. There are many such people. On the plus side, they are glad to hear from us about the development of events and the help we need.

Groundhog Day, communication with donors, and future plans

I don't know how I am managing to put up with everything. I think it depends on the personality. I know many people who have been unable to continue because of stress, danger, etc. My colleagues and I have been through many crises as an organization, so we were prepared.

Two months seemed like an endless Groundhog Day: I handled moderating *Women's March* and *Insight* on Facebook, communication with journalists and international partners, almost all grant management, and communication with donors (by the way, we stopped working with some).

On the downside, people started demanding help. At first, people were grateful. But in a month, many began to write that no one had called them back. There are many such cases, and we now have over 12,000 requests, 8,000 of which have been processed. I see this change even at the state level. For some reason, they have decided that we owe them something. It's like we're taking everything for free from some warehouse and underperforming. I think this attitude will intensify, but I have no idea what to do about it.

We are not a charitable foundation; we have limited resources. So we decided to set the criteria by which we would choose people to help. It is clear that we cannot continue to work at the same pace, given the number of requests we receive.

2022.05.17.

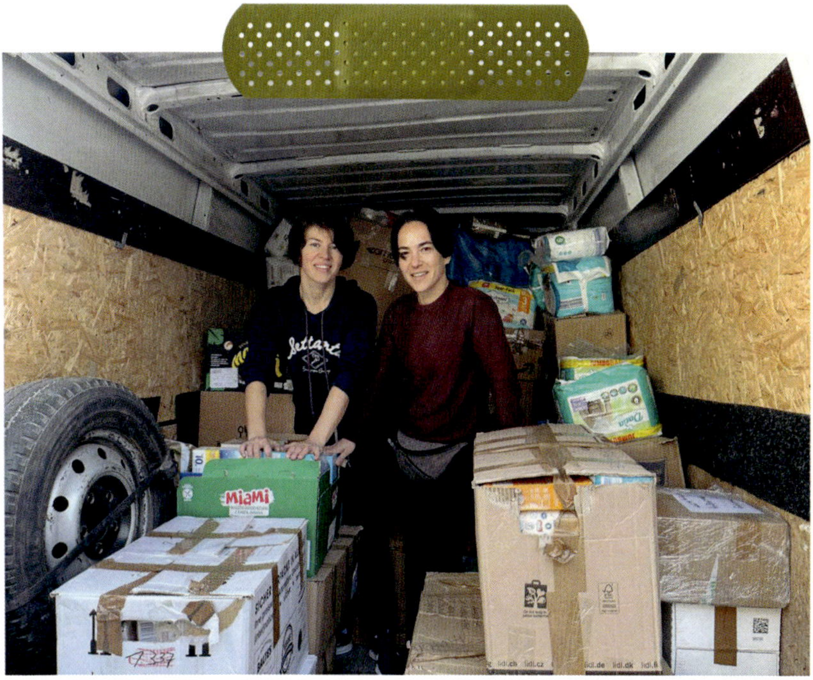
MiaMi

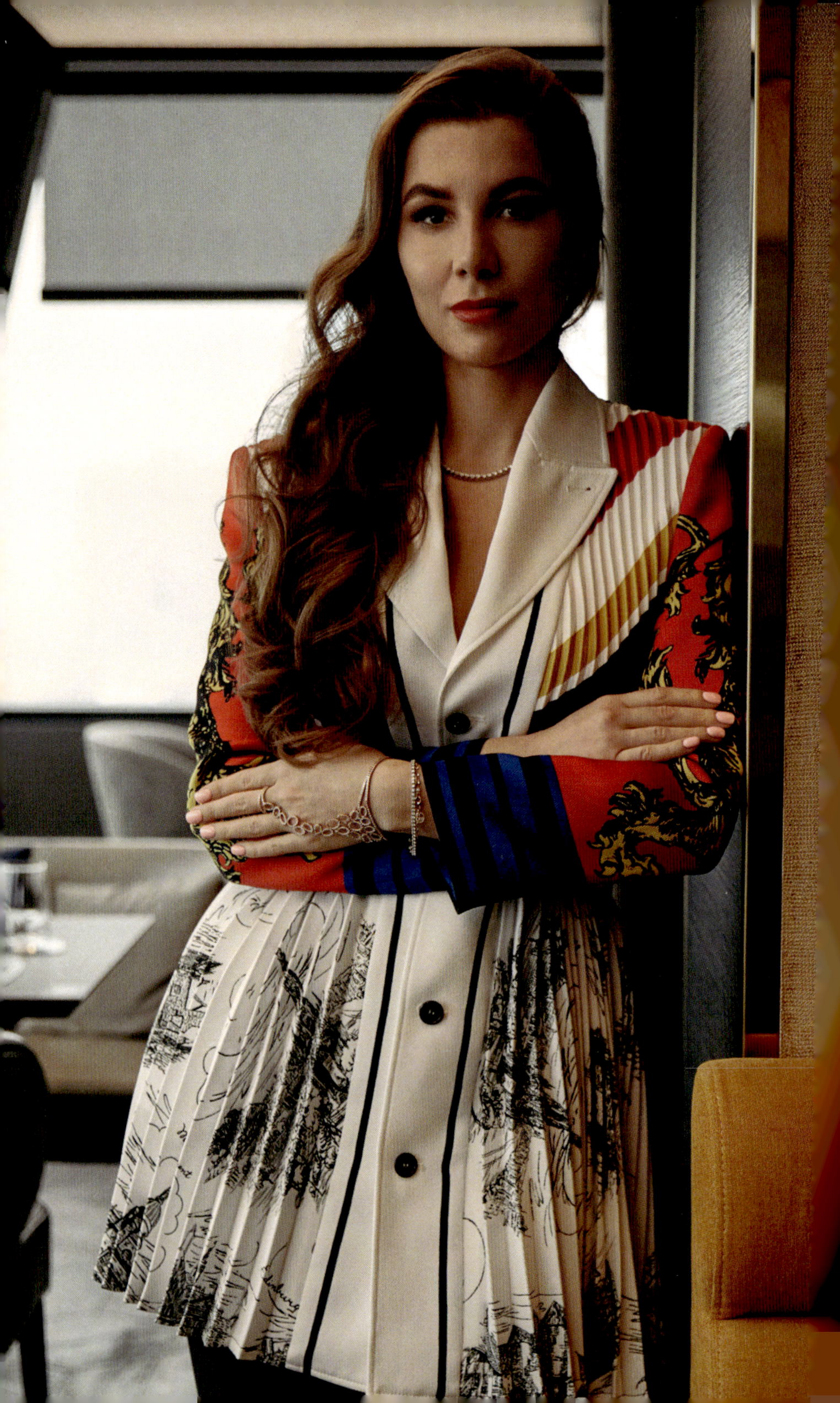

Olena Shevtsova

CEO at LEO, the international payment system, and Chair at IBOX BANK Supervisory Board

With the outbreak of full-fledged hostilities Olena Shevtsova started restoring the business to its prewar state and helping the military and IDPs.

How a running business helps the army

"The first thing I thought about was my family and staff"
The invasion caught me at home in Kyiv at 5 a. m. It was a sleepless night: searching YouTube, I stumbled upon Putin's video message. My children were sleeping peacefully, and my husband was on an urgent official call. I got worried straight away. Every word the Russian dictator said that night shocked me. I realized that difficult times awaited Ukraine. As soon as the speech ended, Russian planes started bombing Boryspil airport, which was close to our house. The first thing I thought about was my family and staff. The main task was to create a safe environment for my children and our employees.

At 5 a. m., I called Mariam (*CBDO LEO*), who was in Georgia, and Viktor (*LEO* developer), who was in Lviv. In absolute shock, involving other colleagues, they began evacuating people from Chernihiv, Sumy, Kyiv, and Kyiv Region. My four children and I started refurnishing our basement into a bomb shelter.

My family and I first stayed in Kyiv because we wanted to support each other, our neighbors, and the country. On the eighth day of the invasion, when the situation in Kyiv Region reached a critical danger, my children and I left for western Ukraine. The road was arduous, but surviving was my responsibility to my children. I also had to think about 700 employees who had to work and earn money for their families. Under such conditions, we relocated our team to safe places with smooth communications.

From the beginning of February, we heard about the impending invasion almost every day. Each company had a plan of action in place to minimize risks and remain as profitable as possible during the full-fledged war. This plan was created just in case, but certainly we were not really ready for the shelling and bombing. My husband and I also had our own family plan, but no one even imagined it would actually come in handy. So on February 24, we followed our instincts, just like most Ukrainians did.

"Back to pre-invasion financials"

As the full-fledged invasion began, I started working harder, finding ways to help our army, following my inner guidance. My priorities did not change much: the main thing for me was to keep jobs, ensure the safety of my team and family, and contribute as much as possible to the economic stability of Ukraine.

My work helps a lot to take my mind off the situation. During the first three months, we were adapting to the new business practices, both online and offline. We were busy moving servers to the cloud, closing *IBOX BANK* branches or providing them with everything they needed, and relocating our team. It was extremely hard, yet fundamental for further work.

LEO and *IBOX BANK* didn't stop their operation. The main goal was to return to the pre-invasion financials. We understood that only a running business would help the state win. The company operated from offices in three cities: Kyiv, Lviv, and Warsaw. In the fourth month of the full-fledged war, we managed to restore about 70 percent of the processes. The company achieved it by expanding the list of foreign partners, adapting to the new working conditions offered by the National Bank of Ukraine, and expanding the staff. At that point, the main challenge was harnessing emotions and feelings to deal with work issues effectively.

"The running business must help the military"

I think any running business must help the army. We're all on the same front, only with a different format of the fight. *LEO* and *IBOX BANK* are working on the economic front and are also engaged in providing humanitarian and military aid. 16 of our employees were enlisted in the early days of the invasion, and we are keeping all our work commitments and their jobs. My colleagues keep in touch with them and provide them with everything they need: walkie-talkies, gloves, uniforms, and drones. In the first month, Ukraine suffered a shortage of helmets, body armor, and thermal imagers. So we looked for them all over Europe.

As soon as part of the team got to Warsaw, we set up a hub to help the army there. Our girls collected everything we needed from all over Europe. That's how we started delivering body armor, helmets, military uniforms, thermal imagers, etc. The hub was located in the Warsaw office we rented for the *LEO* team. In that same office, we restored the company's financials. Nine staff members from HR, PR, and IT departments headed the volunteer work. Our friends with a license to ship military products ensured the logistics. They got the process moving, literally and figuratively.

Helping internally displaced people is of particular importance to me. For example, we help families from Mykolaiv that left for Odesa. They live in the *Alice Place* Hotel, where they get food, clothes, and accommodation. We have a lot of projects aimed at different population groups. In addition to military aid, we fund operations for children with heart defects, provide scholarships for talented students, provide financial assistance to the *First Maternity Hospital* in Odesa, conduct medical training with doctors of the *Dobrobut* clinic, and so on. We invite everyone to join these projects! All initiatives are realized transparently within the *LEO Foundation*, established shortly before the invasion (in November 2021). The *Foundation's* funding and labor force are ensured by the management and employees of *LEO* and *IBOX BANK* and their partners.

I am proud of our team. Everyone found something that brought us closer to victory; everyone found their front: some enlisted, some ensured safe working conditions for the team, and some went to Europe to quickly bring equipment for the military.

"We continue to grow despite the war"

Firstly, the *LEO* and *IBOX BANK* teams are working for the sake of a common victory. We give part of our profits to support the army and help IDPs. We retain jobs and pay taxes. It seems like a small thing, but this approach can keep a country alive amid war.

Secondly, *LEO* and *IBOX BANK* entered the international arena. During seven months, we prepared the legal and technical framework for providing payment services to Ukrainians abroad and introducing domestic services in offers of European providers of payment services. The team also involved new foreign partners in developing payment services in Ukraine.

LEO and *IBOX BANK* are growing. We have expanded by 42 employees since the full-scale invasion. It was related to entering new markets. The war has forced us to accelerate, shift to online mode even more, and pay attention to geopolitical factors in fintech and banking operations. But we faced difficulties related to the occupation of the Ukrainian territories, where we have our service users, and to our refugees in Europe. That's why our plans for the next months include expanding our presence in Europe and helping the AFU to liberate our territory and return the peace.

For us, volunteer work results in military personnel dressed and armed to NATO standards and displaced people well-supplied. We are moving toward that!

The past seven months have proved that Ukrainians are courageous, united, and tenacious. As for me, I have discovered an incredible desire to live: to live on our native land, to live with a common national idea, to live in a prosperous and free state without the vestiges of the past, to live for the sake of all Ukrainians, and build a promising future for Ukraine.

"Perhaps, we have never been so united in the history of independent Ukraine"

U.S. Secretary of State Antony Blinken was entirely accurate, "If Russia stops fighting, the war ends. If Ukraine stops fighting, Ukraine ends."

We are protecting our home, children, and future, so we are ready to fight till the last. Perhaps, we have never been so united in the history of independent Ukraine. On February 24, we realized that only standing side by side we could defeat the enemy that the entire world feared.

Plans after victory

I think, first, we will feel the incredible joy of victory. And then we'll start restoring our country! Our company entered the European market, but Ukraine has been and always will be the center of our interests. Our team works for the future. We popularize Ukrainian payment services in Europe, provide safe and beneficial payment offers in Ukraine, and attract investors to our market.

Europeans learn from us, and we adopt their experience. There is a lot of work, and we are getting ready for it!

2022.10.03.

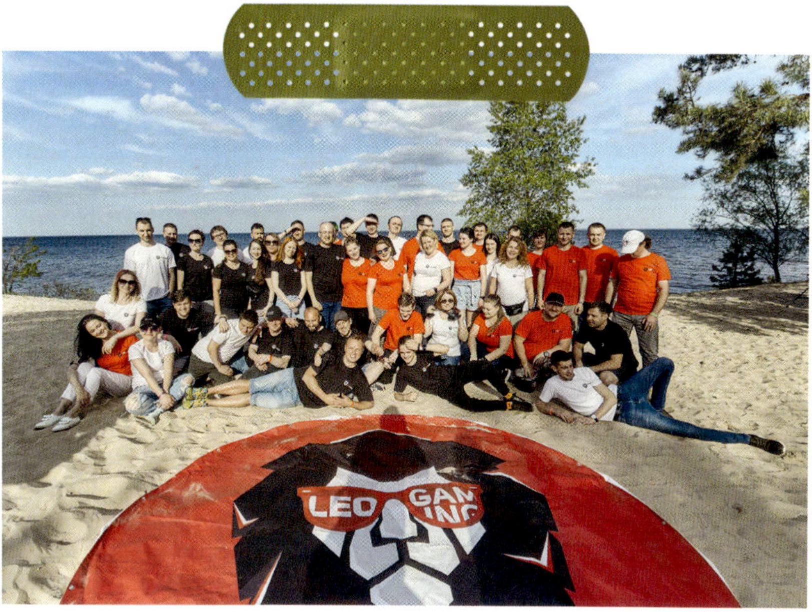
LEO GAM ING

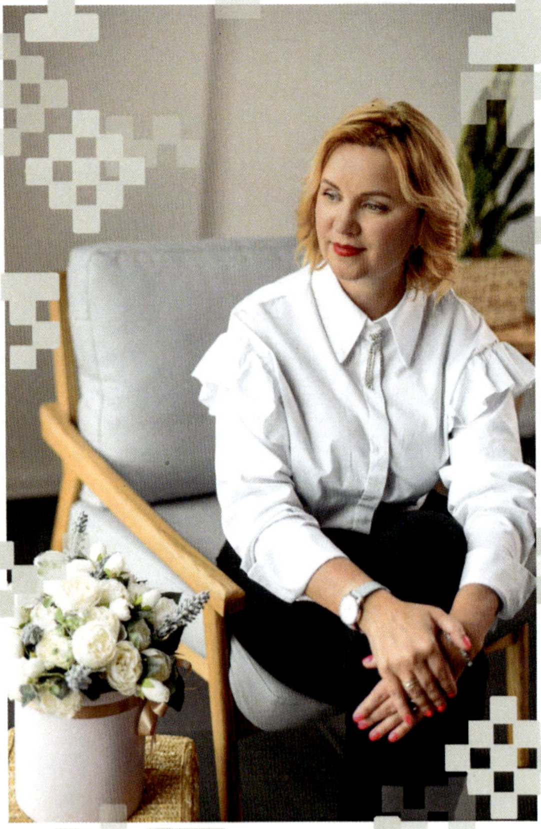

Inna Skarzhynska

Owner of the Vesna cosmetics brand

Inna Skarzhynska is a teacher and a mother of many children. She started making natural cosmetics about seven years ago when she could not find care products for her child, who had atopic dermatitis. That's how the *Vesna* (*The Spring*) cosmetics brand was created.

Healing ointment for the army

No recalling of pre-war life

We lived in a house not far from Hostomel airport. We used to go to work, gather in our kitchen at the dining table, and communicate with friends. Now it seems unreal. We try not to traumatize ourselves with pre-invasion memories. A month before the Russian troops intruded our brand entered the *Amazon* Marketplace. We were to send the first batch of cosmetics to the *Amazon* warehouse on February 24–25. Of course, we couldn't do it those days, so we postponed it for a while... I feel uneasy to recollect it, and I do not want to because we have already turned this page and live in a new reality.

On February 24, we woke up to explosions. We packed right away, got into the car, and set off. There was a general panic around, lines at the gas stations, and traffic jams, but we managed to get away because we did not hesitate. It took us two days to get to the border. First, we lived in Poland and then at a volunteer's place in the Czech Republic. My husband and my son-in-law stayed in Ukraine in Lviv Region.

When Bucha was occupied, we were doom-scrolling the news and worrying about the city. Even though it was hard, we decided we had to work even at a time like that. So my daughter and I started thinking about how we would resume our business because we were sure we would go back to Ukraine. Though, I'm grateful to the people in Poland and the Czech Republic who helped us. We keep in touch, and they even help us sell our cosmetics.

We came to terms with the fact that Russians had destroyed our products in warehouses and laboratories. We started buying raw materials and containers abroad and sending them to Lviv.

We also had a stock of our cosmetics in a store in Mukachevo, that had been opened on February 20. The money from sales was used to buy raw materials, which saved our business. Our products were in demand. When people learned that our production facilities were in occupied Bucha and we couldn't make cosmetics, they started buying our products as early as the first week of the invasion. It shocked me and inspired me not to give up. Even though our production facilities were in the occupied city, we did not stop running the business!

Having returned to Ukraine, I went straight to Bucha

I went to Bucha as soon as it was liberated on April 8. What I saw was awful. Fresh graves in the backyards, identification of bodies, fields mined by the Russians... I felt an incredible hatred for Russian troops and for everything they did. They ripped everything in their path. The whole world should scream about the genocide in Bucha.

After what I saw, it felt like everything froze inside me. I tried not to let my negative emotions affect my physical state, or it would destroy me. Your mind cannot react normally to such abnormal things. Our two premises were ransacked. Some things were stolen, some—just destroyed. Russians took large industrial equipment and small appliances, chairs, smashed microscopes, and even stole flasks and beakers. On top of that, they destroyed what they couldn't take with them. The damage is about 5 million hryvnias. The city had no water, gas, or light, so I realized I had to relocate production to resume working. Volunteers helped us transport the surviving furniture and equipment.

Our house and the house of our daughter, who lived on the outskirt of Bucha, were almost undamaged. Only the windows were broken by bullets. But the house next door to our daughter's was hit by a Russian missile and destroyed to the ground. Russians also burned down the *Epicenter* hypermarket located in the vicinity.

New production in Lviv and cosmetics delivery to the front line

We set up a new laboratory in Lviv and started working straight away.

Raw materials and containers became twice as expensive. We are looking for them wherever we can. Still, we have only increased the prices by 5 percent because we don't have the heart to sell our products at a higher price. We know our people are struggling, and we want to make excellent products for them.

We don't want to make more money; we only want to keep our business afloat. A month after the invasion began, people who had gone abroad started looking for us to order cosmetics again. We started sending our products to Poland, France, Italy, Germany, the Czech Republic, Latvia, Lithuania, and Estonia. I was worried we would lose those customers, but that did not happen.

At first, we were producing shampoo. But once, a female soldier wrote that the military had severely damaged skin on their hands and faces due to the extreme conditions. She complained that cosmetics from humanitarian aid only worsened her skin problems because they were either of poor quality or expired.

We sent her a set of remedies for free and started thinking about how we could help the others on the frontline. At first, we decided to send hand creams and sunscreens for female soldiers.

But then, we started getting letters from male soldiers that their burns and wounds were so bad that it even hurt them to shoot. So we began to send them ointments and protective hand creams. Volunteers from different organizations who went to the front line contacted us. Thanks to them, we have sent over 3,500 healing ointments bearing the inscription "You are our hero" and 1.5 thousand creams to the front line. We add letters and children's drawings to each jar.

Stories like this make me realize that we don't just make cosmetics, we make people feel safe, as strange as that may sound. That's inspiring. We realize we can't give up.

Whenever possible, we help combat soldiers and volunteers to raise funds for pickup trucks, thermal imagers, and drones.

At first, I cooperated with a volunteer who photographed our labs in Bucha. Now he delivers drones, thermal imagers, and military equipment to the front lines. There are several volunteers whom I trust and help with money for various frontline needs. One of them recently registered his charity organization. I tell them that if they don't have enough money to finish fundraising, I can always help.

Before the invasion, I wanted to build a house and work in my garden because I really loved it. Now I have no desire to set up a house because it can just vanish. I don't deem material things important anymore. What you really need is a good car because it was precisely what helped me get my family out in those terrible hours.

The only real values now are hard work and being even more sincere than before the war.

In the early days of the invasion, the only thing that saved me was that I could convince myself of anything if necessary. I tried not to show my children how worried I was but supported them instead. For example, I tried to joke with my youngest son on our way out of Bucha. Though, I clearly understood that we wouldn't have the same life as before. I told my older children that the new country was an opportunity to expand their worldview and make new friends. We neither hid the news from them nor exacerbated their fear not to traumatize them. We should not focus on suffering... stay flexible.

During that difficult time, I realized that the only safe place was my body. Even my country, my house, a bomb shelter, the Czech Republic, or Poland does not give me the desired feeling of safety as my body does. If I feel comfortable, I feel safe and should not adjust even to depressing situations but should take care of my "temple."

2022.07.27.

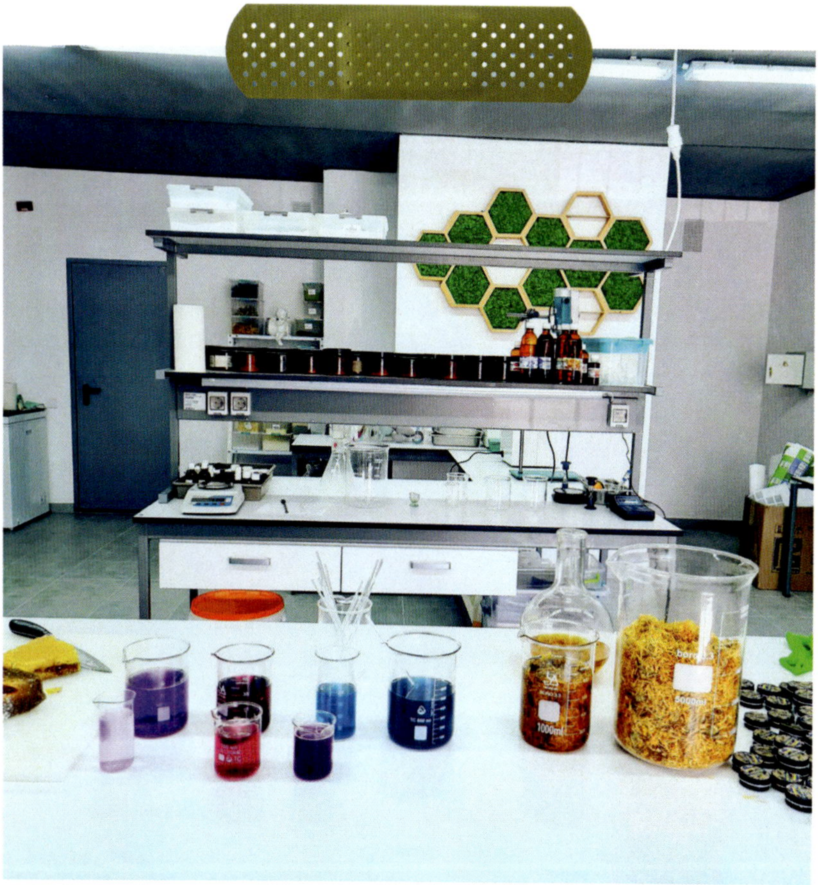

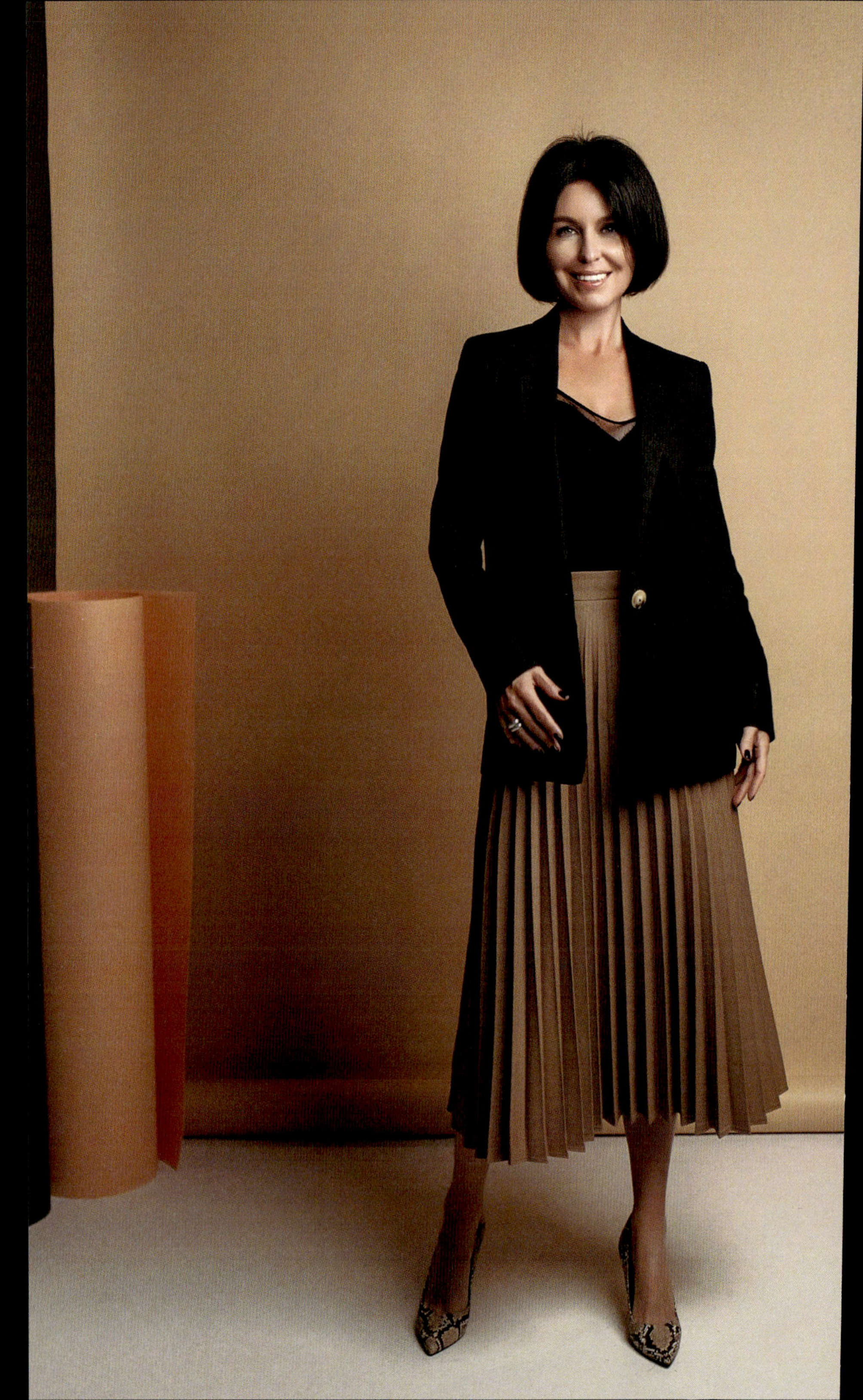

Inna Popereshniuk

*Co-founder of Nova Poshta, co-owner
of the restaurants 100 Rokiv Tomu Vpered and Inshi,
New Run brand ambassador, and founder
of the Komanda Charivnykiv, a project for orphans*

Inna Popereshniuk lives in Poltava and has not left since the full-fledged hostilities began. "Loving your country means being there for your people, taking care of your workers and your dreams, and supporting Ukrainian business," our heroine believes.

How business started supporting volunteers

On February 24, my daughter woke me up. She called me in Poltava from Kyiv saying, "Mom, I hear explosions; the war has started!" "It can't be true. It must be some kind of drills!" I reassured her. I had other concerns at the time: my family was sick with COVID-19. My daughter called again, "I hear an air raid siren. Tenants of the house are evacuating." At five in the morning, I started calling my friends.

Nova Poshta (the leading postal service in Ukraine) had already known what war was and how it unraveled. In 2014, we evacuated our employees from eastern Ukraine. Back then we didn't know what would happen but gradually developed enduring operating procedures.

On the day of the invasion, our offices in the cities, that were the first to get attacked and shelled, did not open. People were shocked and scared and tried to take their families to safer places. On that same day, we set up an operational headquarters.

The company's head office and headquarters were evacuated from Kyiv to a safer location. CEO and managers involved in operations moved with their families. In a few days we managed to sort out the logistical issues. Some branches of our network resumed their operations on February 25, though not all of them. We could not deliver parcels to certain settlements, but we continued to hand out those that had arrived before the invasion.

For instance, we were issuing parcels in Kherson to the last... On the second day of the war, we offered our corporate cars to volunteers and the military. The cars were taken away in a few hours.

The company has lost a lot: on February 26, our performance was down to almost two percent compared to pre-invasion levels. That's 30,000 parcels a day, while we used to transport up to 1 million.

We decided we would help the country and Ukrainians, so we started delivering humanitarian aid from abroad and across Ukraine within the *Humanitarian Nova Poshta* initiative. At first, we did it at our own expense. But the volumes were so large that our resources were no longer enough, so we asked for donations for fuel. We are very grateful to every Ukrainian who helped us back then and is helping us now. Donations from overseas institutions, such as the *ECCT Alliance*, were especially generous. It helped us deliver 5,200 tons of humanitarian aid. That's 81 flights from the USA and 440 cargo runs. The aid came from Poland, Romania, Turkey, France, Great Britain, Germany, etc. By the way, we joined the UN *World Food Program* in April, and now we deliver food packages to troubled areas of the country. Ukrainians have received 700 thousand of such packages from the UN.

Borscht during air raid alert

On March 7, I cried for the first time. I remembered that day because I was frightened by the air raid sirens and worried about my daughter, who was away. I slept in the basement and was afraid to leave it during the day because of the air raid alert.

Then I realized I had to change my attitude toward the news. There was a lot of different information. I noticed that *Telegram* channels gave some information or photos repeatedly, and we were horrified by the same things over and over again. I decided to pull myself together. I really like cooking. It comforts me. So I started cooking borscht. As soon as I started, an air raid siren sounded. I got mad, "When will you stop it, bastard? Let me cook some borscht!" I felt better then.

Working in the vegetable garden also helps. On the first day of the invasion, I set to plant radishes under agrotextile. I had planned this experiment back in peacetime... Quite recently, I have harvested a bountiful crop — it embodies indestructibility for me... like a new life among the ruins.

Nova Poshta at war

Two months after the full-fledged hostilities began, we managed to open half of our offices. 70–80 offices resumed their operation every day. We have 14,000 automated parcel terminals, which means around-the-clock packaging releases. In mid-April, we almost restored the whole network in Kyiv Region and launched mobile post offices in the cities where we couldn't open stationary ones. We even organized address delivery in Irpin, Bucha, Makariv, and Borodianka, which I consider a milestone event. These cities are real martyrs. I could not imagine how people would go back there. It was exciting to see how many Ukrainians volunteered to help restore order, repair roads, and fix running water and light. Starting March 1, our offices resumed operation all over western Ukraine.

We were adjusting to the war and changing formats. During the first weeks of the invasion, people sent heavy and oversized parcels, so we allowed some regular offices to work as cargo offices and accept parcels weighing up to 150 kilograms. We understood that people had to send their belongings due to the forced displacement, so we offered special conditions for the delivery of suitcases for 120 hryvnias in Ukraine and agreed with some foreign partners to deliver belongings at discounts up to 80 percent in 25 European countries.

I admire the courage of our operators who work in the post offices and drivers who often have to wait until the end of the shelling to deliver goods, including humanitarian ones. They are ready to risk their lives during the war. Just imagine: while we are sitting in shelters, these people are in the post offices, handing out and accepting parcels, loading cars, and driving parcels all over the country. I see them as heroes.

We have created a *SOS* HQ to solve any complex problem of our employees. All you have to do is call the hotline or text our chatbot. We can help with loss of housing, medical treatment, rehabilitation, evacuation, relocation, or finding new housing. Even if you need simple help with buying food, we will be there for you.

We evacuated our employees from Mariupol, Melitopol, Kharkiv, and Kherson to our terminals in the West of our country. We bought pallets and blankets and arranged places to stay. If people cannot return to their homes due to the occupation or hostilities, we help them with employment in relatively safe regions.

Two thousand seven hundred of our employees have been mobilized into the AFU. We pay them financial aid of 10 thousand hryvnias, which is 45 million hryvnias monthly.

It is an honor, not just a duty. Unfortunately, we have 38 deceased heroes. We support and help their families and have also established a fund with educational grants for their children. We have been supporting our army since the first day of a full-scale war. We allocated 25 million hryvnias straight away.

Keep calm and eat Inshe

As for the *100 Rokiv Tomu Vpered (A hundred years ahead)* restaurant founded with my partner Yevhen Klopotenko, our entire team stayed in Ukraine. In early March, we started cooking food for the AFU and the territorial defense forces and keep doing it now. We opened the restaurant for visitors right after the liberation of Kyiv Region.

Yevhen and I were planning to open a Ukrainian fast-food restaurant. We found premises in Lviv, had ideas for the interior and menu, and made a business plan when suddenly the invasion happened. At once, Lviv had to host a lot of people, mostly IDPs, who lined up at food outlets. So, let's open! But I wasn't in Kyiv back then, and the restaurant manager was temporarily away, too. Only Yevhen was in Lviv, so we opened it online. We still run our establishments remotely. Not everyone understands how to manage restaurants through Zoom meetings. But it works!

The owner of the premises in Lviv did not charge us for rent in the first month. We sent part of the Kyiv team to Lviv. After a month, we saw that the fast-food restaurant brought in more revenue than the restaurant in Kyiv. Now we are working on decorations and installing a summer terrace. I am really nervous, though, because Lviv has been under an active attack lately. God forbid an enemy's missiles hit here. But we started with crazy enthusiasm, so we hoped everything would be fine. In April, Yevhen and I opened the *Inshe (Others)* project with unusual items of street food in Ivano-Frankivsk city. We plan to create a franchise for our Ukrainian fast-food restaurant so that there will be more national cuisine establishments in the country.

Future plans and dreams

I am a responsible person. I aim at a result and demand the same from my subordinates. Everything you do should bring results. Even this interview will motivate other women to do something and show our resilience to the world. I can be sentimental and cry when I see the horrors of war. But my patriotism gives me the strength to move forward. My own version of patriotism: helping my country in difficult times, supporting people and Ukrainian businesses, and never giving up.

In order to combat dark thoughts, I go for a run. For example, I came up with my *Komanda Charivnykiv (Magicians' Team)* charity project while running. Now we send drawings of children with cancer to the front line. If you don't like running, do about 150 squats, and you'll blow the cobwebs away.

The second piece of advice is to cook delicious food. Get inspired by Klopotenko and other talented chefs, take a bottle of wine, and treat your family to delicious food.

Don't forget your dreams. It's hard to dream about anything right now. But dreams are vital; they inspire, comfort, and give hope.

Last year, I dreamed of growing tobacco. I did it and rolled wonderful cigars! But what can we dream about now? It seems there is no energy for that. But you have to find something to strive for. For instance, I really want peace in our country and to travel again. I dream of driving with my family from Poltava to the Faroe Islands. I am sure that we will do it and all our dreams will come true.

I hope and believe we will kick the enemy out of our country soon! And then *Nova Poshta* will hold its traditional running event, this time to celebrate our victory. When I look at the bombing of Kharkiv, Chernihiv, and Sumy, I realize that the squares where we rewarded the run finishers no longer exist. But we will rebuild it.

I think the recovery of our country is also in the hands of women. Our strength is in multitasking! "Indestructible" is the right word to characterize Ukrainian women, especially female entrepreneurs.

2022.05.25.

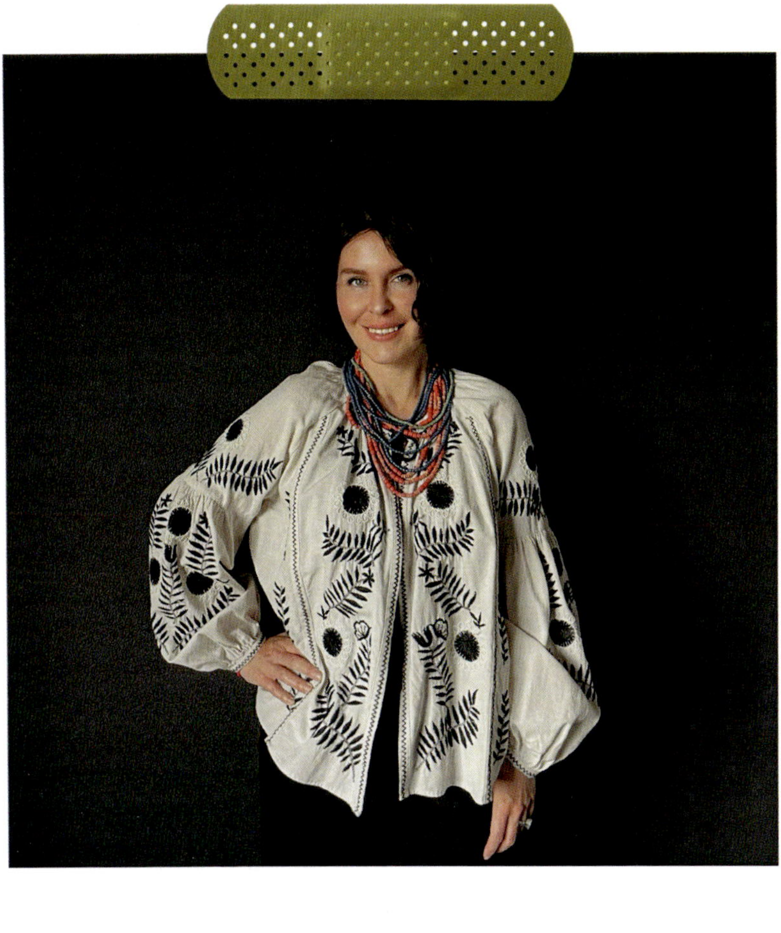

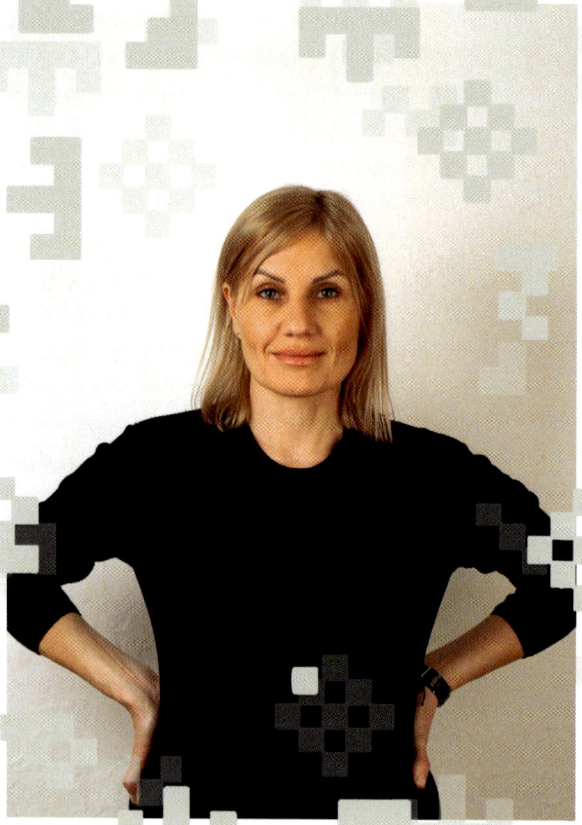

Olena Stryzhak

Chair of the Board of the Positive Women Charitable Organization

Olena Stryzhak is Chair of the Board of *Positive Women*, a charitable organization helping women living with HIV, which started helping all war-affected women and their children after the full-scale war began. The organization's coordinators are still working in all regions of Ukraine, including the occupied territories except Luhansk Region.

Antiretroviral therapy during the war

"I was wondering where to get weapons if Russians came": the first days of the invasion

Before the invasion, I worked in Kyiv and came home to Cherkasy on weekends. On February 23, I visited my friend and colleague Vira and stayed overnight at her place. I planned to go home on the evening of February 24. Vira woke me up in the morning to tell me the terrible news: the Russian invasion had started. I didn't hear the explosions myself because I was sound asleep.

We have a corporate chat room, which includes co-ordinators from all the regions of Ukraine where we work. At five in the morning, they started chatting about hearing explosions and their cities being bombed and shelled. These were employees from Kharkiv, Odesa, Dnipro, Chernihiv, Kherson, etc.

After waking up, my first thought was, "I have to call my family and get to the office somehow." We assumed all this would happen because such rumors had been going around for quite a time. Besides, actually we had been in a state of war since 2014, though it had been raging just a little further away from our regions. In late January 2022, Vira and I held training sessions for civil servants and our female activists from Donetsk and Luhansk Regions. We were in Sievierodonetsk and Kramatorsk and communicated with people living near the territories where the hostilities had been going on for eight years. When the full-scale invasion started, I realized what kind of reality was looming, and there was nothing we could do about it.

I immediately called my husband and told him that the Russians had invaded. He and our son were sleeping peacefully, and the news shocked him. I told him not to take our son to school but to turn on the TV and watch the news. Vira and I went to the office in Kyiv to get some equipment, documents, and a laptop. On the morning of February 24, I had an online meeting scheduled, which eventually took place. At 2 p. m., I was supposed to be at a meeting at the photo studio to discuss an event that was to take place on March 1. March 1 is Zero Discrimination Day, which resonates with our work because society discriminates against women living with HIV. That's why we try to raise awareness among our partners and people in general about the unacceptability of discrimination based on any criteria. Together with the *Center for Public Health* and our partners, we wanted to hold a photo shoot in T-shirts with the relevant slogans and a flash mob. The photo shoot didn't work out, for obvious reasons.

In the evening, I drove home to Cherkasy. It took me 5 hours. My friend Vira and her family came to me from Kyiv the next day.

We immediately started chatting to find out who needed help and what the situation was. We literally gave all our time to these chats and constantly kept in touch with each other. Some of us left for the relatively safe regions of Ukraine, and some for other countries. It was just the beginning of the full-scale war, so nothing had been organized yet. We only managed to arrange for therapy for our displaced women in Poland.

I think such a rapid pace helped us master all our strengths. When you are in the process and know that someone needs your help, it saves you. To be honest, I rarely checked my email in the first week because I spent all the time in messenger chats. Sometimes I got business emails and answered that I had to put off everything for a while because of the war.

I never thought about leaving the country. I only wondered where to get weapons to defend myself if Russians came into the city. I thought about protection rather than an evacuation.

First weeks of work

Back then, we kept in touch with our colleagues and coordinators, who told us what was going on in their city.

We didn't get enough sleep, provided targeted aid, visited a military aid center, and bought fuel and ammunition for the military, etc. We did not know what to focus on first; it was complete chaos.

In a week, we gradually figured out how to organize our work and managed to hold our first working meeting in early March. We started planning where to spend the available funds and what to buy.

Since I am actively involved in protecting women's rights, I take part in international events as a member of various committees. When my foreign colleagues learned about the hostilities in Ukraine, they offered help. We prepared a letter in Ukrainian and English with our details and sent it to those who wanted to help. We just needed funds because Russians destroyed almost all infrastructure in Melitopol and Sievierodonetsk, so we could only transfer funds to our coordinators if any ATMs were working there. They immediately withdrew the money and bought food and water for women. We could do that in the first weeks of the invasion. Here's what we did: we distributed funds received in our account to our coordinators. During all this time, we received about $2,500. I made an arrangement that we would send a photo report for funds, not a written report. All individuals who donated money agreed to that. So we quickly started helping women with basic needs like food, hygiene, etc.

In mid-March, we began submitting requests for funding programs. Our employee translated a project proposal into English while sitting in a basement in Chernihiv Region as they were under shelling. Then she went out to find the Internet connection and sent this proposal to us. Our initiative was supported by the

Women's Peace & Humanitarian Fund, and we launched the *Supporting Women Living with HIV in Crisis Situations* project. As part of the project, we set up shelters for vulnerable women in Ivano-Frankivsk, Khmelnytskyi, Cherkasy, and Chernivtsi. Women can get the help they need in these shelters.

We also apply for grants and accept help from partners who offer it to us in order to get funds to purchase aid. We find out which areas are better off and which need help. For example, Melitopol needs help now. We have established a way of transferring humanitarian aid there through Zaporizhzhia. The coordinator in Melitopol asks for materials to set up shelters because they are waiting for the Ukrainian military to free them from the Russians.

We did our best to make sure women received what they needed to prevent HIV. For example, we provided antiretroviral therapy and milk formulas for their children, which is one of the recommendations to prevent mother-to-child virus transmission.

From the very beginning, I told my colleagues not to deny help to non-HIV-positive women. Our primary focus is to help HIV-positive women, but now we will help any woman who applies to us. We also fulfilled our responsibilities under the projects, although some processes were postponed.

The first official meeting I attended was a meeting of the Committee on Validation of the Elimination of Mother-to-Child Transmission of HIV and Syphilis at the Ministry of Health on June 1. An important talking point was the state laws and regulations on the rights of children born during the war in the temporarily occupied territories to be registered as citizens of Ukraine. We also considered joint plans and algorithms of interaction to provide aid, milk formulas, and diapers to infants born to women living with HIV in temporarily occupied territories.

Shortage of therapy and work in the occupied territories

The most current need that the representative from Kherson told us was for antiretroviral therapy. As of the beginning of August, there were about 50 jars of it were left. It is close to nothing because HIV-positive people take these medications every day. I contacted the All-Ukrainian Network of PLWH, which also purchased and delivered this therapy, and they agreed to solve this problem. Unfortunately, two trucks with medications were shelled and burnt out before they reached Kherson. So we are looking for help again. We know that volunteers deliver small batches of therapy to meet emergency needs. But we have no current information because our representative left the occupied city a week ago with her family and does not have permanent Internet access yet.

In Melitopol, girls look for an Internet connection to get in touch every day. We have found volunteers and deliver humanitarian aid through Zaporizhzhia. Our representative says it is hard to work in Melitopol because if the occupiers see our organizations delivering humanitarian aid, they make threats. But our girls still deliver aid to women. When they need to take therapy to a village, they give it to the driver who delivers bread. It's the only way. They say that keeping in touch with us saves them. It is like a breath of fresh air while living in a vacuum and waiting to be liberated.

They have basic needs now, like housing, food, and work. We help them with that, but as this need for help is permanent, we always look for funds and bring in donors.

We're also launching a new project to help women who have suffered from sexual violence. We will have counseling centers in several regions and involve local partners so that women who have suffered sexual violence can seek qualified assistance. The topic is very sensitive, so assistance must be professional.

I still have no schedule, but then I have days off

When I think back to the beginning of the invasion, I realize I didn't even notice the days of the week. It seemed like one endless day to me. I just processed appeals and even forgot to eat.

The turning point was when my kids went abroad. My 13-year-old son's soccer coach texted that they would take the kids abroad temporarily with the soccer club. We agreed because, first, he would be able to train there, and second, it was safer that way. On March 10, I took him to Mukachevo, and then he went to the Czech Republic with his team. My 20-year-old daughter went with a friend to her relatives in Poland.

Once the kids were safe, I sighed with relief and fully concentrated on my work. I didn't have any definite schedule, but I already knew what I had to do, and I thought about nothing but work.

In June, I had my first days off, my work gradually became more structured, and the kids came back. We managed to go for walks and even to the beach.

I have been in Kyiv since April 22 and try to go home every week.

Sometimes I have too much to do and don't know how to prioritize. In that case, I stop myself, let the situation go, and things happen on their own. I let some fears go and stop thinking of the situation as a problem to be solved. I just do what's up to me and be as it may. All things are difficult before they are easy. If I get distracted, I realize that I need to rest. So be it.

You should take things lightly, do what you feel, and live in the now.

International AIDS Conference in Montreal

Two weeks ago, the 24th International AIDS Conference was held in Montreal, Canada — the largest event on HIV and AIDS in the last four years. This major conference is usually held every two years. About 25 thousand participants attend such events. The last large-scale conference took place in Amsterdam in 2018 and was supposed to be held in San Francisco in 2020 but was held online due to the pandemic. The online format didn't really work out. There were a bunch of sessions and parallel events that were hard to perceive, so I don't think that format is very effective.

In 2022, the conference was held in Montreal. According to the organizers, there were about 12 thousand participants, but at my estimate, there were about five thousand. The latest conference focuses on the decriminalization of HIV transmission. Many countries still have criminal liability for HIV transmission, which is a violation of human rights. Today, thanks to therapy and certain prevention methods, people with HIV do not transmit the disease to others. It's the same with women: if an HIV-positive woman takes medication, her newborn child will not have the virus.

The conference was also about long-acting drugs that can be taken once a month rather than every day, as is the case in Ukraine today. There was also a great deal of attention to our country. On the first day, the *Emergency Response to HIV and TB in Ukraine* session took place, where the Ukrainian delegation presented the achievements our government has made in responding to HIV during the war.

Representatives of all communities spoke about the challenges they faced because of the war and how they managed to keep providing help and services. On the fourth day, the *Inclusion Means Involvement: Community Engagement in Research* symposium was held, where I spoke about the role of female activists and women in research, best practices, and recommendations for agencies funding research related to safety issues.

There were no Russians at the conference for the first time in years, and the aggressor was not mentioned at all. There used to be a lot of Russian representatives at this event, and Russia had always been the focus of discussion but in a negative way because of its repressive drug policy, high rates of HIV transmission, etc.

On restoring resources

What helps me at work is that I recover quickly. Of course, I get tired, but sometimes six hours of sleep is enough.

My family really helps and supports me. They free me of housework altogether, giving me much additional time. I only do chores when I want to. It may be relaxing sometimes. My colleagues and friends are also very supportive. That helps me move forward.

I have always liked sports: as a child, I played basketball and liked skiing and bicycling. When the pandemic started, I began bicycling a lot because life went online, and we went out less often. I enjoy bicycling along the promenade and watching people, so I try to do it every evening. I also like walking my dog along the Dnipro River and watching movies with my family.

My friends and I went to the mountains when we were in Canada. Those experiences somewhat altered the reality we were in during the war. It was inspiring and energizing. In Canada, we met Ukrainians who asked where we were staying. We explained we were only there for a week and were going back to Ukraine. One man said it was the first time he had seen Ukrainian women returning home during the war. Now, many people are returning to Ukraine, which is a good sign.

Plans after victory

I wanted us to hold a School of Feminism this March because I participated in several schools held by the Eurasian Women's Network on AIDS. These were regional meetings with professional trainers, including from Ukraine—Olena Shevchenko from the Women's March and Nina Verbytska.

I wanted to invite them as trainers to our school, too. But when the invasion began, the money we planned to spend on the school was used to create a psychological support service for women. We conducted individual and group psychotherapy and supervision. But when Ukraine wins, we will all come together and organize this school. I've already told my girls it would happen anyway.

2022.08.17.

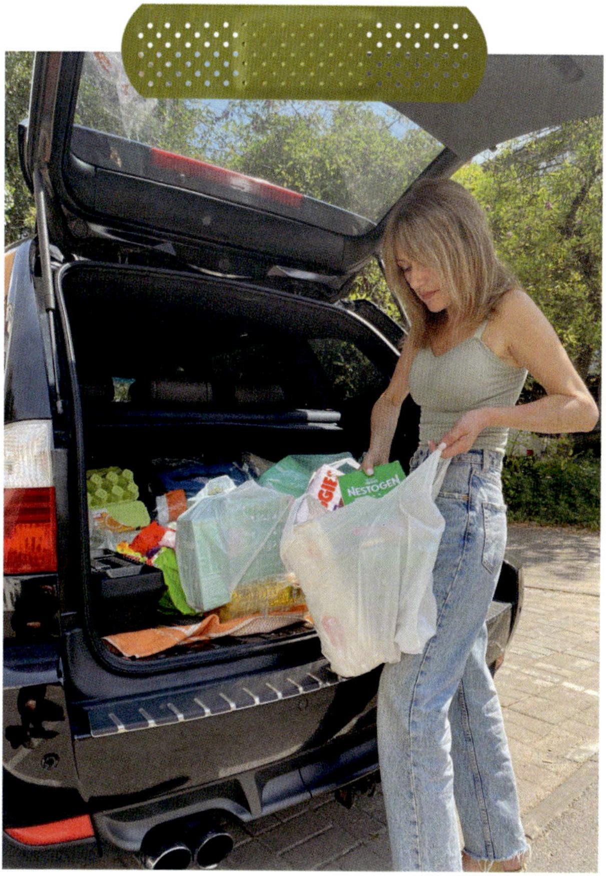
NESTOGEN

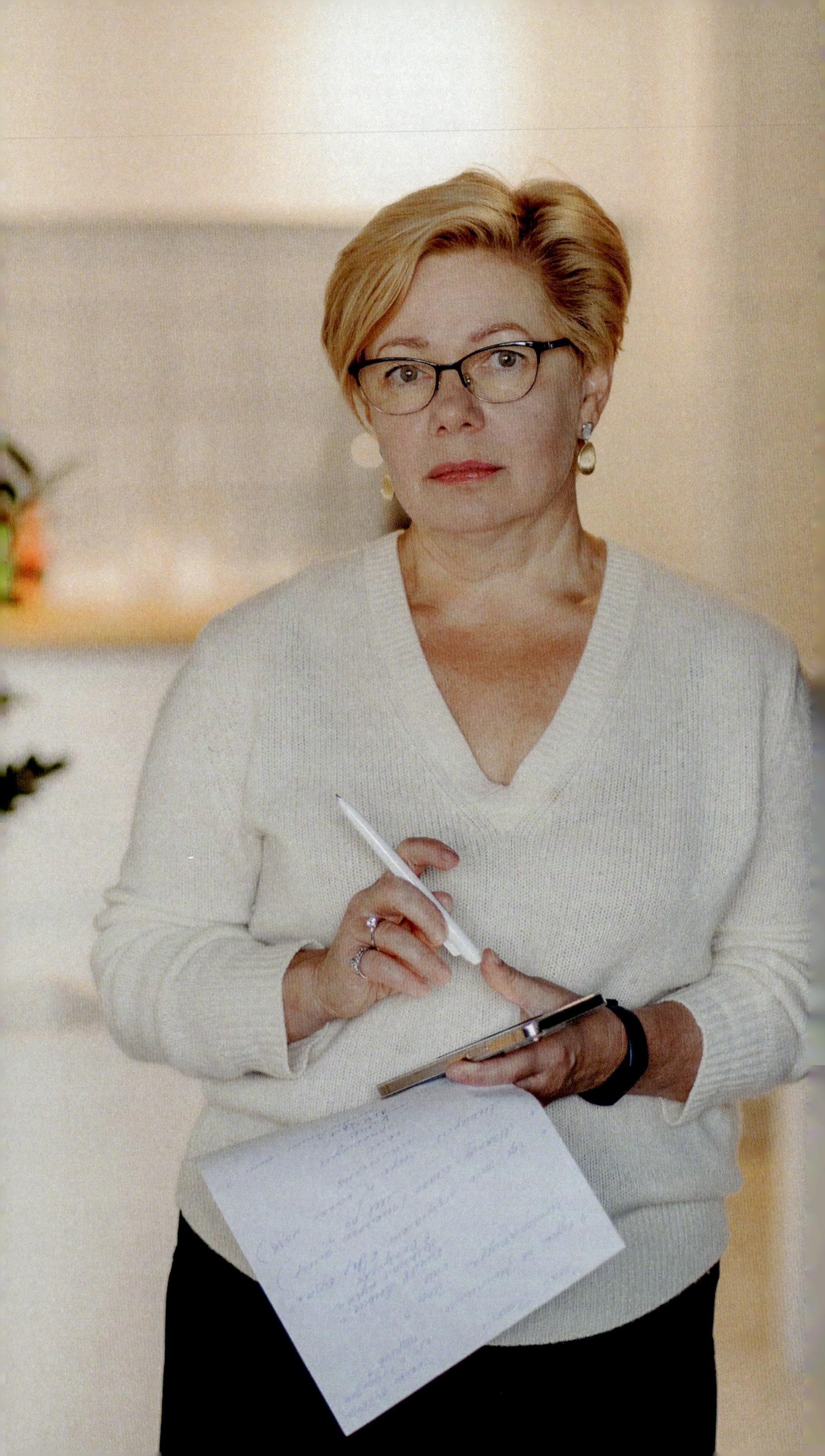

Iryna Ivanchyk

*Co-founder of the Believe
in Yourself Charity Fund*

The price of social investments during wartime is much higher, Iryna Ivanchyk, co-founder of the *Believe in Yourself* Charity Fund, believes. A person's life depends on how timely, transparent, and effective humanitarian aid is organized during wartime.
Iryna told how she managed to reorganize the fund's work, launch new humanitarian projects with an extensive network of regional hubs, and build cooperation with Ukrainian and Western donors.

From business to charity

New dimension of social responsibility

The war instantly moved all of us into a new dimension of social responsibility. Thirteen years ago, my husband Viktor Ivanchik and I founded the *Believe in Yourself* Charity Fund to invest in education. Thanks to the fund's grant programs, hundreds of talented graduates from Ukrainian villages have obtained quality education in Ukrainian and foreign universities. We provided financial support not only to students but also to teachers at the Ukrainian Catholic University and the Kyiv-Mohyla Academy.

With the beginning of the war, the philosophy of charity in Ukraine changed and set new goals for the society: to help the country stand out, survive, save, and keep Ukrainians alive. That's how *Believe in Yourself* established a separate humanitarian project, *Common Help UA*. We focused our efforts on helping war-affected Ukrainians. Subsequently, tens of Ukrainian and international partners supported us, which made it possible to scale up the project and transfer over 28 thousand tons of humanitarian aid. Over 716 thousand evacuated Ukrainians, and 407 social and medical institutions in 16 regions of Ukraine have already received our help. The financial assessment of charitable donations and humanitarian aid within the project has already exceeded UAH 575 million. The work continues.

A consistent, effective, and transparent approach to charity is a must

Charity requires a lot of resources: human, time, financial, and other. Given the scale of problems charitable foundations face now, charity is a second full-fledged job, a much more responsible one. That's why consistency, efficiency, and transparency of processes come to the forefront. We understood that from the beginning, so we considered the project design to the core. The skeleton of volunteers responsible for all the operational activities of *Common Help UA* — the work of two warehouses and eight regional hubs, fundraising, logistics, financial, legal, and IT support — included the highly professional specialists of the *Astarta* team.

Logistic chains of humanitarian cargoes from international and Ukrainian donors are maximally optimized. First, they get to the central warehouses. Then, they are transferred in equal parts to regional hubs, whose teams sort and send them to recipients based on requests from communities or civil-military administrations. Depending on the situation and the distance, delivery takes 1 to 14 days.

Our IT company, which developed a digital platform for the project, ensured transparency and accountability. Every single cargo is entered into a common database, including using a barcode reading system. The receipt of aid is accompanied by documentation, photo, and video recording. The donor receives a detailed report on each batch. It is an essential and sensitive issue. Our first international donor, the Portuguese volunteer organization *Ukrainian Refugees UAPT*, was disappointed with the cooperation with Ukrainian partners because they did not understand whether their aid really reached people. So when we received the first 40 tons of medication from them, we made a detailed report right after the handover. They were pleasantly surprised and said that transparency encouraged them to seek more and more help for Ukraine.

The project relies not only on international partners. The Ukrainian side also provides the lion's share of aid and donations. Apart from ensuring the project operations, the *Astarta* team donates a part of their salaries. Even though we conduct fundraisers, we pay a lot ourselves and transfer food and other humanitarian aid.

How to help and whom
We set clear priorities and help three categories of people: war-affected local communities, evacuated residents,

and people with disabilities. Experience shows it is impossible to be effective by spreading ourselves too thin.

We provide evacuated residents from the East and South of Ukraine with food, clothing, medicines, and education for children. We supply local communities such as Bucha, Borodianka, and Velyka Dymerka communities with food, medicines, generators, and building materials to repair what they can.

We initiated a project to provide the communities with seeds to plant vegetable plots. That way, people would have jobs, prospects, and an opportunity to support their families despite the economic downturn and the loss of their homes and jobs.

Together with Carlsberg Company, we provided the necessary products for almost 300 people living in the Paralympic Rehabilitation Center. Our regional hubs contacted the families and learned about their needs. Carlsberg made a donation that we used to buy all the necessary help and deliver it to the people.

My friend Alina Shaternikova, GBU World Champion 2005, has joined our project and involves the Ukrainian and world sports community. Together with our team, she is working on providing targeted assistance to families from Velyka Dymerka affected by the occupation.

International support

The Western world (mainly humanitarian and religious organizations) refocused its efforts on helping refugees who had come to their countries. For example, the Paris Eparchy of the Greek Catholic Church has announced that it had sent its last shipment to Ukraine and would now focus on helping the Ukrainian community in Paris.

The state will have an increasingly more significant role in receiving and distributing aid. Western countries have more trust in the government and large, well-known, and established organizations.

Small volunteer initiatives are fine as they come together and provide the required assistance. But large foundations like ours can help much more effectively.

We have logistics, warehouses, transportation, and people who can do everything fast. Besides, I believe you cannot be a volunteer only. You should work and earn money and help in your spare time. Then there is a balance.

It is possible to attract private international donors only with the help of companies with a proven track record. Our cooperation with the Swiss Embassy in Ukraine, the Danish Ministry of Foreign Affairs, the *International Labor Organization*, and the UN *World Food Program* indicates that one can trust us with their humanitarian aid and help us with donations. That's how it works, I guess.

We can say that during the nine months of the *Common Help UA* project, we managed to create a full-fledged humanitarian ecosystem that unites the efforts of Ukrainian producers, international organizations, local communities, and temporarily displaced people to assist those in need, develop local business, create new jobs for displaced people, and support Ukrainian producers and the national economy.

War as a revolution of values

War is a severe test of human will, decency, and indestructibility. Many Ukrainians find it difficult to maintain a psychological balance, and that's fine. Helping others and participating in charitable projects can return the purpose of life and make it full and colorful even in times of war. Constant learning and new knowledge will help, too.

The war was a catalyst for changing life values, especially regarding material or social status. I can say that I am already at the age when material things somewhat lose their meaning and become secondary.

People and social relations as a resource for social development come first. When it comes to any activity, I am firstly interested in its humanitarian or social component.

It is not just charitable projects but also psychological counseling, the creation of cultural space, and many other things.

War destroys the world around us. But it is also an incentive to try to change the world for the better, even more than in peacetime. That's why, along with humanitarian projects, we continue to provide educational grants for our students even during the war.

Ukraine's victory and the period of its recovery will bring us new social projects. But I am sure that the educational project, which was the starting point of our philanthropic work, will remain the most important to me. I believe that supporting Ukrainian education is a key social investment in Ukraine's future. Our task right now is to reach a global level which will help us attract more investment into Ukraine and bring Ukrainians back home. I'm sure this is how we'll cope with all the challenges and be on par with the most developed countries of Europe and the world. And maybe we'll become even better.

2022.05.19.

aksa POWER GENERATION
PORTABLE GASOLINE GENERATOR
Villager
VGP
7900S

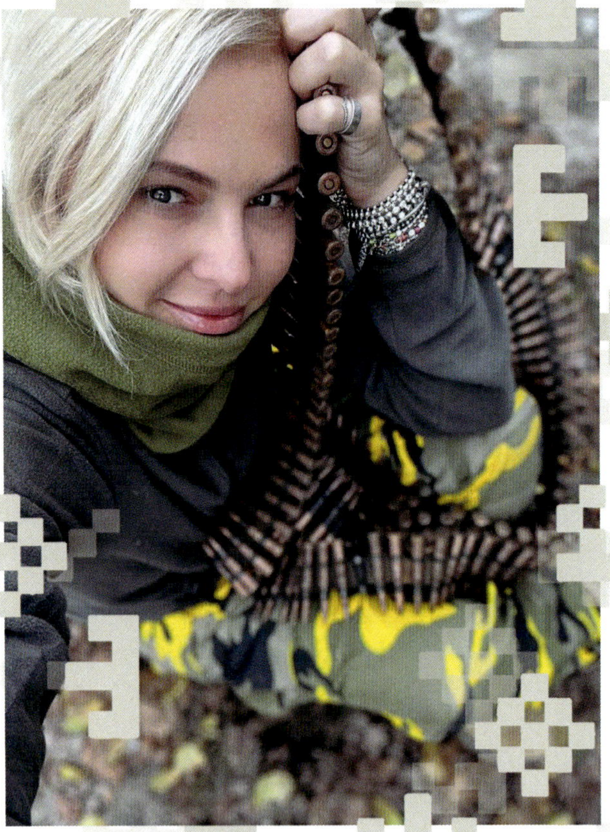

Kateryna Zirka

*Volunteer, founder
of the Buongiorno UA Foundation*

Kateryna Smirnova is a Kharkiv resident who moved to Italy a few years ago. Before the full-scale war in Ukraine, she ran her own gastroblog and worked in the tourism business. Since the beginning of the Russian invasion, she has focused on helping the military on the front line.
Thanks to her *Buongiorno UA* Foundation, Ukrainian defenders have over 12 thousand pieces of clothing, over three thousand military gear, 26 *Starlink* terminals and vehicles, eight ambulances, a mobile ICU, an all-terrain vehicle, tactical first aid kits, medical backpacks as well as vacuum-assisted closure (VAC) devices and supplies, medicines and humanitarian aid.

How to gather over 12,000 sets of clothing for the military in six months of the war

The first days of a full-scale war

At the time of the full-scale Russian invasion of Ukraine, I was in Italy. I woke up in the morning to a call from my friend Marta who told me that Russia invaded Ukraine. I was horrified.

On the first day, I was doom-scrolling Telegram channels, following the news. On the second day, I went to Vienna to participate in a rally of Ukrainians who took to the streets holding Ukrainian flags and wearing national costumes. But I realized I would not make much of sitting in Italy and going to the rallies with the flag. Crying is not for me. I thought I could be of use to my country in this war.

"When we started entering a global level, we initiated the Buongiorno UA Foundation"

We've helped with humanitarian aid since the first weeks of the invasion. I work in the travel industry in Italy, so I have quite wealthy acquaintances whom I asked to help gather several trucks of humanitarian aid. I made sure it was quality food, medicine, and clothing for children. These were our first steps. This is how a team of volunteers and those willing to help both in Ukraine and Italy got organized.

I am an organizer by nature, so these people knew I could organize any process and trusted me. I have a degree in business process management, so I know what I'm doing.

My contact details spread by word of mouth, so the military called and wrote me all the time. We decided to work in three areas. The first one was humanitarian aid delivery. The second was gear and assistance to the military. In the beginning, Ukraine experienced a shortage of helmets and body armor, so we had to look for them. Besides, the gear was of poor quality sometimes. So when we got sets of body armor, we had to test them in Italy. In case the military needed thermal imagers, we looked for exactly the model the particular unit asked for. I got wise to stuff like that rather than spending donations from people on any random thing.

The third area was medicine. I had help from people developing tactical first-aid kits for NATO. At the beginning of the war, there was a need for VAC devices used to heal large wounds and burns. It's a quite specific device that is not used in peacetime but is a must for military and civilian casualties of shelling during the warfare. We've bought quite a few VAC devices and consumables required for their proper operation. When we realized that we were entering a global level, we established the *Buongiorno UA* Foundation (which means "Hello, Ukraine" in Italian).

I came to Ukraine in May for the first time since the invasion. I couldn't come earlier because of my kids. My eldest son is a grown-up and studies at a university in another country, while my younger son lives with me, and I had no one to leave him with. When my friend Marta, who later became my partner in *Buongiorno UA* Foundation, came to me, I asked her to look after my youngest son. She agreed, even though she had three kids of her own. So I went to Ukraine to get in contact with the military, get to know their needs and find out what to deliver. I traveled across a significant territory: Odesa, Mykolaiv, Kherson, Dnipro, Zaporizhzhia, Kharkiv, and Donbas. I also visited the front line.

The military feels the need for cars now. We not only buy and deliver many cars but also repair them. No one wants to repair cars because people are happy to donate to something big and beautiful to have a good report later. Besides, I spend a lot of time on the front line, so I am well aware of the needs of the military. And one of those needs is car repairs.

We also get a lot of drones for our defenders because they're badly needed right now. We have drone instructors as our partners who come to the front line and teach soldiers how to operate this equipment. We buy a lot of medicines. We even have our own daily production of tactical first-aid kits because such kits and backpacks are required all the time. The combat officers say the backpacks we buy in Italy are the best. We have two types of backpacks: the classic one and the big one, which I call "the over-the-shoulder hospital". We give the latter to medical professionals who know how to use it.

"The thirst for victory keeps me going at times when I'm tired and feel absolutely done in"

In the first months, an adrenaline rush fueled my work: I woke up at 8 a. m. and went to bed well past midnight. But then I felt that my body could not cope further without days off, so I started running. I have been doing sports all my life, and running is what I like most. When I'm in Italy, I try to run 10 kilometers a day. It helps me recharge. I spend my free time with kids because they give me a lot of energy, support me, and are proud of me, which is of great importance to me. The thirst for victory keeps me going at times when I'm tired and feel absolutely done in. I wake up in the morning and realize

I can do it and have to move on. We have to get through it to spare our children from having to do it instead of us.

Being hyperactive helps me not fall by the wayside. Nothing is impossible for me. If something came up that seemed impossible, it only made me more interested in making it real. I don't have fear. There was a time in my life when I was afraid to die, but after working with a therapist, that fear vanished.

I move forward, and if I have a goal, I will reach it. My goal now is prosperous, great, and unitary Ukraine.

You can cry, you can call your friends and complain looking for getting comforted, you can open a bottle of wine, you can eat a dessert, you can go for a run, you can sleep. But in the morning, everything changes. When everything goes wrong, I can whine, put things off until the next day or for a few hours, and then deal with them anyway.

War is terrible. Everything happens very quickly in war, both good things and bad things. Everything is fast-moving. So if you really want something, you get it.

My social circle changed a lot during the war. I only communicate with the military, partners, foundation employees, and medics because I have no time for friends. My friends know what I do, so they understand everything. They text me more often and ask how I am doing and what I need right now because I mostly text them when I need something for our soldiers. We will communicate as usual after the victory.

Fundraising

It happened once that everyone got tired, both those who needed help and volunteers. On the bright side, only idea-driven volunteers stayed, who figured out a way to find funds and continue the work despite the downturn in donations.

We work in two ways. First, we receive funds as a foundation from large patrons in Europe and Ukraine. Some of them just cover our needs. They may call me and ask what the Foundation needs now. I answer that we have a bill for 10 thousand Euro for tourniquets. And they transfer the money to our account.

Second, we have urgent needs: say, a car for the military because the previous one was destroyed. In this case, I use social media.

I used to run a gastronomic tourism blog called *Totallyitaly* on Instagram and Facebook and had several thousand followers and friends. Almost 10 thousand users on Facebook and about 80 thousand on Instagram follow me. So I use this resource to post about the army's needs and ask to raise a certain amount of money in a few days. So far, we have been able to fulfill all requests.

"After we victory, we'll have a lot to do"

In Italy, I took a military *TCCC* course, meaning Tactical Combat Casualty Care. I went to Rome, where my Italian military friends developed a personalized course for me. They knew what I was doing, so they let me use their military base to get the necessary knowledge. The first part of the course had practice, theory, and partial reproduction of scenarios. The second one, which I am going to take, offers the simulations of military scenarios when you have to save a person's life in certain settings.

I want to pass this experience on to our defenders, who often arrive at the front line unprepared because of the lack of time for that. My dream is to do a project where instructors would train the military at the front line on how to provide medical care to the wounded during combat. Big cities like Kyiv offer similar initiatives and opportunities to take such courses, but I'm talking about small towns and villages.

I also want to develop the foundation to have more patrons. Now I'm in negotiations with our partners. I have a friend and an assistant in Europe, Andrii Prokhorov, who developed Ukrainian games *Stalker* and *Metro 2033*. He helps us a lot, particularly in looking for patrons. We're bringing in Ukrainians who are now in Europe and can help. After we win, we will rebuild Ukraine using the skills and contacts we've acquired.

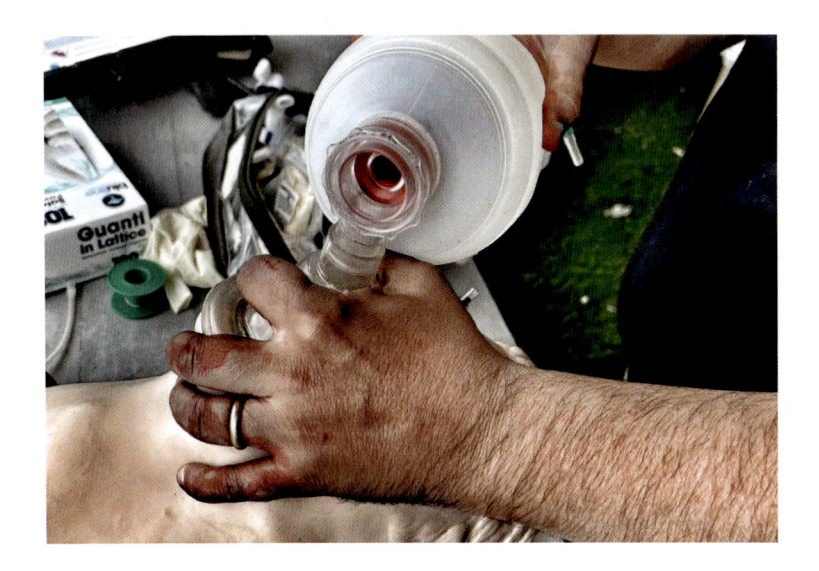

There will be a lot of psychologically affected people who need help. After the victory, I want to open free rehabilitation centers for war veterans. I'm talking about the military because I know them better and work with them more than with civilians.

Some time ago, we started working with people who returned from the front with injuries such as loss of limbs. But we temporarily postponed this project for some reasons. I still want to get involved in helping these people in finding prosthetics. So we keep working for our soonest victory.

2022.10.18.

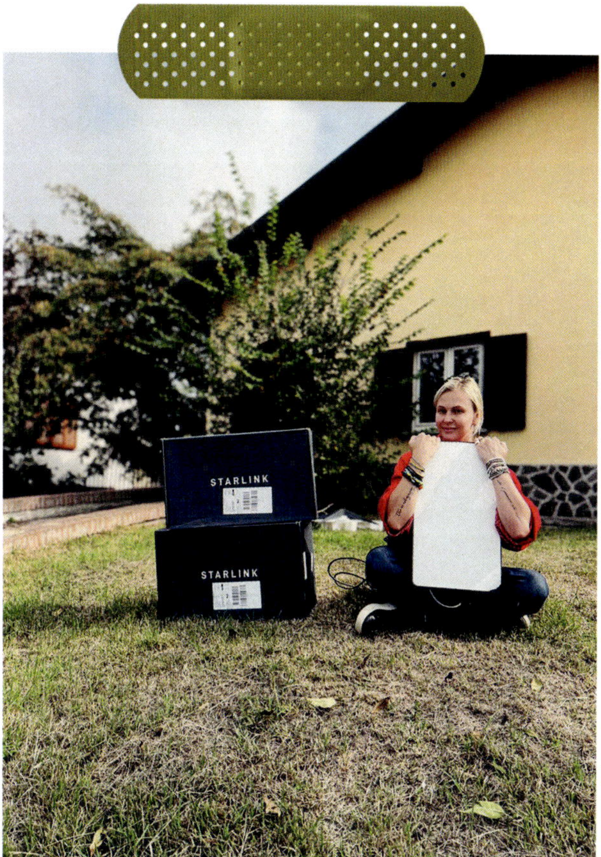
STARLINK
STARLINK

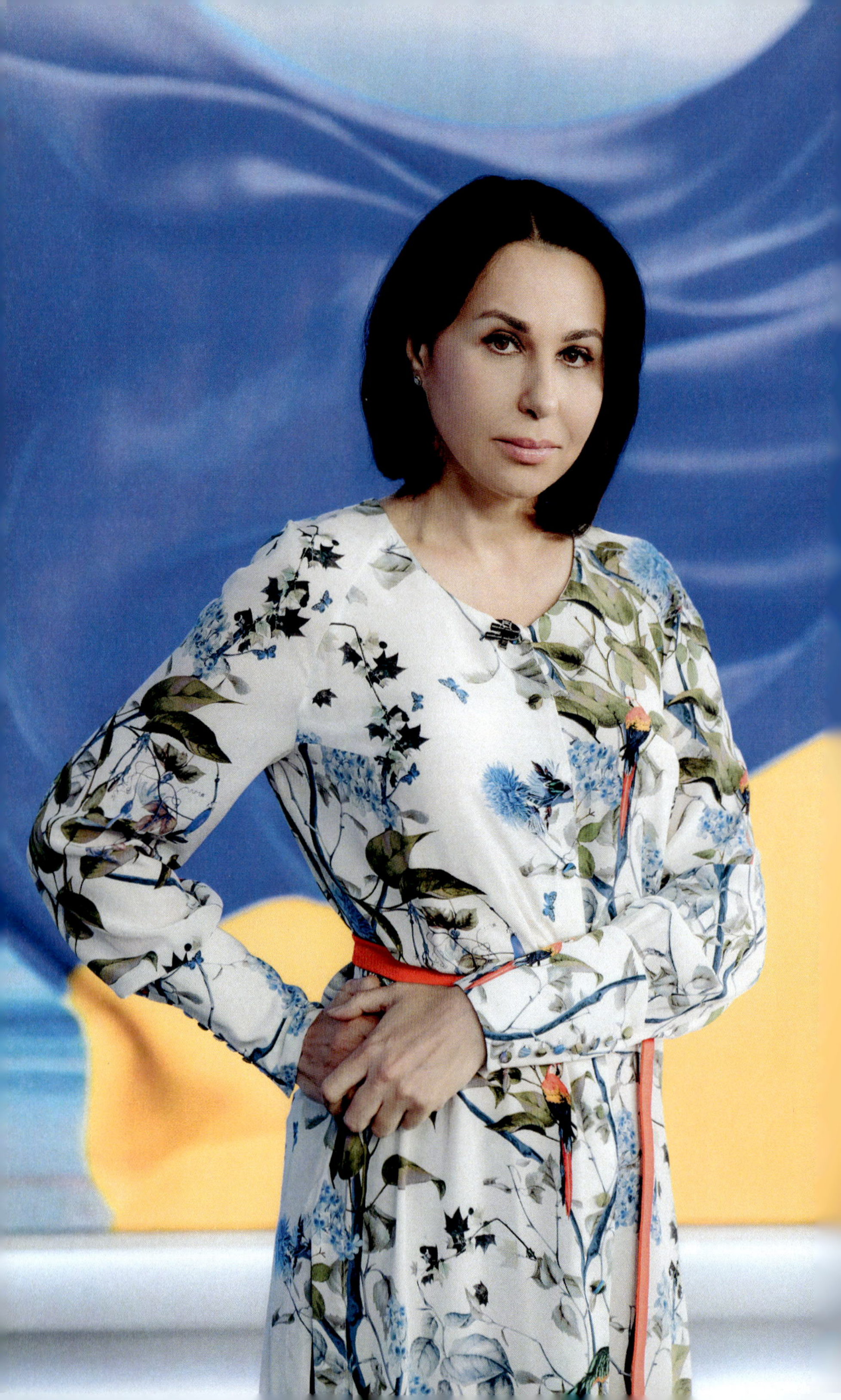

Nataliya Moseichuk

TV hostess

Nataliya Moseichuk is a TV hostess of *1+1* TV channel and *United News Marathon*, YouTube blogger, monitor of the *Right to Education* project, *Superhero School*, and the nationwide *Global Teacher Prize Ukraine*. Here she recalls the premonition of invasion, the focus of the news in February 2022, the fight against fakes and threats. Also she tells us about the wartime censorship she had to master from scratch, about the values that united us in the early days of the war, and about the motivation to fight.

The indestructibility gene is in our blood

**Before the invasion:
plans and premonitions**

Newsrooms naturally have a bit more information than the average person. It came from different sources and was very controversial. So the reactions of our staff were no different from those of the citizens. Some believed in the invasion and psyched themselves up for it. Others said this was a fake and that Putin was getting on our nerves.

There was no shortage of fakes from Russians that seemed like viral diseases attacking both political parties and citizens. That is why we needed a TV show that would get across what was really going on. *1+1* TV channel made such an offer to its viewers before the invasion. I'm glad we felt such a need back then. So when I hear somebody saying, "No one warned us!", I'm frankly surprised. All we talked about every night was the possibility of an invasion. We warned people over and over again to get their documents, necessities, and medicines packed. There is nothing noble about Russians, so we shouldn't expect them to warn us about the warfare. Intelligence data is always a ballpark estimate. "Anything can happen" was our main message to our viewers. We have to be prepared.

There was an escalation phase right before the invasion when we decided to make a TV marathon, a series of broadcasts on *1+1*. We combined two projects, *The Right to Power* and *Your Evening*. Yehor Hordieiev and I had experts, politicians, statesmen, and opinion leaders in our studio every evening. Back then, we considered it our duty to be with the audience. We discussed the probability of certain events and what all of us should do. I have always liked the idea of a round table at which experts and power holders can discuss and develop ideas. This is how we tried to work: to support and provide maximum information and expert opinion.

I remember the last broadcast on February 23. We had an MP from Luhansk Region, Viktoriia Hryb, and Oleksii Arestovych in our studio. Back then, the Ukrainian parliament introduced a state of emergency due to the escalation in the East of Ukraine. After the broadcast, I asked Oleksii whether the situation was that difficult. He believed an offensive was imminent.

I am not prone to panic. I got home deep into the night after the broadcast, scrolled through the news feed, and went to bed. Two hours later, I heard the first explosion. It seemed it was just around the corner. We lived not far from where the Russians had attacked, so the explosions were distinct. I remember myself saying, "The war." And I posted on social networks: "War". Just one word...

The invasion: first weeks

I had no hesitation about leaving or staying. On the first day of the full-scale invasion, I was going to work. But I told my parents right away that they had to leave. Two wars for one life are too much. It wasn't easy to talk them into leaving. Dad flatly refused at first. But I packed their things, made them get into the car, and told them to leave. On February 24, I had a broadcast of *The Right to Power*. I remember it well: Pavlo Klimkin, Fedir Venislavskyi,

Julia Tymoshenko, Oleksii Arestovych, Yevstratii Zoria, mayors Terekhov and Martsynkiv, Serhii Rakhmanin, Valentyn Hladkykh. The gunnery was heard everywhere as Russians were advancing from all around.

At the beginning of the broadcast, I said, "They're not going to win anytime soon. They're not going to win at all."

On February 25, as I was planning to go to work, I got a phone call saying that bridges towards Kyiv had been blown up and it was impossible to get to the city. I was instructed to take alternative route. Some other employees also received the same instructions.

That's how our evacuation to the West of Ukraine began. The day lasted forever for me. It seemed like it was 24 hours multiplied by three. It took us ten hours to get from Kyiv to Zhytomyr. You could actually walk next to your car because a stream of cars was moving at 10 kilometers per hour. Many cars were parked on both sides of the road; some gas stations were out of gasoline. People walked with backpacks over their shoulders, rode bicycles, and some brought their cats and dogs along and gave them water during stop-overs. It was a nerve-wracking quest.

I was just stunned by how everyone behaved: no one was pushing one another, no one was breaking the rules, and no one was fighting in the gas lines. People were tolerant and united, sympathetic and helpful. In short, it was a human sea of horror. We had no idea back then that this road from Kyiv would turn from "the road of horror" into "the road of death" in a few days.

While following the situation on TV, we came across a report from Stoianka village by my fellow *TSN* journalist Oleksandr Zahorodnii. And we lived nearby: in the area near Irpin, Vorzel, and Bucha. Seeing the familiar road dotted with shelled cars and burnt bodies of women and children was unbearable.

In the first weeks of the invasion, I tried to do my best on the air to get across to people that the Russians wouldn't steamroll us, they wouldn't destroy us, we were all fighting, the political leadership was on the same side as the people, the AFU was holding firm. It was very important to convey this message. And it was important to really believe that. If you believe what you're saying, people will believe, too.

Now I get messages from people saying, "Nataliya, thank you for being with us and for being on the air in the first days." And I realize what a great job all the anchors of the national marathon did.

We won't be able for a long time to wrap our minds around everything we all managed to do back then... I mean all the people, the military, the territorial defense, the volunteers, the country leadership, the TV people. We can't appreciate it yet because we are living it now. Over time, we will give ourselves an "Excellent" grade. We were at our best as a nation. I am beginning to miss what we were like in the early days of the invasion.

Whether I had strength was not in question back then: you just have to work. That's why I really wanted to go on the air. My emotional state was far from normal. I felt anger and hatred rather than worry. These feelings overwhelmed me. That was what I felt on the air: terrible anger and humiliation. It felt like they were trying to crush me. I knew what they were trying to do to our country. I also had a frantic desire to survive.

We began to work under military censorship. Or rather started to learn to work like that. That was the main difference from working in peacetime. In the context of war, every word and every frame were important. Channels united into one nationwide marathon to start joint broadcasting.

As for values... In the last 30 years, we have managed to adopt certain values that unite us all. And they came in handy in the early days of the invasion. These values gave us a powerful impetus to fight for freedom, identity, and ourselves.

I started my YouTube channel in March. Since then, I have almost 300,000 subscribers, although I still feel a bit uncomfortable asking them to press a bell icon and like the videos. I'm a TV person, so I've mastered a new format right before my viewers' eyes. What makes life easier for YouTubers only makes it harder for TV people. I had days off between broadcasts, although before the invasion 24 hours a day were just not enough to do all work planned. Besides, I really wanted to be there for people, let them listen to wise speakers, and uphold their spirits. So YouTube has become a new platform for opinion exchanges. We started making videos right in the office kitchen. And I still don't make my videos in a TV studio. I follow the rules of TV format, though, so we adjust the light and set up the special sound.

I publish exclusive weekly videos, comments, expert opinions, appeals, and petitions on my page. My videos have got over 20 million views since I created the channel. Interviews with Volodymyr Povorozniuk, Valerii Kur, and Angela Pearl reached over one million views.

I try to invite people who will give viewers points to ponder. We should listen to the pundits to make our choice. Right now, we are in search of our own unique path and audience. We are also looking for new and interesting guests. I am very grateful to the viewers for their comments, suggestions, and criticism. Several videos have already reached a million views. There's a certain paradox, though, in that people don't rush into watching videos with experts whose opinions I find most valuable, such as the linguist Pavlo Hrytsenko or the historian Yaroslav Hrytsak. These people really inspire me to think deep.

The invasion: 100 days

The full-scale war made me cast off illusions regarding friends and enemies. The war has torn off the masks and even rendered enemies some of our relatives who do not share our values. Our social circle has narrowed to people who head for victory and see no other way. I have become more violent, yet sentimental. I hate our enemies and love our people.

Adapting to war may be challenging when you have children and parents of venerable age. You are always on your toes because the war goes on. The fact that we can move around Kyiv freely right now doesn't mean the city is no longer at risk.

Adaptation is out of the question when you live knowing that you might get hit by a missile or a bullet. War is war.

The same emotions, the same order of life. I feel sorry for every city, for all suffered Ukrainians, for mothers, wives, and children of our guys who are now defending us at the front. The unspeakable horror. Pain. Rage. Hatred.

Volunteer projects

We continue and expand our work with schools in hospitals. Teachers come to the little patients because they want to learn.

Schools of Superheroes resumed their work in Kyiv, Kharkiv, and Zhytomyr. We hope we open a *School of Superheroes* at the Cancer Institute in Kyiv. But now we focus on providing psychological help to young patients and on training and extending the network of educational psychologists. For example, Ohmatdyt Children's Hospital now has many children, who were wounded, who experienced all the horrors of the Russian invasion, and who saw the death of their parents with their own eyes. When the girl who managed to get out of Mariupol says she wants to revise for exams no matter what, you realize how wise our children are. And you want to support them, inspire them, teach them to overcome adversity, rise to the occasion, and grasp for every chance.

Our teachers are the real heroes in that regard. They are outspoken, good, and sincere. They are holding the educational front with courage. And it makes me happy that despite the war, we will honor teachers in my nomination, "Following Your Heart," within the nationwide *Global Teacher Prize*. This year, together with the *Right to Education* project, we want to honor an educational psychologist who works with war-affected children.

(As the ones who heal children's hearts, psychologists have an incredible workload now and need special attention). We also want to honor homeroom teachers who, despite the bombing, did not leave their students, set up online work, and supported their children all these days. We are now looking for such stories to share with all Ukrainians.

I would especially like to note our state of mind, which is far from normal. It is important to take care of our mental health and that of our children. In September, the *Order of the Phoenix* psychological support project will launch a training course for psychologists and educational psychologists and a crisis help program for children and teachers in hospitals and educational therapists. We provided funding to launch the course with the *Right to Education* team and the *OneUkraine gGmbH* partners. It is a free online training course certified on the *EdEra* platform. The course is about children's souls, love, care, and invaluable support.

Threats and family support during the war

I did not pay that much attention to this episode of the war because there were far worse episodes. But the threats and accusations were insulting, especially those concerning my parents. The threats to my mother were beyond cynicism and morality. In Soviet times, my mother taught the Russian language, reading, and mathematics. There were many Russians among her students. They are about 50 years old now. She taught in Hungary and Germany, where my dad had served at the time. Mom taught the children of pilots. They must have followed in their parent's footsteps to become commanders. So, I appealed to the Russians, hoping they would understand that they were bombarding their first teacher, who taught them nothing but good. I sincerely wished that my appeal would stop these pilots. Or that their wives or children would stop them. I made it clear that they were committing terrible crimes and would surely pay for that. Ukraine will avenge its children. It will!

I despise people who build their reputation by hating someone. It always hurts when someone puts more resources into hating and harassment than, for example, into helping the front or children. I call them parasites. It would be better to work and do more than the one you hate, despise, and offend.

It's important to remember that you don't always have to pay attention to little fish swimming next to the big one. We should focus on our common task and goal: victory.

Ukrainians do not care about the aggressor's special services and the fact that they initiate some criminal cases. It's our neighbor's own funeral. We mind our own affairs. That's what our mindset is.

The indestructibility formula and motivation

The formula of Ukrainians' indestructibility resides in our faith. We all believe in victory! And we realize we don't have a second string. Many Ukrainians have lost their homes and jobs. And yet, they strive to live and make money in their own country. It makes a difference. All Ukrainians are fighting for their country. End of story.

Female volunteers have the courage that comes from an inner strength that no one has ever suspected. It is a courage that has yet to know its limits. It is a power that has not yet shown its limits. These women are holding on and will stand their ground, and so will the front and the AFU.

My primary motivation is life, which is the same for everyone. I want to live in a beautiful European country which had to see and live through a lot. I wish the days in Ukraine belong to the elderly and youth. It's when the elderly sit in the cafés of Uzhhorod, Kyiv, Sumy, Chernihiv, Krolevets, and Zhytomyr in the daytime and then give place to young people who come to the same cafés after work. I wish for such a change of generations, for a lot of smiles, and for people to be happy with themselves, their environment, and their country. For people to be proud. We have one more step to go. We have to win and stay united. Not much, yet so hard...

2022.08.30.

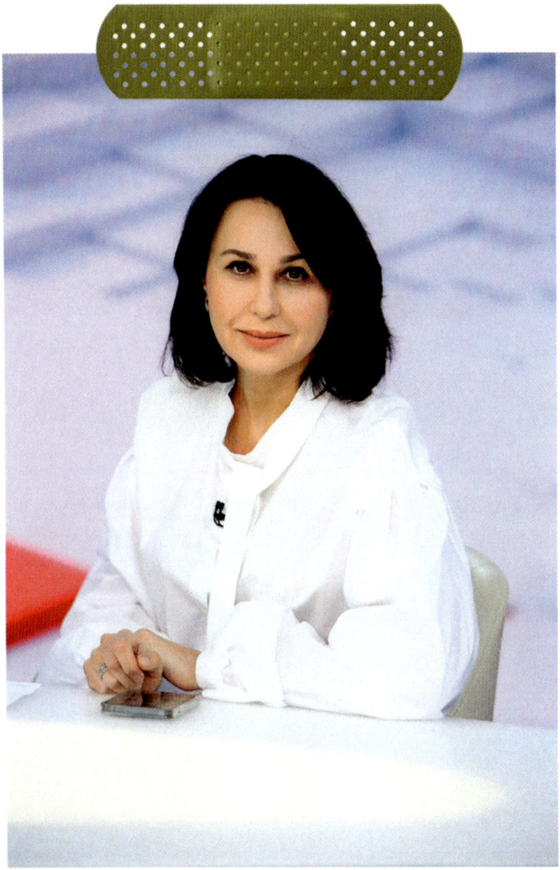

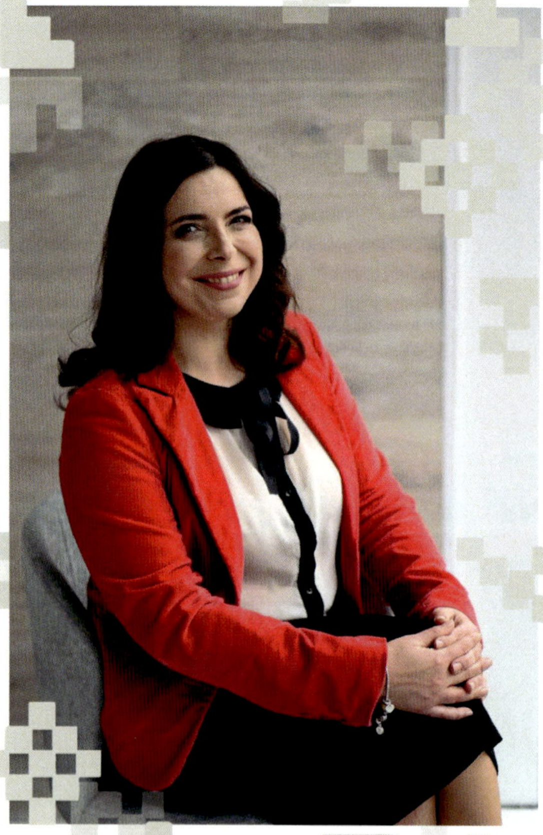

Oksana Misiura

Volunteer

Volunteer Oksana Misiura has been helping the military since 2014. It's when the war started for her. She and her sister chose the most complex areas: tactical medicine and optics delivery. She also started a uniform and eco-bag business.

The importance of optical systems in combat

For me, the war started in 2014, and that's when I engaged in volunteering. Over the years, a lot has changed in my career and business. I ran the *Veneto* company and founded a new business in partnership with Oleksandr Sokolovskyi (founder of the *Textile-Contact* company) just under a year ago. We launched a new brand of eco-bags, *TakaSumka*, and specialized uniforms, *TK Uniform*. Production was at a standstill in the first months of the full-fledged invasion. We have already resumed work and stuffed up to make up a lot of military uniforms and gear.

Like most people, I learned about the full-scale invasion at 5 a. m. on February 24. We all woke up to loud explosions near Kyiv. I realized that a large-scale war had begun. It was terrifying to hear the roar of fighter jets and helicopters, explosions, and air raid sirens. It reminded me of 2014 straight away. Except back then it had been happening far away, and now it's right over your and your children's heads. We left Kyiv pretty quickly. Now, my family is in a relatively safe place in Ukraine, and I am engaged in delivering drugs for tactical first-aid kits and optics for our military.

I believe optics and medicine are the most complex areas that require knowledge to procure medical devices, transfer them, and provide training courses. I knew many people would prefer to buy cars or boots as it was much easier.

In 2014, I was terrified to hear from soldiers that they used four tourniquets for one person who lost all limbs as a result of Grad shelling. It was shocking, so I decided I would take on that. Besides, I had some experience in wound care after the Revolution of Dignity. At first, I bought whatever the guys said. But I searched into the matter and got versed in it myself. I also learned from paratroopers from the 95th and 25th brigades, who had expertise in weapons and accessories.

We knew what a NATO-style first aid kit was and bought everything we needed in the USA. Our friends transferred it in suitcases by airplanes, and we kitted it out: tourniquet, bandage, hemostatic gauze, and film to stop pneumothorax.

In 2015, the Defense Ministry decided to create Ukrainian first aid kits, so the AFU was well supplied with them around the end of 2016.

Just like before, each volunteer does what they can and understand. For example, knowing that we were short of hands and money, I decided I would take on complex matters. My team can buy body armor and helmet for those in need. Still, our priority is tactical medicine and tactical equipment (thermal imagers, optics, laser rangers, night vision devices, scopes, etc.). We focus on preserving lives and increasing the combat effectiveness of our army.

On the cost of the first aid kit

A low-budget Ukrainian NATO-style first-aid kit costs 80–100 dollars. A unit has 60 soldiers, so we need 6 thousand dollars to provide all of them with first-aid kits. The American or Swiss tactical first-aid kit has the same equipment but is of higher quality, so it costs about

200 dollars. A tourniquet alone costs 30–50 euros, depending on where it was purchased.

One backpack for a tactical medic (and a unit has at least two of them) is worth 5–6 thousand dollars, which is quite an amount.

On army supplies as of February 24

By the time of the full-scale invasion, all active units were equipped in full. So we provided first-aid kits mostly to mobilized soldiers. The problems were the same as in 2014, but then again, you have to replenish first aid kits. Let's say you have a tourniquet, and your comrade-in-arms is wounded and doesn't have one. You will use yours. Combat medics must have a bunch of tourniquets, systems, IVs — everything you need to stabilize a wounded person and get them to a hospital. The need exceeds what the army can provide, and that's where volunteers come in. The military also needs helmets, body armor...

Some volunteers take care of a separate unit because they have, say, a brother there. So they supply everything that the unit needs: uniforms, collimators, etc.

We've been working since 2014, so we have a lot of units. We use all our contacts to provide soldiers with what they need. We also take under our wing newly formed units that apply to us.

"Guys have zero experience now": providing first aid

Experienced professional soldiers, who have been at war since 2014, know how to use a first aid kit and help themselves. They have learned that either from volunteers, paramedics, or through their own experience. Now, guys have zero experience, which is not good because you can't just give them a tourniquet — they need get instructed how to use it.

There are actually two of us on the team: Anna and me. Large volunteer foundations cover large needs, and we continue to work with our guys from the 25th and 95th brigades.

Anna Varich has a lot of experience in teaching how to provide first aid to yourself or a wounded comrade-in-arms on the battlefield. That's what she's doing now.

The Defense Ministry had eight years to teach the military how to provide medical care but, unfortunately, never did it. When we tried to call attention to it, no one listened. By NATO standards, soldiers learn this for over a year until applying a tourniquet and clearing the airway become their second nature. But we haven't done it, and our soldiers must learn it now.

On post-victory plans in volunteering

I hope that after our victory, I will bring the issue of tactical medicine to the state level. At least, I really want to do it. Tactical medicine is the kind of paramedicine you may need anywhere, including in a car accident. People shouldn't just watch a person bleed to death but should help save her or his life.

For example, my car first aid kit changed after 2014 because I realized that the Corvalol and Analgin that used to lie there were complete nonsense. My present first-aid kit can really help save a person's life. I've already had some bad cases when I managed to stabilize a person and waited for an ambulance.

It can happen anywhere and to anyone, so we should know how to help. I would like to see a mandatory first aid course in high schools and universities so that students can develop the basic skills in providing pre-hospital emergency care. People die not only in war. So we all should know how to provide medical help, for example, in case of a heart attack or epileptic seizure.

It is also necessary to take the production and strategic programs of tactical first-aid kits for the AFU under public control. We have manufacturers who have made great progress in 8 years but found themselves without assets, government orders, and raw materials at the beginning of the invasion. It is unacceptable whatsoever. I think the Defense Ministry had not created any strategic stock of tactical first-aid kits.

On the funds and necessary components for first-aid kits and optics

It's great when volunteers ask what to buy. Otherwise, they may buy something useless or of poor quality. Of course, they do so because they want to help. But such an approach may result in delivering tourniquets that don't stop bleeding or tear or plastic helmets that may be shot through with traumatic weapons.

We've had the same suppliers in Europe since 2014. We had a chance to purchase hemostatics and materials for field surgeons quickly. We gave them to different organizations: to *Shpytal Maidanu*, to *Pravyi Sektor* medical professionals, and to medical professionals from our AFU units. People help us with this. After all, volunteering is a bit of a brain and a lot of hands. Ukrainians inside our country and abroad really do everything they can: give funds and help find everything we need.

Now Ukraine comes short of everything. For example, some military unit makes a list: 30 sets of body armor, 30 helmets, 5 thermal imagers, 12 walkie-talkies, etc. You read this list and realize you need 200–300 thousand euros! And that's just one subunit. It is impossible to cover this by and at the cost of volunteers, so you should set the priorities. We decided that the army provides the weapons, and we provide the optics for these weapons to work effectively.

Foreign foundations are not very helpful in supplying optics. They play it safe and want to help, for example, only children. And I need our soldiers to score a hit. So does the military. Diaspora in Manchester, New York, and Switzerland help pay for optics.

Back in 2014, we established the *VulykUA* Fund, but it was just a formality. We had to do it because Western foundations tended to help a certain organization, not just some volunteer named Oksana.

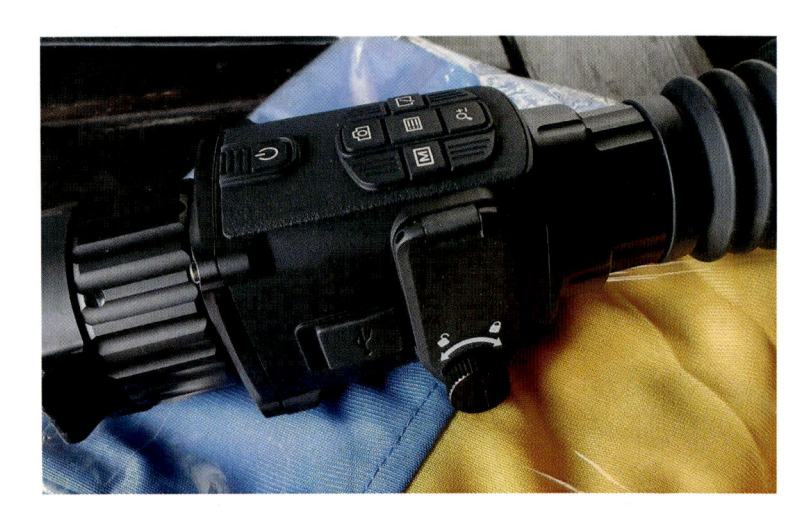

In fact, my volunteering is something like six degrees of separation: everyone helps each other, and you see how it pays off. For example, a Ukrainian pilot we knew used to help us bring tourniquets for first aid kits in his suitcase. So mutual aid helps volunteers get everything done quickly.

On volunteering and change of priorities

I couldn't help volunteering. What does it give me? Confidence in the future of Ukraine, above all. It's an opportunity to say "thank you" to our defenders. That's how I contribute to beating the aggressor and approaching our victory. The war started in 2014 for me and made me change my priorities completely. Almost nothing has changed since then, except that the scale has grown highly.

On business plans

I think that after the victory, Ukraine will confidently move to Europe, fighting corruption, paying taxes, and teaching children tactical medicine…

Once we win, I want to develop our business of producing eco-bags, *TakaSumka,* and uniforms for employees of restaurants and services, *TK Uniform*. This business idea came up while my friends and I were standing on the bank of a river in Switzerland. We haven't noticed a single piece of plastic there, unlike in the Carpathian Mountains, where we see piles of plastic bottles and bags all around. I realized we should do something about it because we produced an incredible amount of plastic. Besides, eco-products are now on trend, so it's worth doing it.

We bought a sewing shop and created new jobs for over 20 women. Women in Ukraine present a less protected group, so creating jobs for them, especially those having small children, is also one of my priorities. They can earn money and be financially independent.

We'd been doing this business for about a year. We partnered with *Epicenter* (construction supermarkets network) and supplied a lot of bags there. We also had contracts with *Mehamarket* and sewed uniforms for employees of *Nova Poshta* (the all-Ukrainian commercial post service). Ukrainian designers created designs, and we sewed the first batch. On February 23, we met with the employees of Nova Poshta to make adjustments. Unfortunately, adjustments were made by the war. I hope we will return to sewing this batch of clothes after the victory.

Now production is suspended, and some of the women have left Ukraine. The rest work solely for the needs of the Territorial Defense Forces and a bit for the Armed Forces of Ukraine. Women sew military uniforms in Boryspil, so they are also holding their front.

On burnout

I am very focused and don't have time to burn out. I have to work. It's not the time for burnout yet because it's a kind of marathon. After the start of hostilities in 2014, the first burnout happened to me in 2017. And now we have a powerful army, so I hope it won't last that long, and we'll rout the enemy quickly.

When the burnout did happen, I had the help of psychologists and my kids. That's what saves me. Traveling with my kids also works for me. I hope to go on a journey after the victory. Now, we have to keep a positive stance, not dream about something big, but keep our feet on the ground, be happy about the sun and the sky, and believe in the AFU. Our task is to support the military from the rear and help them in any way we can.

2022.08.20.

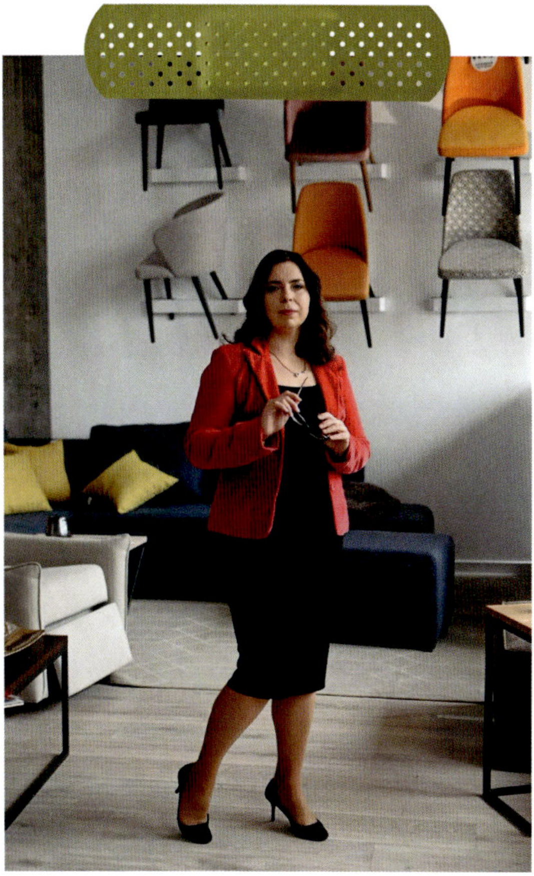

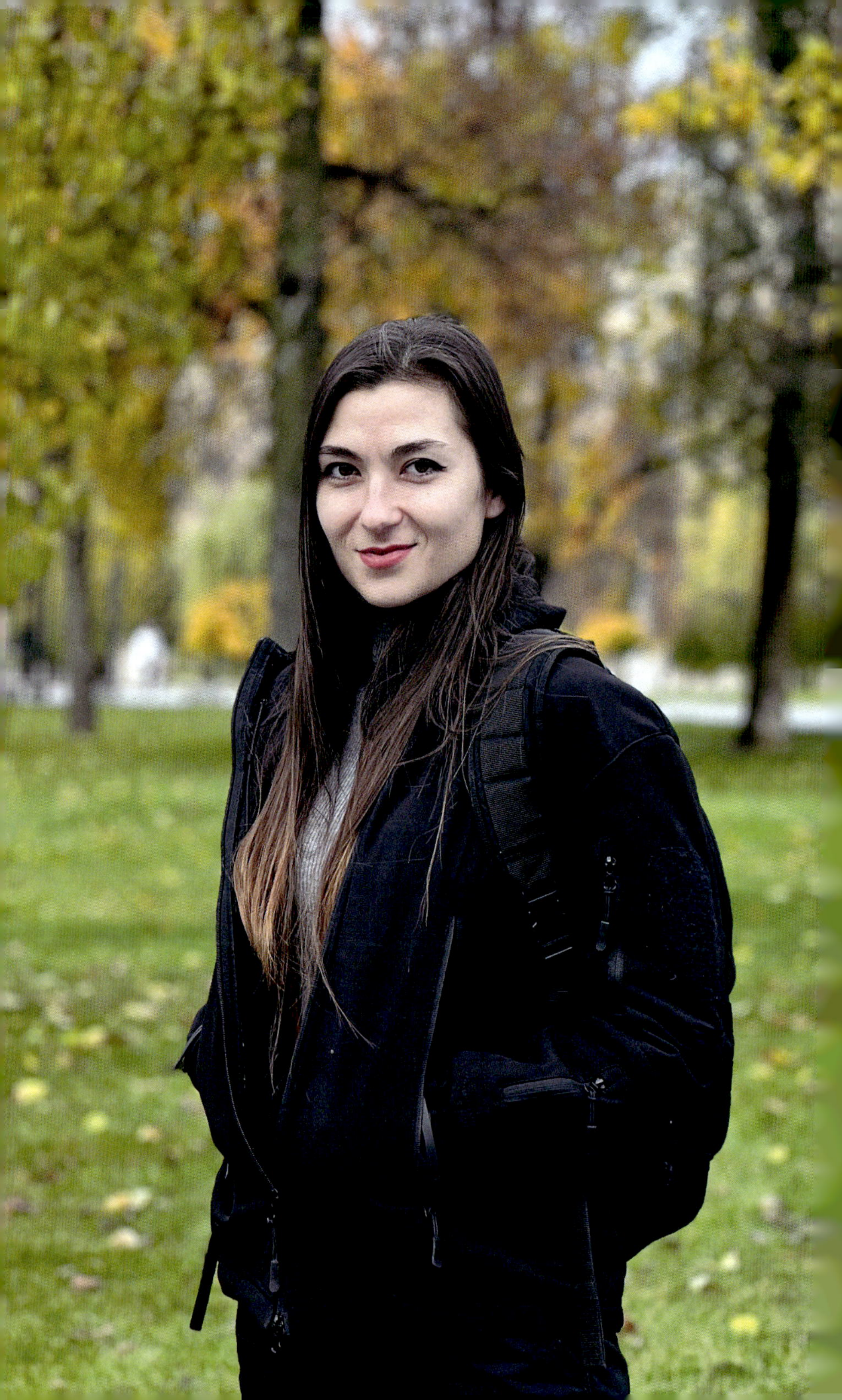

Iryna Sampan

War correspondent

Iryna Sampan is a war correspondent who decided to become a volunteer and deliver cars for the military because she believed Ukraine needed it the most. Four months later, she returned to journalism and now brings war stories from the front line.

Recruiting motivated and experienced people for the war

From journalism to volunteering

The invasion caught me when my son, my friend, and I were in the UAE. Tickets for February 23 happened to be at a discount, so we went on vacation. We learned about the full-scale invasion of Ukraine only upon arriving in Dubai. The only comforting thought was that my child was safe and had not seen the horrors of this tragedy. At first, I thought about returning home, but we stayed in Dubai for my son's sake. Even there, we were surrounded by Russians and Belarusians who came on vacation. I tried to make some broadcasts on *Hromadske Radio* remotely, but most of the time, my friend and I were on our phones monitoring the news.

I started tracking the movement of Russian equipment: civilians sent me information, and I forwarded it to the relevant authorities that knew what to do with it. I was doing this almost around the clock. That's how I got a tan sitting with my phone in my hands: my belly stayed pale, and my back got tanned.

Later, I took my son and my friend to Georgia and left for Ukraine on March 3. I returned with nine soldiers from the *Georgian Legion*, who headed to help Ukrainian defenders. In Georgia, they were organized by the sister of the *Legion's* commander I had previously interviewed. Volunteers met us in Warsaw and took us to the border. I remember the cold night and the long lines of children and women at the Polish border. Crying and terrible racket came from all around, and the men were breaking the gates to get the border guards to let them through. It seemed like the apocalypse. And then everyone saw nine stocky soldiers striding confidently in the opposite direction, with me by their side. Everyone fell silent and stared at us open-mouthed. I exclaimed, "Glory to Ukraine!" and heard a loud and unanimous "Glory to Heroes!" in response.

We arrived in Lviv, where they were already waiting for us. After bringing the first soldiers, I started organizing the coordination headquarters.

Georgian Legion and recruiting of soldiers

I helped the commander of the *Georgian Legion* recruit foreigners. I interviewed him three weeks before the full-scale invasion, and he told me there would be big war. I didn't believe him.

He urged foreigners to fight for Ukraine. He even appealed to those who had no experience, saying they would be taught in Ukraine. And if they had experience, they could share it with the newcomers. He got calls from all over the world: Taiwan, Arab countries, the United States, Japan, and Korea. He hardly had time to process the requests and filter out the soldiers, so I proposed to systematize it and launched a coordination headquarters and a hotline staffed with volunteer students from Lviv who knew English.

We communicated with soldiers and those who wanted to come to Ukraine via WhatsApp. We worked around the clock in four shifts because we got calls from different countries and time zones. There was an incredible influx of people: 60–80 calls a day. We had to explain to them which route was the best to take to Ukraine, across which border, and what they could bring along. Many American and British veterans could have brought weapons, but they would not have been allowed. So we had to systematize that. For our own staff we wrote down answers to the frequently asked questions, such as how to properly refuse foreigners and filter out and screen them. People wanted to come to Ukraine with different intentions, like getting citizenship or arranging their romantic life, but we needed only those who are able to help us defend ourselves against the Russian aggressor.

Initially, we accepted everyone regardless of combat experience because we needed people. But we understood that we should take only motivated and experienced people. Not even all of them could stand it: some joined the *Red Cross* instead, some went to clear mines, and some just left.

Then we put the recruitment of soldiers on hold, focusing on recruiting foreign instructors with combat experience. There isn't much of an influx anymore.

When I set up the headquarters, I assigned a deputy to work for me. As for myself, I decided to drive cars for the army.

"I had a driver's license but no driving experience": transporting cars to Ukraine

At the beginning of the invasion, a lot of volunteers went to defend our country. We had so many needs but came short of volunteers who would deal with those needs. There were cargoes to deliver, but no one who would do it. A press officer from one of the units contacted me asking to help transport valuable aid to the front line: scopes, walkie-talkies, and optics. I agreed, but I did not know how to drive back then and did not have a car. I found a driver and a car, and we took this cargo to Pisky village in the East. I established contacts with other volunteers and started transporting aid.

Later, my friend wrote that he figured out the best way to transport vans for the military. It should be women because men couldn't leave the country. That's when I realized that I was the right woman to do it.

I had a driver's license, which I got two years before, but no driving experience. I only drove my dad's car a few times to the store not far from our house and while dad sitting by. As for now I have already covered almost 50,000 kilometers.

I had to go to Kraków to take the first car. I looked for a car through my friends, who sent me photos of cars available in Poland. I specified that I needed a car with automatic rather than mechanical drive. I spent two days driving around Poland to take a look at these options. I was exhausted and wanted to eat and sleep. Finally, I went to see a Pole who showed me his car. He opened the door, and I saw… three foot pedals. I almost cried. It was despair. But I had little time and couldn't look for cars for another day, so I just drove to Ukraine.

I have a track record of only five cars: four from Germany and Poland, and one was found in Ukraine. It is very exhausting to transport cars. Besides, every country has its own laws. I had to bring two huge *Mitsubishi L 200*s and a *Hyundai Terracan*. These are two five-meter-long "tanks" with a huge engine capacity. Back then, they were the biggest cars I'd driven in my life. I've already mastered both the *Bogdan* bus and the *Volkswagen Transporter Technik*.

Once, I drove for over two days from Germany. I was on the road for 24 hours and waited in a 6.5-kilometer-long line at the border for another 40 hours. I hadn't had a chance to sleep because the line was moving really slowly but steadily.

Later, my colleague from *Hromadske Radio*, who had over 10 years of driving experience, joined me. It was more fun with her, but I realized that my resources started running short. Besides, other volunteers did a better job: they managed to transport several cars at a time because they had been doing it for almost eight years. I was trying to figure out where I could be useful and what kind of help I could provide best, and I came to realize I was a journalist, so why try to change myself?

Going back to journalism

As a volunteer, I didn't get a salary. Naturally, my resources, both physical and financial, started running short. I could not spend the money people sent me to buy a car for the AFU on my own needs. Sometimes I even wondered if I could take 50 hryvnias for a hot dog as long as I was driving a car. But I did not dare to take even that amount because it was not my money.

Also, constant long-range movements really exhausted me. So I realized that I wanted to go back to journalism and do what I do best.

I decided I would write stories about the people defending our state. At this stage of the war, I realized that it wasn't just physical help that was important to win but my journalistic work, too. I wrote a post that I was returning to journalism. Yurii Butusov, Editor-in-Chief of Censor.net, responded. He wrote he needed me because I had done my program there before. The Executive Director of *Hromadske Radio* said the organization had a certain budget for my trips, and I could shoot for them, too. I thought that if they needed me, I should take it on.

Women in the army and a duty trip to the front line
Now I focus on the stories of those who defend our country, from the soldier to the company commander. These are people who fight on the front lines. Many mobilized people not related to the military joined the army at the beginning of the war. They are musicians, teachers, and miners. Some units were renewed by 80 percent. We can call it a people's war because ordinary citizens are fighting on the front line. So it is fascinating to find out who they are, that is, to see the face of today's Ukrainian army.

As for women in the army, there are not so many of them — neither in combat positions. But I was told (by journalists, among others) that women are taken away from the front line. It is a kind of unspoken relocation. It is a shame that women are still trying to fight for their place in the sun, win authority, and prove that they are worthy of fighting. But I hear more and more often that their commanders do not allow them to go on combat missions. I wouldn't want anyone to devalue women's contribution to this fight and victory. They do military service on par with men, get wounded, and, unfortunately, die.

In the first months of the war, I did nothing but move to keep myself resourceful. So I had no time to think about whether I was tired. I felt an emotional uplift, and the adrenaline was going through the roof!

But as early as in May, I started having a hard time: I was physically tired and missed my son, whom I had seen only once since the beginning of the invasion (now he is in Kyiv). I was also worried about my husband, who was in the East of Ukraine. Emotional, financial, and family factors started to undermine me, and I needed to feel useful. So I had to see a therapist who worked with me on the phone, even at two in the morning. I believed

I did not have the right to get tired and have a rest, too. Now I get my resources from journalism and the stories I work on.

A week on the front line, a week at home: weekdays of a war correspondent

Every week is different for me. Recently, I was in Zaporizhzhia Region, then in Donetsk Region near Avdiivka and Pisky. That's where we got under fire. Pisky is one of the most dangerous spots after Lysychansk and Sievierodonetsk. But I knew one of the unit commanders, who let me come to the unit, meet the soldiers, and stay there for a few days to talk to them. Seeing soldiers in their everyday life makes it easier for me to identify which story I should work on.

So I got in my car and drove to this unit near Pisky. I left the car near the village, which was quite far from the front line. I got to the front line and stayed in one of the companies for 24 hours. That night, the Russians opened terrible fire. They wanted to cut off one of our groups of soldiers. First, they shelled with heavy artillery, then threw incendiaries and tried to break through, but our guys beat them up.

During this battle, all I managed to shoot was darkness and sounds. Then one fighter with the last name Zelenskyi and the call sign "Legitimate" helped me take pictures of the phosphorus shells. He held me by the belt and told me if any shells suddenly flew, he would get me into the dugout. Covering the camera screen with my hand because it wouldn't go out, I was shooting phosphorus shells.

When the battle ended, we went to rest, hoping for a quiet night without shelling. At 8 in the morning, we went back. I had just started to film a story 300 meters away from the enemy positions when one soldier came running in and asked for the keys to my car because the enemy had started shooting near that location. He wanted to take the car to a safer place, but I refused because I did not want to endanger our guys.

The shelling continued for twenty-four hours. The Russians fired everything they had, sparing no ammunition. Now they can open mortar fire even at one soldier they see. Nothing like that happened for 8 years. For example, the occupiers can fire 208 shells at an area as big as a large café.

But I managed to meet amazing people there and do great interviews. I met one fighter there, a tractor driver from Rivne, who told me, "I would sow these shelled fields with grain." That's my inner resource, which gives me the strength to move on and keep going there.

Tips for journalists caught up in the war

There are three basic rules that I follow while shooting.

The first is not to shoot the equipment location or number; always check the footage with either the press officer or the commander; ask if you can publish such material. It's not censorship but military safety because you will leave, and they will stay. So you should be extremely prudent in this regard.

The second is to present people as they are without adding artificial heroism. You don't have to show the tractor driver as a cyborg. His heroism is in the fact that he is there, and, being from a distant region, he cares for the fields of Donbas. And that goes for everyone.

The third is to keep in mind the words of my teacher Mykola Veresen, who always said, "A dead journalist is of no use." You shouldn't take risks if you can avoid them. You shouldn't take risks for the sake of taking risks. It's important to understand whether the material you get in hazardous conditions will be valuable and help others. Or maybe it's worth waiting a while and finding another way to get there. It may not be as expeditious, but everyone will stay alive, and you won't endanger yourself or the military.

2022.07.05.

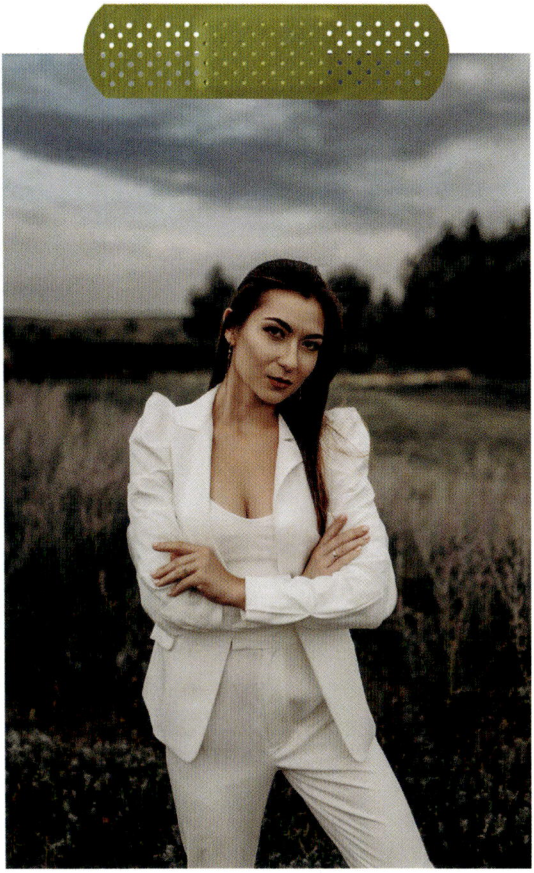

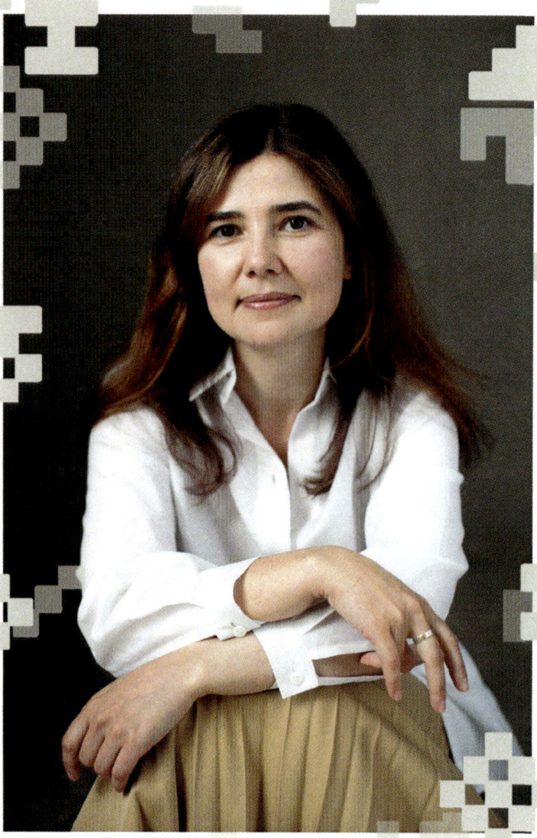

Nataliia Yemelina

Editor-in-Chief of the Yedyna women's magazine, volunteer

Nataliia Yemelina has long been the Editor-in-Chief of the *Yedyna* women's magazine and the *Tvii Maliuk* magazine. At the beginning of the war, the journalist was in Bucha with her teenage son. They were under Russian occupation for 15 days. For about three months, Nataliia tried to recover from her experiences and then decided to join the army as a volunteer fighter.

How can a woman defend herself and help the country

Life before...
A month before the full-scale invasion, I was preparing the March issue of the women's magazine. I did various interviews; our editorial office discussed the cover.

On February 17, the day the invasion was rumored to start, I was at a concert in memory of Misko Barbara, the frontman of the *Mertvyi Piven* band. All the showbiz stars joked a bit, "The war was supposed to start, but here we are all together now." The day before the Russian troops entered, I also interviewed Ukrainian actress Olena Kravets. It was timed to coincide with the premiere of *The Big Walk* comedy, which took place on February 23 and which I attended. The day before... Such a usual life for the glamorous glossy I used to do.

"I saw people's bodies in supermarket carts": life under occupation
On the morning of February 24, our house in Bucha was shaking with explosions. We heard the noise of helicopters in the sky because Hostomel airport was nearby. And in a few days, my son and I found ourselves under occupation. I didn't think about leaving Ukraine because I was sure that my country needed me. No one realized the scale and horrors that the war would bring.

In the first days, we believed the news we read. We were assured that there would be a turning point in three days and everything would get better. On the first day, we heard distinct explosions. Our cat didn't know what to do with himself, crouching at every loud sound, running from the window to me and back again. I added new Telegram channels and joined the neighborhood chats because being in touch poured oil on troubled waters. And my son got on his laptop to harm Russian channels online. Students from his university quickly banded together to do that.

Around the third day, the lights went out. Our neighbors told us that a store nearby would open to sell leftover groceries. We waited in line to the horrible sounds of explosions for almost an hour. We tried to guess how close it was hitting. Back home, I began boiling potatoes. I had just finished cooking when the lights went out, but we still had mobile Internet. I drew some comparative conclusions from what was on the news and what I saw with my own eyes. We were told several times that Bucha had been liberated, but we knew it was not true.

Then the occupiers began blocking communications as well. The only option left for communication with the outside world was text messages, but due to weak mobile network signal we could only send them in one place in the apartment. And we needed the news to understand the situation.

I contacted my friend, who used to be my deputy at work. We understand each other without words. She became my connection to the world. We got in touch once a day via text messages. She gave me brief information about situation around our town and communicated with friends and relatives who were worried about me and tried to find me via social media. She also topped up the account on both SIM cards because the money kept running out.

I have been working as a manager for a long time, so I am aware of the responsibility for other people.

Besides, I sincerely believe that if you find yourself in chaos and don't know how to deal with it, you should lead it. So I was busy all the time collecting information from locals about where to get water, where Russian soldiers were (to avoid danger), who had a generator, etc. I cautiously walked around the city to get what I needed. And what I saw was astonishing and horrifying. It will be just enough to mention destroyed houses, burnt equipment, and supermarket carts with... human bodies lying in them!

I cooked food using candles in my apartment and later over a campfire in the backyard of our apartment complex. There were no utilities anymore. A bucket of snow served as a refrigerator: we put snow in the bottom, then food, then snow again. We ate frozen and thawed vegetables and fish simply by pouring soy and Worcester sauces over them. Leftovers were used to make salads. I checked the "for-later" food every day, salted it, covered it with balsamic vinegar, and pickled it. Melted snow was used to get technical water. We charged phones using my neighbor's generator. We got by as best we could, and our tenting camp experience helped a lot.

Subsequently, we arranged a bathroom to live in because it got cold and too dangerous in the apartment. We brought travel mats, blankets, pillows, water, candles, and headphones to listen to the radio (at least some news!). We even tried to read books. We took backpacks to the bathroom and clothes to wear in case we had to pack quickly.

My son was "lucky" to always stumble upon Russians. As soon as he left the apartment, he would immediately meet either them or their equipment (with them inside). Russians treated our boys terribly. They searched them, undressed them, took their SIM cards, broke their phones, and threatened them. So I was afraid for my son.

Perhaps the elite squads of Russian fighters were transferred to our area because we saw strong, trained, and well-armed soldiers — not those young, confused, and hungry guys depicted in the media.

"We left on my son's birthday": evacuation from Bucha

One day, Russian soldiers with machine guns and crowbars came to our backyard. They told the residents to line up at their entrances. Everyone had to open their apartment for the Russians to search it. That's when I decided to leave. On that day, a "green corridor" was supposed to be arranged for those who wanted to leave, but we had no official information. People gathered near the City Council, but Russians didn't let the evacuation buses through, so we decided to walk across the neighboring town of Irpin. We managed to sneak through Bucha to avoid meeting Russian soldiers patrolling the streets. Eventually, we came to a multistory building on the border with Irpin. But the locals told us that the occupiers shot a car and unmounted people a few minutes before. They suggested that we stay in their basement because loud explosions could already be heard all around.

But what was the point? We needed to get out, not sit in there. We went back to the City Council. But the news was disappointing: the occupiers would not let the buses in Bucha. The city administration offered to come back the next morning for another attempt because there would be no evacuation that day.

We went back home and put out the things that attracted the most attention from the enemy. We worked on our mistakes, packed again, and went to bed. In the morning, I made salmon sandwiches, opened canned pineapple, and put a toy-plane with a candle in the center of the table to congratulate my son on his birthday. That was our "luxury" breakfast in the occupation. But I had to make him happy somehow. The fish had been in the marinade under the press in the hallway the whole time. Then we started dressing. I taped my phone to my calf and put some money into my shoes and underwear and into my son's backpack in case we would get separated for some reason. He also had copies of my papers. I wrapped his phone in diapers and put it under the feed in the cat's carrier.

We took all the remaining food out into the hallway and let the neighbor and friends know about the supplies. We were about to walk but, luckily, we got an offer to leave by car. That was real luck! We attached a "CHILDREN" sign and hung up white rags and our T-shirts. It was scary to see a lot of destroyed houses, people's bodies, remnants of shells, and even mines along the road. The Russian military aimed guns at us at their checkpoints, but finally, we reached a Ukrainian checkpoint. We showed our documents and sighed with relief. I congratulated my son on his birthday once again. We decided to visit my friend in Berdychiv town, where we ate, showered, and stayed for a few days.

I was struck by the fact that people, who were just 30 kilometers away from the occupation zone, weren't too frightened. As if everything was happening somewhere far away. But it wasn't true! It was really close! We paid the price for this feigned calm: while in Bucha, we were clearly aware that we would be sacrificed to save Kyiv.

First, in Berdychiv, we found a craftsman to make new holes in my son's belt because he had lost a lot of weight. We were sent to the workshop, where we met a nice man. He was surprised because he had to shorten the belt by 20 centimeters. He asked where we were from.

We answered that we were from Bucha. He asked us to wait and went to the service room. He came back and said that our payment was to eat two candies each and take care of ourselves. For the first time in a long time, tears welled in my eyes.

While in Berdychiv, we were buying something in the stores, walking along the lake, and planning how to get to my sister, who had settled in a village near Kamianets-Podilskyi. Finally, after coming across several frauds, we found a real driver who agreed to pick us up from the station and take to Kamianets-Podilskyi.

Life in the village and the decision to become a volunteer soldier

I found shelter with complete strangers. The old man, whose house we moved into, immediately took us in his charge. He said, "I'll give you a piece of the vegetable garden to plant potatoes." But I understood that the first harvest was in the summer, and I wouldn't be able to stay there till then. That is why I did not even go near the vegetable garden.

We lived near Kamianets-Podilskyi for two months. At first, people there were eager to know about the war. But then, they asked me to stop telling them about it. They want to help and sympathize with us, but their war is on TV and in the news and stories of people who came from the occupied territories. Even in Bucha, different facilities are already opening, and children are walking around. One might think the war is over. But that's not true… Many people do not understand why I do not go abroad. I want to be useful here. If everyone leaves, who will the Ukrainian military defend?

After the liberation of Bucha, I registered for medical, mine safety, and first psychological aid courses. You need to know how to survive.

I wanted to understand and influence the situation somehow, so I became a volunteer soldier. Few friends and colleagues were surprised to see me in uniform.

Of course, I'm not rushing to the front line because I'm not that brave, although I've seen off those who go there. I am very annoyed with the fact that children have to study in schools and universities offline. It looks like people have cut themselves off from the war as if it's happening elsewhere. But it is here and now! We are not supposed to deny reality. The danger is near us. And we should not let our guard down!

Sometimes, after curfew begins, I stop individuals or even a group of people and ask them why they are on the street at inappropriate times. And they say, "We didn't make it on time, what's the big deal?" Don't make it harder for the military to do their job!

I hear a lot of complaints from the locals, too, who say we scare them and their children by wearing uniforms. They reproach the guys in uniform for being an eyesore, patrolling, and enforcing a curfew. People complain, scold, and threaten. You get really scared when you see a Russian coming to your house with a gun. But when you see our soldiers, it's good because they protect us. Amazingly, people don't realize it! They should be thankful, not quarrelsome!

People should also remember that volunteer battalions are self-sustaining. The state does not help them with anything except training while requiring a lot from them. Just realize: people joined the Defense Forces at the call of the heart, not for money!

Toils and realities in a volunteer unit

Days are different. Sometimes, I have to show up quickly on full alert in a certain place. Sometimes, I have drills.

Sometimes, I go to thrift stores to find a uniform or look for it from volunteers. Whether you have everything you need depends on your money or the money of your family and friends. There are no specific volunteers who help. I am always looking for everything by myself. Besides, military gear is really expensive. That is why we often hand over some parts of the uniform or necessary devices during drills.

Almost all the guys in our battalion were small business owners, and when they went to the army, they gave almost everything they had to the military. Some gave a house for the soldiers to live in, some gave cars, some gave a store for the headquarters, and others gave all their money to help the front.

I come home quite rarely now. My son and cat are also with me. I have a lot of issues to deal with in my work. But I try to be on the beat. I make at least some time for writing texts.

Right now, I am looking for shoes for the guys because they wear what they have: slippers, gumshoes, sneakers, and canvas boots. I can tell from experience that civilian shoes are no good. If you wear sneakers for a single patrol, your feet will be nothing but wounds. Socks stick to the wounds! And that's not even the front line!

Dress as a protest

Sometimes, I guess, as a protest and a breath of fresh air, I wear a dress. After all, why have so many in my closet? Most of them are inappropriate, so I wear them rarely. Looking at my clothes, I realize that a person doesn't need much to survive. I came to realize it many years ago when a fire started in my rental apartment, and the first thing I grabbed was my son and cat. I laughed at myself later that I didn't even take my money and papers.

It's still the same for me because I do the same thing again, but I'm tired of leaving home for good every time. When they let me go home for a leave, they always say, "You're packing as if there was no tomorrow." I always take the essentials with me.

But every time, I need something new because life goes on, and I can't live on the rims all the time.

After we win, I simply plan to live. I'm already trying as hard as I can. There's no telling what's going to happen next. And life goes on! Also, the little things matter! No matter how trivial or absurd it may sound, sunscreen is the number one remedy for me. I invested so much effort into my appearance, so it would be unacceptable to ruin it in a few months. And I love being beautiful! As soon as I got home, I immediately made an appointment with my hairdresser and beautician. I also try to do some feminine procedures, even under field conditions. You can't focus only on the war, and you still need to enjoy life. This is a marathon, not a sprint, so you should keep a positive stance.

2022.08.01.

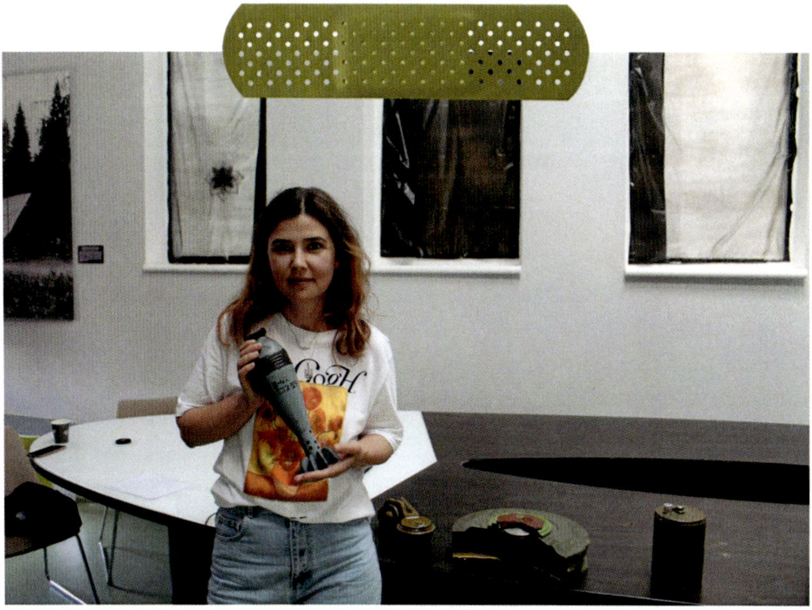

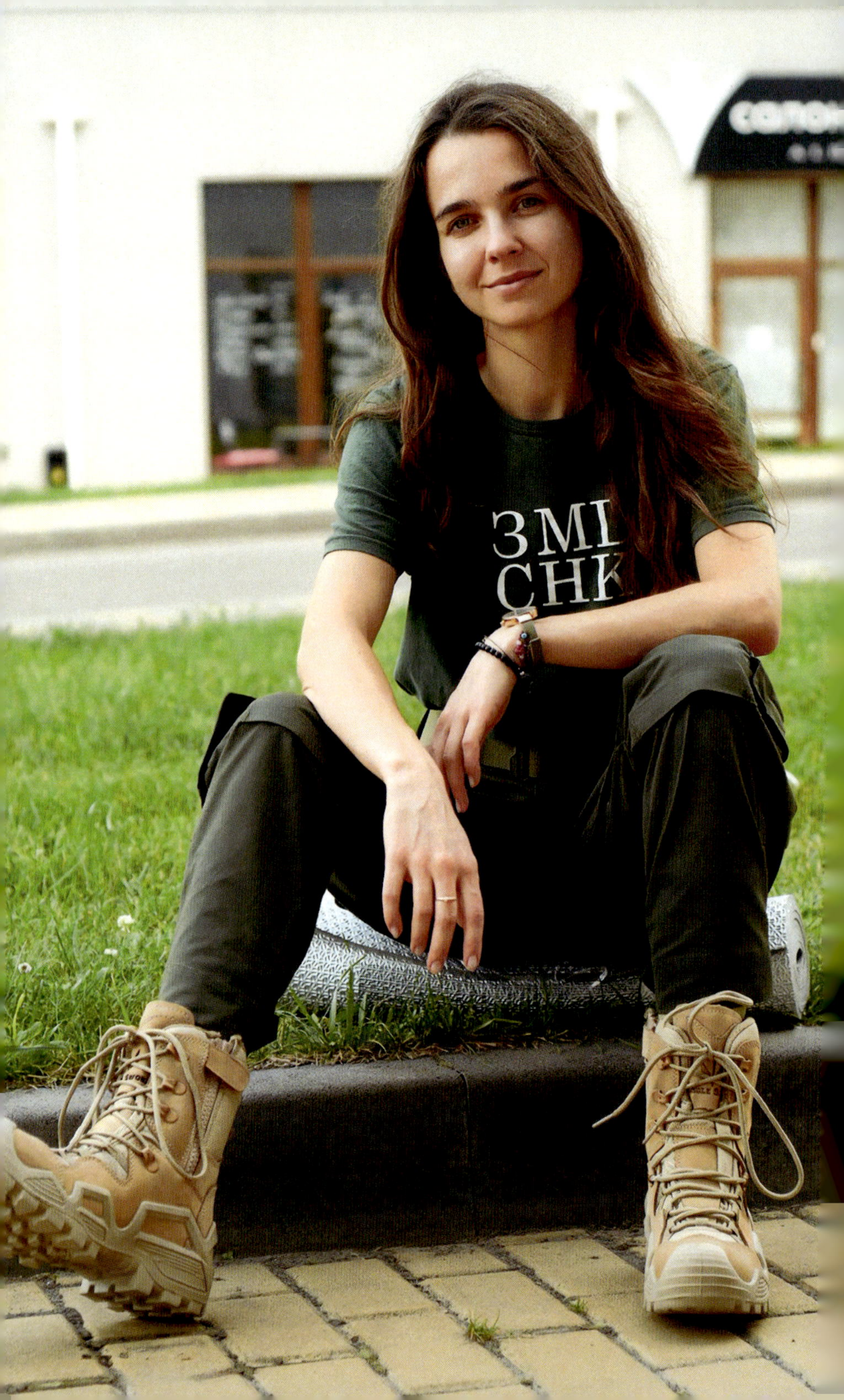

ЗМІ
СНК

Kseniia Drahaniuk

*Co-founder of the Zemliachky.
Ukrainian Front NGO*

Kseniia Drahaniuk and her *Zemliachky Ukrainian Front* (*Female Compatriots Ukrainian Front*) help female soldiers who defend the Ukrainian land. Kseniia and her team accommodate requests for women's military uniforms, gear, shoes, and "women's humanitarian goods," which they deliver anywhere around the country. The organization also publishes stories about women at the front in an effort to develop a culture of "female soldiers" in Ukraine.

Helping
female soldiers

"I went back to Kyiv to be more useful."

For the first three days of the full-scale invasion, we lived in the basement because of the loud explosions in the Obolonskyi district. We were scared to leave by car but even more scared to sit still. After three stressful days in the basement, we set off.

First, we left for a village in Vinnytsia Region, where we stayed for two weeks. We lived in a house that no one had lived in for eight years. It had no heating, so we had to burn wood in a stove. We made camouflage nets and baked cookies to help the military.

Then we decided we wanted to help more and started thinking about organizing the *Zemliachky Ukrainian Front Foundation*. I came up with this idea because I was a journalist before the war and had a TV project about Ukrainian women with atypical professions. I have long been involved in helping and supporting women. I presented stories about female blacksmiths, pilots, and soccer players.

Before the war, my husband's sister, Nastia, was a manager and had nothing to do with military service. But on February 24, she enlisted in the Territorial Defense Forces while we were sitting scared at home. Once in the Territorial Defense Forces, she started talking about women's needs at the front: uniforms, underwear, and shoes.

I am originally from Mukachevo town and have many relatives in Uzhhorod city nearby. So we went there and started sending humanitarian aid to our female defenders. But we soon realized we didn't get really effective away from the capital, so we had to return to Kyiv. In the capital, we were able to meet with partners, rent a large space for humanitarian supplies and headquarters, and send packages faster.

The culture of "female soldiers" in Ukraine and the first humanitarian kits for women

The culture of women in the military is still developing in Ukraine. We are only now starting to get used to it and understand that a woman can be a gunner, an artillery officer, and a paramedic. Now women have many military professions at the front. While previously we did not talk about it much, now the culture of women in the army is developing rapidly. So far, women are given men's uniforms a few sizes larger than necessary because we do not yet have uniforms for women. Many people are working on this now, but it is a long way. So we accommodate these requests for now. Female soldiers cannot go to the store and buy the hand cream or underwear they need because they are at the front. For example, the first thing my husband's sister asked us to pack was a set of "women's humanitarian goods": hygiene products, lip balm, hand cream, underwear, etc. Then, we started sending the same kits to her sisters-in-arms.

Shortly after, other female soldiers asked us for the same products.

At first, we filled these kits using our own resources. We went shopping and looked for what we needed because you could hardly find anything in the stores in late February and early March. Then, our partners started to join us. Now we cooperate with the Eva company that sends cosmetics to women for free.

The package for female soldiers consists of 30 items, such as shampoo, shower gel, soap, intimate care gel and wipes, baby wipes, dry showers, moisturizing creams, lip balms, underwear, pads, tampons, etc. If we can, we purchase manicure scissors, files, tweezers, and razors. We also add a basic set of pills: Loperamide (for upset stomach), Paracetamol (for fever and acute respiratory infections, the flu), Ibuprofen (for menstrual pain), and pills for vaginal yeast and cystitis.

We also put goodies we have: candy, cookies, coffee, etc. We have a tradition of writing something on each box. For instance, "You're awesome!", "Kill the enemy!" and things like that. There's a girl Liuba on our team, who finds very original inscriptions, something like, "You're cooler than HIMARS." Women sometimes send me pictures with these cut-out inscriptions. They keep them as mementos and hang them near their sleeping places. We can send expensive things like plates, uniforms, and shoes that are hard to find. And girls send these photos in return, thanking us for the goodies and inscriptions because such little things make them feel supported.

The girls receive parcels by post or from volunteers in case there are no post offices nearby. We have several trusted organizations that travel to the front line. But still, we send over 90 percent of the parcels by post. By the way, we partnered with Nova Poshta about a month ago. So we send parcels for free now. We used to spend three thousand hryvnias a day to send parcels, and now we can spend the saved money on, for example, two sets of uniforms and shoes for our women. Eventually, we save about 20,000 hryvnias a week.

"We operate thanks to the support of people and partners"

The *Zemliachky Ukrainian Front* NGO officially opened a month and a half ago. It coincided with the release of Oleksii Durniev's show, who told everyone about our organization. We started receiving help from many people: subscribers, donators, and just individuals who want to help. For example, a person owns a soap store and sends us a pallet of soap. Recently a lingerie store provided us with several thousand underwear for female soldiers, and another store provided us with fifty pairs of sneakers, T-shirts, and sports tops.

From the very beginning of the project (six months ago), we started telling stories about women defending us. We publish mini-interviews on our *Zemliachky. Ukrainian Front* Instagram page. We are telling about their everyday life, food, sleep, and how they became soldiers in the first place. We don't do big interviews for safety reasons. Girls can't tell much about their activities, as it is dangerous. But this brief information is enough to get to know them better and for people to understand whom they are helping. We wouldn't be able to organize the whole process without people's support.

The Zemliachky team doesn't have many people. It's just me, my husband, and close friends. We communicate with female soldiers on our own and don't allow strangers in this. The girls can always write us as friends to tell us what they need or just talk. They know they have strong support.

We have a lot of partners who help us with our work. For example, the PR manager Alina and *COMMSX* agency who help us tell about our activities, or foundations, which help us buy the necessary gear, humanitarian aid, etc.

Also, the *Alexey Stavnitser Charity Foundation*, which we get to know about thanks to the former Director of the *Olena Pinchuk Foundation* and the guardian angel of charitable projects Olha Rudnieva.

Olha offered to unite our efforts in support of female soldiers and create *Try on Her Boots*, a joint project with the *Alexey Stavnitser Charity Foundation*.

We also have a so-called *Sewing Batallion* consisting of women from Dnipro, who sew T-shirts and buffs for women and send them to us for free from time to time. Recently, employees of the jewelry brand *Zarina* created a project to support *Zemliachky*. We developed three videos for social networks. They sell bracelets and give part of the money from the sales to our foundation.

We are starting cooperation with a clothing factory in Kharkiv to create Ukrainian women's military uniforms. Turkish uniforms we order for women are good, but we would like much better quality. Production in Ukraine will allow us to hem the uniform if necessary. Besides, we want to spend all the donations to support the Ukrainian economy, not a foreign one. Plus, we will create new jobs for Ukrainians.

People who want to help us also text us on Instagram. They send parcels with several sets of military uniforms, pallets of hygiene products, or goodies. We receive such support from different parts of Ukraine, and it's inspiring.

**Winter military uniforms:
needs of Ukrainian female defenders**

As part of the *Try on Her Boots* project, we created an online form where we stated everything we help with. A woman fills out this form and chooses what she needs. Then we verify the request, contact the women, and find out where to send the package. We send a set of "women's humanitarian aid" to all women, even if they do not ask for it, because it is always relevant. We also send underwear, socks, sports tops, panties, thermal underwear, women's military uniforms, shoes, tactical backpacks, paramedic backpacks, tactical and paramedic first aid kits, helmets, lightweight armor plates, plate carriers, sleeping mats, sleeping bags, etc.

We never get idle because, first, more and more people learn about us, and second, all these things are always relevant.

It never happens that we get a request one day and forget about it. We always keep in touch with women.

Donations help us accommodate the individual and urgent needs of female defenders. Here's an example: a girl recently wrote us that a shell hit their dislocation, and the light went off, so they needed a generator. We had never bought one. But just a few days before that, we got some money from the IT people. We used some of the money to buy headphones and left some for the next batch. But when we got the letter from that girl, we decided to spend the money on the generator.

Now, we are getting ready for winter and realize that the amount of work is enormous: our women need winter uniforms. We have bought 1.5 thousand sets of summer uniforms, and now we need to buy the same amount of winter uniforms, which are twice as expensive. People can officially donate to our accounts indicated on our social pages or to *Monobank "Jar"* (that is "*Military Money-Box*"). First, we want to raise a million dollars to meet the needs of at least two thousand female soldiers, and then we will continue raising money for the needs of other women.

Attitudes toward women in the army and psychological aid to female soldiers

This is a very sensitive topic. I can tell you there is no such thing as "I'm a woman, so have some mercy" in the army.

In the army, you are not a woman but a fighter! Female defenders do not define themselves as women in war. They call themselves "women warriors," especially those who have been serving for several years. When women perceive themselves as military, their comrades-in-arms treat them respectively. If you constantly point out that you are a female, you will not be perceived as an equal. There is no real differentiation in the army, all of us are just the military.

Although, it depends. Just like in civilian life, sexism may or may not be present in a team. It all comes down to the commander and each fighter. It's just a human factor. The culture of women in the military is now evolving. That's a given. While in 2014, women were not allowed in any combat positions, that's not the case now. So this culture is developing.

For example, I once interviewed a 20-year-old woman in the military. I asked her if she had any difficulties at the front. She replied that the most challenging part was when they told her she was like a granddaughter or daughter to her comrades-in-arms. But here's another story. There are three women on the five-person intelligence team working out of Ukraine, and they experience no sexism toward them. I also have a girlfriend who works in air defense and shoots down enemy missiles on par with everyone else. In the army, how you are treated depends on how you present yourself. You can flirt, or you can define boundaries. We often emphasize this and even published an article in which our psychologist Hanna Havrysh talked about these boundaries.

We knew that not everyone could go to a therapist because they may not have time to find one or not even be aware they need that kind of help. At first, we made posts on this topic in social media because when you flip through the newsfeed and come across such material, you may learn something.

Sometimes I refer female soldiers to psychologist Oksana Votum to get the psychological support they ask for. Oksana and her team work with our female defenders for free. As for the questions that they ask the psychologist, I can only say about the anonymous ones, like how to present oneself in the team; how not to forget about normal life, living under fire; how not to lose a woman in oneself when you are in the military; how to build boundaries.

When women return to civilian life, there will be a long process of rehabilitation waiting for them. War makes you change drastically or you cannot survive there. They toughen up, so they are going to need help to get back to normal life.

We recently met girls from New York who raised two thousand dollars. We used these funds to buy 350 copies of *The Choice* by Edith Eger, recommended by psychologists Hanna and Oksana.

It is a fiction book with motivational overtones. We send books along with humanitarian aid to the front line. Mobile communications may not work there, but you can always read a book.

"I realized I don't need much": the war changed values

I used to want everything at once, so I did a lot of projects, but now I've learned to live gradually moving forward. I do not expect any particular result except our victory. The main thing is to keep moving and do your best to help.

Now I accept any reality. I realized I didn't need many things. When we decided to leave, we took two warm suits, a few other things, and some face wash. I had one backpack. When we got back to the apartment, I told my husband I wasn't taking anything because I didn't need it. It's such a turning point when you don't need a bunch of stuff. I didn't miss the photos or the laptop. I appreciated that I was alive, that I had my loved ones by my side, and that my cat was safe. That was the most important thing to me, and material goods took a back seat.

"Communication with our girls keeps me going"

We are in the hub 24/7. We work there in the morning, then have meetings, and come home late at night (our house is next to the hub). We hardly ever leave the neighborhood because there's a lot of work. But such productivity makes us efficient.

Communication with our female soldiers supports me. They can make stories about how they hit the occupiers or tell us something about their lives. That's what keeps me going because I know they need me. If someone really needs you, you can move mountains.

Sometimes I text with girls for hours because I understand they need someone to talk to. I'm like a friend to them, and I love each of them. They're like family to me. Knowing that they are alive and feel my support makes me feel better.

I'm sure this kind of internal communication will help us win because Russians do not have anything like that.

"Our project will go on after the war"

We will not close the project after victory. We will still have a lot of work related to the rehabilitation of the girls. Besides, they will need to find a job and an apartment and return to civilian life. We will initiate new major projects, which I don't have time to think about yet, but I know for sure our mission will live on after victory.

I do not make personal plans now. I just live and try to be effective in this war. I try to do my best to hold on and support my loved ones and head for victory.

2022.09.09.

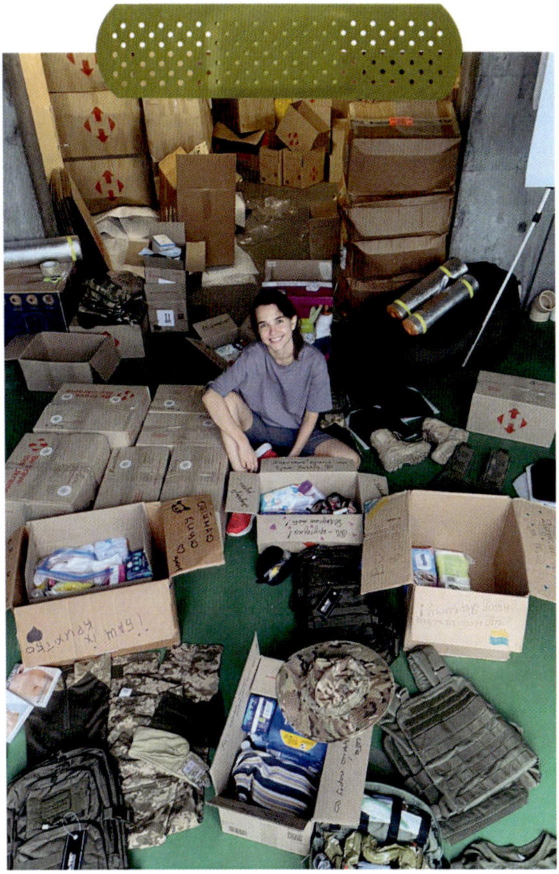

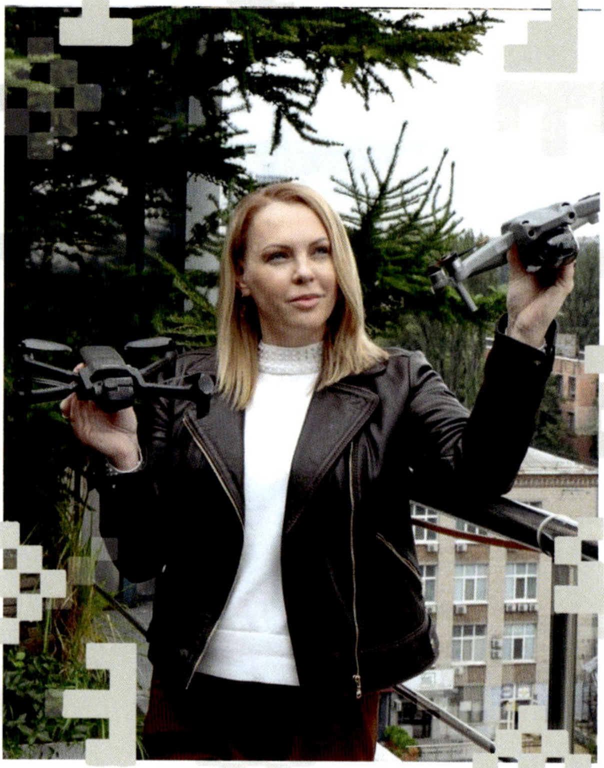

Nadiia Omelchenko

*Vice President
of IT Integrator Company*

Raising funds for tourniquets, tactical first aid kits, reconnaissance UAVs, boats, and jeeps for the military; helping units of the State Emergency Service, the Armed Forces of Ukraine, and the Territorial Defense Forces; organizing the logistics of protection equipment, gear, drones, radios from abroad under rough conditions; working in warehouses with humanitarian aid. And all this was in between full-time work. And also taking care of the family and employees, moving the office to Lviv and organizing relocation for the team, becoming the number 1 volunteer in the company, setting up the *R&D* center to help the army and the front. This is Nadiia Omelchenko's war days.

Volunteer projects for technological victory over the enemy

Since February 24, my schedule has not changed much: my workday starts at nine in the morning, as always. Except that, since the first day of the war, I stopped drinking coffee because caffeine stimulates the nervous system. I am jittery as it is, so the working day begins without coffee. I work and run volunteer projects at the same time.

Putting the business on a wartime footing

Like many businesses in Ukraine, we tried to develop scenarios for different courses of events. In January, it became clear that we needed to get ready for a military invasion, so we made a few important steps, including opening a backup office in Lviv for our team and an alternative technical platform for all the IT services we provide to our customers. But that wasn't enough, and on February 24, we promptly set up an additional intermediate evacuation base near Kyiv for the team. Most of our colleagues were so shocked and confused that they could not decide where to go. They were also trying to take care of their families. It was almost impossible to work under such conditions, so we put the business on hold for a few days at the beginning of the war.

In this setting, we consolidated all the remaining IT equipment in our warehouses and in the warehouses of our partners and competitors in order to respond to requests — mostly from the military and security forces — as efficiently as possible. Unfortunately, many IT equipment manufacturers had stopped supplying their products to Ukraine, so we had some difficulties with new supplies.

Our key task now is to support the IT services of our customers, supply PCs, rugged laptops, and radios, and adapt solutions of famous vendors to the realities of military operations in our country. We work as a hub, looking for the necessary things (protective uniforms, helmets, body armor, and medical supplies) for the military and rescuers.

While the basic needs of the military we work with are now met, requests for radios with the required parameters, scopes, thermal imagers, strike and reconnaissance drones, and protection against UAVs keep growing. New needs also arise when our military enters liberated territories. We have many requests for civilian protection solutions.

We also try to take care of our team members as much as possible. Right after the full-scale invasion started, we launched a fund to provide mobilized employees with basic gear. We also help those who joined the Territorial Defense Forces.

It was hard to keep the business afloat, but we are proud that almost all our employees are back to work now, with 50–60 percent working full-time, including the branch offices. We have stopped work only in the occupied territories. The most harrowing story is about our office in Mariupol...

The work format is mixed, but if we work in offices, we always go to a bomb shelter whenever there is an air raid alarm.

We continue developing important Corporate Social Responsibility (CSR) projects no matter what. Together with *MIM-Kyiv* Business School, we launched *Survival English* courses for team members who went abroad. Together with *SCR Ukraine*, we have completed the pilot project *Freedom English* and have been presented as one of the most courageous Ukrainian IT businesses in their video project *Brave Ukrainian Business* in front of the guests of *ESG Spain 2022: Corporate Sustainability Forum*. Before potentially difficult autumn-winter period, as a part of the CSR project *Knowledge that Saves Life*, we launched the production of twenty thousand thermal blankets for children and adults at our own expense. Thanks to our *Educational Initiatives Foundation*, they will be donated to protect Ukrainian children and adults, especially in the liberated territories.

All our team works as volunteers in all our projects and donates to help the military and civilian victims of war. But we also need help, both material and informational. We are open to any collaboration, actively cooperating with international organizations, donors, etc., but we always need more because the requests for help from the army are only getting bigger.

Impetus for volunteering

My husband and brother have been in the AFU since the early days of the invasion, and I was the first person they called when they needed help. Besides, I have many military friends whom I have helped since the beginning of the hostilities in Donbas in 2014. After February 28, 2022 I wrote to one of them that I could do volunteer work. They needed to organize the delivery of twenty tons of dual-use military goods. Volunteers couldn't deliver such goods. It was an extra credit task that served as the impetus for me to start looking for opportunities to supply such goods. It was hard to deliver such goods quickly. Together with several team members, we began to learn shipping routes from the USA. I consulted with my colleagues from the *Come Back Alive* Foundation. Then I started working with the AFU leadership. They gave me a list of the needs of military units. I looked at this endless list and did not understand how I could get all this. But it turned out to be quite real!

I also volunteered at humanitarian warehouses in Lviv and helped sort food in my spare time. That's how I became part of a community that dealt with aid and transportation. Later I got acquainted with Lviv IT specialists, who do a lot of volunteering, and now our company is also a member of Lviv IT-cluster, which works on different projects to help and develop IT infrastructure.

The main thing in volunteering is to believe. I believe that my work brings us closer to victory. So does my whole team.

First meeting

I had a little easier time getting started than others: I have a business reputation, understand how logistics work, speak English fluently, am a member of the business community, and know where to get everything we need for our soldiers. Volunteering is all about trust. People who help with things or money need to be sure that you will deliver the goods or send the money as intended.

So when we were out of funds, I had to ask for money from donors and acquaintances. The first things I collected money for were tourniquets and other items that were not so expensive.

We buy almost everything in Poland. Flash coves, radio sets, hemostatics, and tourniquets are hard to find now. It is much easier to buy computer equipment. Besides, we have a lot of requests to develop and protect infrastructure and support IT services for the military.

In other words, if you help someone, it's a never-ending project. I even get orders like "five SUVs for AFU fighters" or "a thermal imager for the State Emergency Service". Recently, in one warehouse, we accidentally came across ten fire-fighting protective suits which we delivered to rescue workers in Kharkiv. Once, we saw a lot of stray dogs near Kyiv and contacted one of our customers, an animal feed manufacturer. They gave us feed, which we delivered to Kyiv for hungry animals. We are now raising funds for four Ukrainian-made *Leleka* UAVs. Although it's really challenging, our team is about to finish it.

Volunteering is when you must keep knocking on someone's door to find things you need. Volunteering brings together people who need something and those who can provide it. We have to ensure a reliable rear for our military to protect us.

And we really appreciate the feedback from those we help. Someday we will show all our awards and commendations, but today we work 24/7 and welcome any help.

Who are the people who send the money

Employees, the community of *MIM* business school, and businesses make donations. I recently found contact details of the Canadian community and plan to contact them. I stopped being afraid to ask. I just realized people trust us. At the same time, we are not used to not being able to solve a problem on our own.

My business team helps me volunteer all the time. It always happens clearly and systematically, which means we keep being digitalized, as befits the IT business.

The power of Facebook is striking. People I have not contacted for years due to lack of time respond. For example, one longtime acquaintance called me, offering the military significant financial assistance and twenty pairs of quality shoes. His company appeared to be our customer.

People donate both large and small amounts of money: as much as they can. And they help not only with money, equipment, or clothes. For example, under our *Goodnight* project initiated by the *Educational Initiatives* Foundation, everyone can present a Ukrainian-language book of fairy tales for children who had to go abroad.

It is worth noting that world manufacturers provide us with equipment, *Starlinks*, radios, etc. It is really important for our country, and we are grateful for such help.

Tips on how to pull yourself together during the war

Keep in touch with the community so as not to be exhausted. Trust in your own strength and understand that even the smallest effort counts. Be that drop that brings victory closer. Do something instead of waiting for something.

As for women's leadership, I see how girls hold the economic front, especially in technology industries like ours. When we now talk about such things on international platforms, it generates a lot of interest among our foreign colleagues: how it works and how we've achieved it. And it also inspires to do more.

To be a leader in Ukraine today is a great honor. To be with strong and indestructible people who are firmly heading for victory makes you an awesome person. We can be proud of ourselves.

2022.04.18.

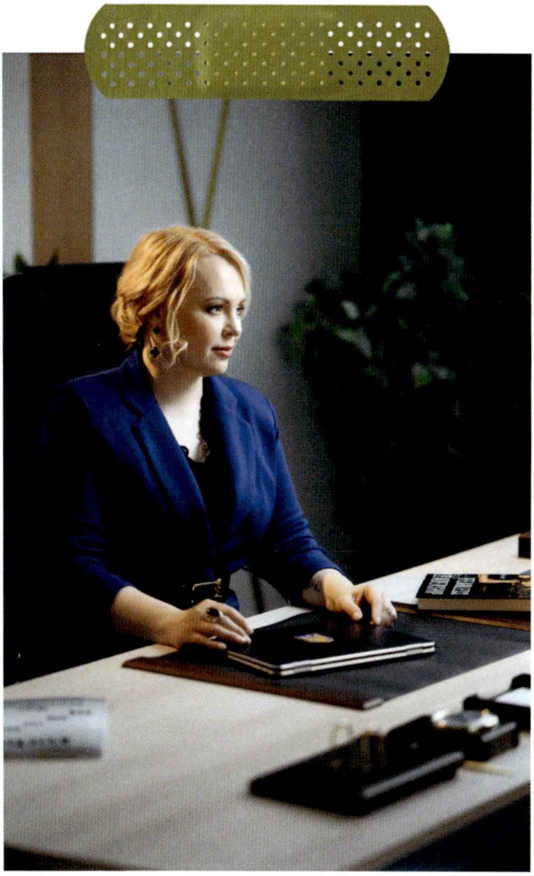

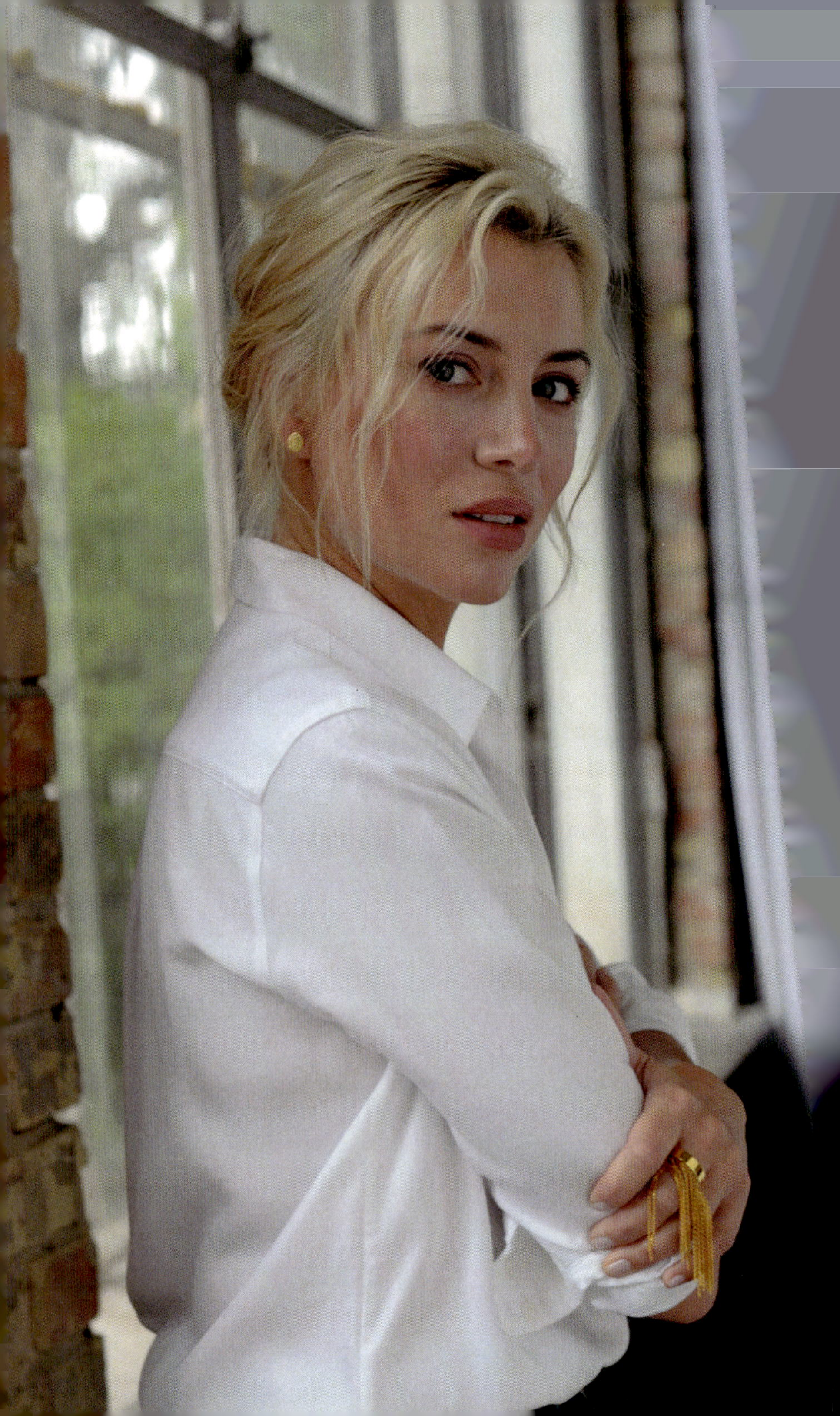

Oksana Lebedeva

Founder of the Gen.Ukrainian initiative

As the founder of a public organization, Oksana Lebedeva is engaged in pro bono rehabilitation of Ukrainian children affected by Russia's full-scale invasion. A health and educational camp for psychological rehabilitation of the first 30 children aged 7 to 12 has begun operating in Spain. This initiative is implemented under the patronage of the First Lady of Ukraine, Olena Zelenska.

How to restore psychological health of children

"I dreamed about war"

Back on January 6, I had this terrible dream. I didn't understand how a war could break out in the center of Europe in the 21st century! But I still did a few things in advance to protect myself a little. I relocated production, reduced staff, and withdrew funds. Of course, I forgot about this dream, blamed it on neurosis, and went to the United States. So at the time of the invasion, I was in America, and my child and mother were in Kyiv, hiding in the basement. The trip to Kyiv lasted from February 24 to 27, which seemed like one day to me. I didn't look at people or pay attention to anybody or anything. Some friends said the capital might no longer exist in a few days. There were two people with me in the compartment of the Warsaw–Kyiv train: a 72-year-old professor of the University of Cologne, who taught nuclear physics and now rushed to help our soldiers fight the Russian aggressor, and a woman who was also on her way to pick up her children. Her husband defended our country and died on the first day of the invasion.

On February 27, we arrived at the Kyiv railway station. Due to wartime restrictions it took me twenty-four hours to cross the Dnipro river dividing Kyiv, and I sighed with relief only when I hugged my son. But I know that my harrowing journey and border crossing are nothing against the torture and humiliation people endured during the occupation.

"Watching children suffer is unbearable": the idea behind the creation of *Gen.Ukrainian*

It all started with a trauma I got as a witness of the events in Irpin and Bucha. At that time, I developed an acute desire to help. At first, I was chaotic and spotty in helping those who needed it, but I realized that such a great number of victims of the war required a systematic approach, which would help control the process and monitor the results. It gave me the idea that it would be better to gather children in a safe space to create conditions for the grieving process. So that children can cry after everything they've been through, relive all the events, get qualified help and support, and we can monitor this process and continue to guide them after the program is over. It is clear that when children return home, we can no longer fully control them, but we continue helping them and giving advice to parents or tutors to prevent re-traumatization. After all, children return to a country at war. I established *Gen.Ukrainian* to provide psychosocial assistance to children and their tutors. The camp in Spain is one of the main offline initiatives of our project. It has proven to be a perfect model for working with children, and we can scale it up. So far, it's a 30-day program for children aged 7 to 12, but we also have two six-year-old brothers who are orphans. The camp involves 6 psychotherapists, one of whom is in Kyiv, and six teachers, healthcare workers, organizers, and managers.

As a public organization, *Gen.Ukrainian* was established in the summer when it became clear that someone had to sign documents, take on responsibilities, etc. After all the paperwork was done, I contacted my friend, a private patron, who entirely financed the creation of the first camp. He is still helping us, but we will look for other sources of funding to cover more affected people. I had strong emotions when organizing the first camps, so I needed time to figure out if I could keep doing this and if I would be strong enough to do it.

We signed a memorandum of cooperation with UNICEF, which helps us work with the children who come to the camp. We work under the patronage of the First Lady of Ukraine, trying to join the state program for post-war society reconstruction, one of the main elements of which is mental health. Everyone helps us when we ask for it. For example, the Ministry of Internal Affairs and social services helped us look for affected children who needed help. There is a problem with the documents, for example, when a child became an orphan after her or his parents were shot in a car. We must draw up the appropriate documents about what happened and the authorization documents to take the child to Europe. And all of this has to be done in the midst of the wartime.

Of course, it is kind of a risk to take a child from adults during this difficult time. When collecting the first child files, I asked for help from the Ministry of Internal Affairs, the First Lady's Office, and social services.

Now we are literally being bombarded with child files. Some requests are even more terrible than it was at the beginning of our project because there is a difference between the month-long occupation and the one that lasted half a year. During the whole occupation, the Russian military did nothing but hurt people... not only those who were in the occupied territories. It affected us all because many people had relatives, friends, and acquaintances in occupied territories. The worst thing is that most traumatized people don't want to talk about the trauma, and I understand them perfectly because this is the typical behavior of the victims: they think no one will understand them.

"We created a safe environment for children": about the work of *Gen.Ukrainian* camp

In the camp, we use different tools for overcoming trauma, such as art therapy, bibliotherapy, hippotherapy, group and individual therapy, cognitive behavioral therapy, innovative technologies, etc. We find a personalized approach for each child because sometimes the child cannot open up during individual therapy, but group therapy helps. Group therapy is the best for children. Art therapy — drawing, puppet theater, etc. — also gives good results and helps children open up.

We had a boy from Mariupol who didn't say a single word for a week. We didn't even hear his voice. And now he is laughing, swimming with all the children in the pool, playing chess. Even his gait has changed. It once again proves the power of psychotherapy. These specialists are like magicians who cannot change the past but can change a child's future.

Bibliotherapy, especially books about Harry Potter, also helps children a lot.

Books have a healing power because a person can find some advice there. We chose special literature for each group of children depending on their trauma and age. I saw children crying while reading the books in the first days. We will eventually post online all the literature that has a healing effect for parents to read. There is an intelligent reading method when you discuss everything you read with your child, see their reaction, what conclusions they draw, and what worries them. Chances are your child is concerned about something personal, and you can feel it. I was amazed when I saw how this works with children. Even the story of Harry Potter is relevant because when his parents died, and evil tried to kill the boy, he countered it despite his young age and supposed lack of power.

When we say goodbye to children, we give each child a bracelet with a personal inscription associated with the child. It all makes a difference because when a child no longer has a supportive environment, she or he have to go through difficult periods of her or his life using the acquired skills and knowledge.

Now I am in Kyiv, solving organizational issues, and the camp participants went to PortAventura Park because the last days in the camp are days of enjoyment. We cancel even individual therapy for the children to enjoy themselves, calm down, and say goodbye to each other. It is important in order to prevent re-traumatization because children and adults have bonded with each other during the month-long camp experience.

Working with children, processing requests, and selecting psychologists

We are scrupulous about selecting psychologists. I had no financial constraints, so I tried to find the best team because it's not just some 30–40 random kids. It is a therapeutic group. We keep watch over these children and record all our actions. We give all these materials to the Ministry of Health for approval.

The mental program we apply in the camp is based on previously developed protocols "The Joy of Growing Up" and "Children of War." We want to refine these protocols and share them with our colleagues who are willing and able to restore children's health. And there are thousands of such children. Trauma doesn't choose you, and it's deeply personal. A child may not see shootings or lose loved ones but may have mental trauma from, say, being in a bomb shelter or hearing constant explosions. Such a child can have nightmares, cognitive disorders, and aggression. We work with children who are traumatized and have no one to help them, children who have severe trauma and need qualified help, or children whose parents ask us to help them. Once, a woman saw the news about a car shooting on a Telegram channel and recognized her husband in the photo. After that, she didn't know how to keep going because losing her husband affected her greatly. The woman retreated into herself, stopped talking, and wrote letters to her deceased husband. She had a child who had also seen the news and, on top of that, observed her mother's behavior. The child also withdrew into herself, became aggressive, and avoided talking. The mother understood that the child needed help but couldn't provide it herself because she wasn't able to cope even with her own emotions. The woman applied to us for help, and we managed to stabilize their condition. That was one of the most difficult cases.

Predominantly, we "pull" the child out of an acute psychological condition and then have to keep working to maintain a stable condition. Often, children have no one left except for tutors or siblings. Close relatives sometimes do not understand the meaning of psychotherapy and downplay it. It is really one of the main issues we have to cover now because adults don't care about both their own and their children's psychological health. We have individual therapists assigned to each child. Also, we create an individual profile, which we share with the child's relatives and advise them on how to work and communicate, what to pay attention to, and what they should and should not do. If there are two children in the family, it does not mean they need the same approach to overcoming trauma. Here's an example: a brother and sister have only a year and a half age gap but are poles apart in personality and need a completely different approach. We found this out during psychotherapy and then told their mother about it so that she could deal with it. In any case, we do not forget about the children after therapy. When they are back home, they and their relatives can contact us 24/7.

Except for psychological help, we also ensure a lot of entertaining and cognitive processes in the camp. Children cannot constantly be engaged with the therapists and talk about trauma, so we developed entertaining activities according to a specific program. For example, if we work with fear, all activities throughout the day are set up so that the child is not frightened. It's all in sync with the therapeutic part, which involves all the workers, even the cooks. Some children make connections through food. Every child needs an individual approach. We discuss together what the child said to the therapist or a friend. And from that, we draw conclusions about how to work with the child. For example, one of our boys told us that he dreamed of working in IT because it was the only thing he was passionate about. We decided that I would provide him with training at the academy, another person would buy him a laptop, etc. We process requests whenever possible, but we haven't finished this camp yet and haven't finalized the protocols for the children we've worked with. We want to finish all of it, discuss the conclusions, and only then decide what therapeutic group we will gather next. Not all children are ready for therapy. If a child has a complicated anamnesis, i. e., cognitive impairment, and losses and war added to this, we cannot work with such a child in the camp because they would disturb others. That's why we refer such a child for individual work with specialists. We also plan to shorten the camp duration, which is 30 days now.

"No one can help us but ourselves": about the mental recovery of affected Ukrainians

I am the manager of this project. I put people who need help in contact with those who can provide it and create the required conditions. For example, you must sign a bunch of documents to take a child to the camp. Besides, it's a big risk because the child is traumatized, and anything can happen on the way to camp, say, if the child demonstrates suicidal behavior or something like that. You have to take personal charge of everything and be sure you can handle it. Besides, this is the first time we're all doing this. Even the therapists haven't worked with such cases before. And it's not fixed-hour work. We have to work around the clock.

The issue of mental health in society is complex. Being in other countries, I realized that their specialists would not help us and our children overcome the consequences of this war because they had never been in our shoes. These therapists have not yet worked with such traumas. The very time and conditions have brought us to the forefront of psychotherapy, so no one can help us but ourselves. There is so much crisis counseling, the concentrated grief we go through, and the affected children and adults that we could do research around the clock. I don't plan to engage any foreign psychologists at all in the second camp. I don't see any advantage in that. We look for empathic specialists who understand our children's language. So it seems we have to count only on ourselves.

Military trauma, for example, is a little different. Israel has tremendous experience and advanced technology in this respect. But as for the psychological rehabilitation of children, Israeli specialists are not so effective.

"I learned from other Ukrainian's experience that I have to do something"

I do a lot of things now but don't feel any fatigue. On the contrary, a lot of energy and strength came from the children and their results. Understanding the scale of the catastrophe, I know I will have to play a long game.

Before the full-scale invasion, I had my own business. I still run it, and it is doing quite well. To be honest, it did not interest me at all for a while. But I understand that I have to recover, bring people back, and find new markets.

I experienced different events in different ways during the war. Of course, I need psychotherapy. Everyone requires a "container" to dump all these thoughts and emotions. I believe we will grow and become one of the best countries in the world. I learned from other Ukrainian's experience that I have to do something, not just sit in Europe. You don't live your life abroad anyway. Mentally, you are in Ukraine. And you follow the news non-stop, waiting for the war to end. I have a lot of girls I know who went to war, so I feel like what I do is the least I can do. I can't take a gun and go to war because I don't know how to do it. They defend our borders, and I will fight for our children's personal boundaries because they have also been trampled. It's only a matter of time before we restore our country's borders. But we still need to restore the boundaries of our children who survived all these horrific events. We cannot change it, and children must not forget it. But we have to teach them to live with it so that aggression and pain do not overwhelm them. A soul wound kills just as much as a physical one and can ruin a whole life. Sometimes adults think that if the child eats and drinks again, even though before they refused to eat, everything must be fine. But it doesn't work that way:

you have to find out why the child stopped eating, find the reason, and experience it together with her or him.

Honestly, I felt much better when I started the project. We want to teach the first link of interaction — doctors, social workers, and teachers — how to work with victims of war. Everyone should know how to rehabilitate a child. We put online a lot of advice on how to talk to a child about the war, whether you should lie to a child about what happens, whether you should take them to a loved one's funeral, etc. We all live in hate now. It's a sign of the times. I have felt this sentiment first-hand, and I am sure that only a traumatized child can be raised in hatred. We must take our children away from this environment and show that they have a future because they don't see it yet.

"The program will go on after the war because rebuilding will take a long time"

The program will definitely go on after the war. We need to think about the recovery of the whole country because the traumatic events have affected us all. No one can tell what happens next. But it will definitely take a long time to work with children. It may be necessary to change the training system. The existing one needs to be improved. We will gladly share our protocols with anyone who wants to work with children. I know that Olena Zelenska is working on this, studying the world experience and looking for tools. Her team is very open and supports us.

We definitely won't be working with adult mental health because that's not what we do. We work only with children and their caregivers. That is, those adults who are connected to children under our care. We provide psychological assistance to caregivers because they create a supportive environment for children. I believe in the unlimited healing power of psychotherapy and that children recover because their psyche is flexible and prone to self-healing. You invest in a child, and he or she brightens up. If this does not happen, you need to change your approach. Adults have many factors affecting their psyche and condition, particularly childhood traumas. Adults are able to make their own choices, take care of themselves, and visit a therapist if necessary. Children do not have this choice, so they need to be helped. For example, those children in the camp do not even understand why they are there. Of course, we tell them what they're doing here, why they have individual and group therapy, and why they should do it, even when they do not want it. We explain it all. We have a lot of kids who lost their parents and buried them right in the backyard, like in Bucha. They don't understand why we ask them about it because they prefer to forget about it as quickly as possible.

Not the entire population will require special assistance after the war, only about 25 percent. But even that is a lot because we're talking about millions of people. We need to create spaces as we have in the camp all over Ukraine. The whole country has to be a supportive environment.

I am a proponent of the post-traumatic growth theory. As individuals and as a society, we can follow two scenarios: either get aggressive because of trauma or survive tragic events, become a better version of ourselves, and go on living. We need collective resilience. This is what we cherish in children: the ability to survive challenges and psychological stability. All of us need psychological stability.

"These children teach me resilience"

Watching children suffer is something awful. But children are so resilient that we have room for improvement: in relationships, work, and even compulsive shopping. I watch them and learn from them.

If a seven-year-old boy can handle such horror, I can too. Of course, you can't compare your emotions to other people's emotions. We are all different and experience the same events differently. But when you see a boy who buried his mother in Bucha and is now able to play, love, and enjoy life, you want to take your cue from him.

We have each other, and it's important. When I left the country, people helped me a lot. I realized everyone needed it. At that time, my situation wasn't that bad, so I decided to shift the focus from myself to those who were worse off.

Compared to the children I help, it seems my son is doing well. But when we were abroad, I saw how hard it was for him without his dad, how hard it was to communicate exclusively in English and to make contact with strangers. But people were really helpful. Some would come up to me at my son's school and just hold my hand and talk. One day, a woman from my son's school called me and offered to bring furniture to my empty apartment. I got a lot of help like that, so I decided I needed to respond to the challenges the best I could.

2022.09.25.

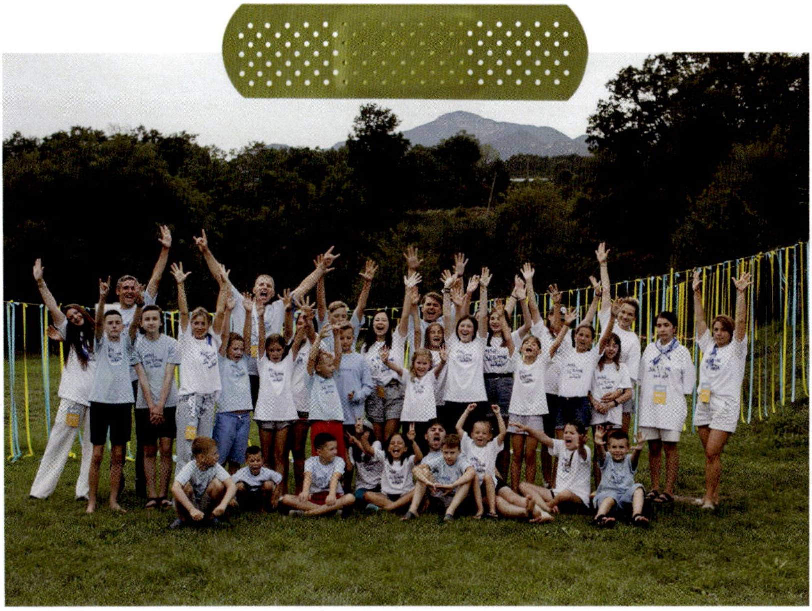

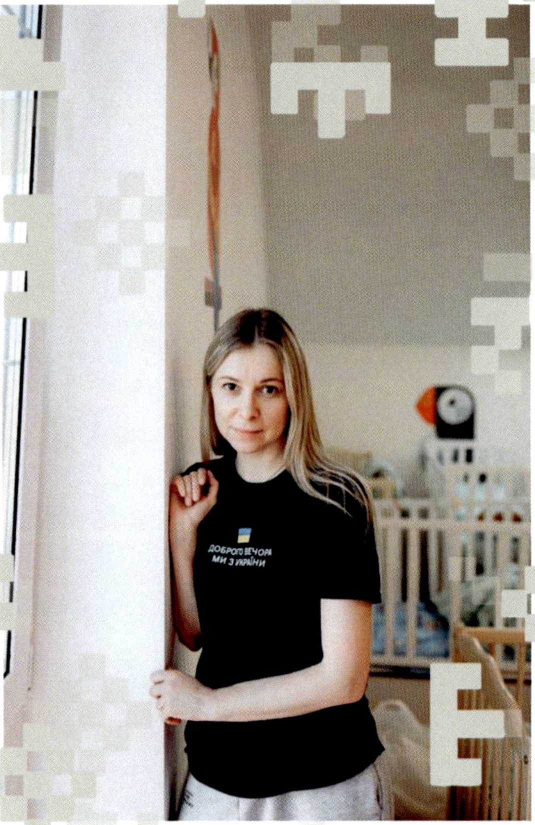
ДОБРОГО ВЕЧОРА
МИ З УКРАЇНИ

Marta Levchenko

Founder of the I am the Future of Ukraine Foundation

At the beginning of the full-scale invasion, Martha Levchenko expanded the activities of the *I am the Future of Ukraine* Foundation and the *City of Goodness* Crisis Center. Before the hostilities, the Center housed children and mothers on the verge of losing their parental rights due to domestic violence, homelessness, or poverty. Now it also hosts families and children from orphanages that had been evacuated from areas of active warfare.

By the time of the invasion, there were about 90 people in the Center. Now there are over 300.

Lives of children who lost their parents during the war

Our country needed a *City of Goodness*

Helping those in need has been my thing since childhood. At some point, it turned into a deliberate engagement in charity. And in 2011, my husband, as a businessman, said I should do everything properly and officially. That's how the *I am the Future of Ukraine* Foundation appeared.

In 2016, we realized it was no longer possible to help low-income families on-site. Many women we met needed to be urgently taken away from their abusers to save their lives and the future of their children, but they had nowhere to go. Sometime before that, I went to Kolkata, India, and worked on a mission that helped children. I remember wondering: how is it that Mother Teresa is dead and her mission still lives? I had a volunteer with me from the U.S. who said she had never heard of Ukraine. I told her about our wonderful country, the mountains, the rivers, and the canyons. She asked if we had a mission or a place where mothers and children could come. It gave me the idea that we should have such a place. That's how the City of Goodness came about.

We rented a house, which became our first *City of Goodness* for three years. We knew right away it wouldn't be just a shelter to hide in. It would be a place where women could start with a clean slate: learn how to run a household, how to look for and get a job, put their lives in order, and learn to be a mom. Most of our graduates grew up in orphanages or families that did not give them a chance to learn these usual things. We learned everything in the process. There was no one to ask how and what to do in a center like this because no one had done that before! Over time, we developed a system that yields results.

After a while, we realized that more and more families who needed help were coming to us, and the house was not getting any bigger. The rent was really high-priced. So we took the risky yet necessary step of building our own facilities. The first house opened its doors in 2019. Then we opened the second and third ones, and now we're talking about the fourth and fifth. So I would say, we now need to build rails and run a small train between the buildings.

I hope this place will exist for hundreds of years. It is the place where a person can get help, a roof over her head, food, medical care, necessary things, advice and help from professional lawyers and psychologists, and most importantly, get sympathy, love, and acceptance. That's what gives people a chance for a new life.

Just before the war, one of our followers gave us a gift of land in Odesa. We already had a finished project and all the documentation. On April 1, 2022, we were supposed to start construction. But the war made us put the project on ice. We also had to freeze another construction project in Lviv.

After learning to shoot, I decided I would defend my City of Goodness if anything happened

When the Russian invasion began, everyone was scared because no one knew what to do with the children. We went down to the gym built in the basement and sat there in shock at what was happening and in total ignorance of what would happen next.

But I did not even think of going abroad because you can't put the *City of Goodness* in your pocket and take it with you.

When the first shock subsided, we realized that the country needed us even more than before. We began to accept people who had fled the attacked territories. A house intended for 80 people hosted 90 people, then 100, then 120, and then 150. We were frantically preparing the second building, where we planned to make a school for mothers and a kindergarten for babies in the spring. As soon as we opened it, almost 200 people moved in. Now we have 300 people living in three buildings. But we keep receiving calls and requests for shelter.

I learned how to shoot. I got an assault rifle and a gun license and passed the training. I decided that I would defend my *City of Goodness* if anything happened. I won't leave the children behind.

My children are also by my side. My 8-year-old daughter takes all these events to heart. She cannot understand what is going on. She is always asking why Russia attacked us. My 21-year-old daughter, whom we once adopted from the orphanage in Kherson, is also with me.

We continue to help children in difficult circumstances.

Our work has not changed since the beginning of the active warfare; just new circumstances have emerged. We help children stay out of orphanages and help their mothers become successful so that the children can stay with them. Our shelter for mothers and children is the largest in Ukraine. Thanks to our work, over 3,000 children have been kept out of orphanages. When the full-scale invasion broke out, we took several orphanages under our care, so now we have 186 more children in the shelter. We are also waiting for children from another orphanage. The shelter will host a total of three orphanages.

Over 30 children who had lost their parents were already adopted. The youngest child is six months old.

In the city of Chernivtsi, we have created a space of total love. Those who have been there are convinced it's better than at home. We are nothing like a social center. We provide psychological support and development opportunities for mothers and children. It is our main activity so far. We host evacuated children, children and their mothers from the occupied territories, and children with disabilities. We are trying to give these children their childhood back. We have gray-haired children coming to us now, and our work is precisely to protect children affected by Russia's actions. We also take in their pets. This is new for us, but these animals remind the children of home, and we had no choice but take them in. Our employees who are allergic to animals take medication to minimize the effects of their allergies, but we don't refuse to take anyone into the shelter. We have cats, rats, rabbits, and dogs.

"Being under stress and fear, you start running faster"

Our shelter is a beacon of love with 300 people, including 200 children and 64 evacuated employees. The war didn't stop us from completing two more buildings and finishing the fourth and fifth to be able to accommodate even more people in need. One of the buildings has a three-story bomb shelter, which the children get into by driving down a wooden slide. They say it's their favorite place now. It's a really cool place with different aisles to keep the kids interested. When it's interesting, nothing is scary.

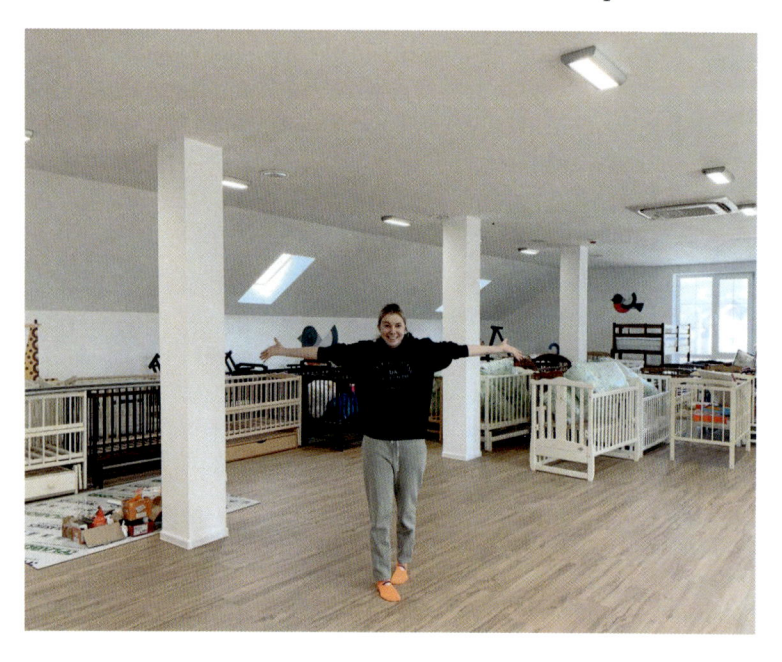

Our staff works three shifts. It's a round-the-clock job because you can't leave a child because the working day is over. It's night work because you have to take care of children with disabilities. We have taken in a specialized orphanage where the children have quite serious health problems. The war made us turn to security staff to protect our *City of Goodness*. So now we have guards, which gives us peace of mind because we don't know what to expect and what will happen.

We get funds neither from the state nor from religious organizations or political parties. The local budget can't fund us either, because we accept people not only from the city and region. The only prerequisite for admission to the shelter is to want to be a better mom.

We get help from people. An older woman walked 8 kilometers to bring 10 barn eggs for the children, and the *Data Group* company sent 805 thousand hryvnias to help the children and keeps looking for partners to provide even more help.

"If you left your home in your slippers and have nothing, come to us"

We provide legal, social, and psychological support, humanitarian aid, treatment, rehabilitation, and transportation. Often, women who have no documents come to us.

We have an individual development plan for each woman. Some need just a month of training because they have two higher education degrees, and some can't even read or write. We had women we taught to write words. We had a 16-year-old mother who did not know how to read the clock so couldn't feed her child on time, which caused her child to be taken away from her. Everyone is to blame for what happened to this girl: her parents, who did not give her a normal childhood; the school, which should have taught her basic knowledge; the state, which should have cared for her but turned a blind eye to her; the maternity hospital, where they should have explained how to take care of the child. But instead, the state takes the baby away because it doesn't want to deal with these nuances. Some mothers say they know where they want to work, and some have no idea. We cooperate with the employment center and refer women there to get career guidance. Then we determine what she can do and what she likes.

For example, if she wants to become a pastry chef, we look for a mentor, a successful woman. She advises what to read, what to watch, how to start a business, and where to study. Often, these mentors take their students to work at their companies or help them by giving them money to start a business. When a woman realizes she has grown out of our center, she looks for a place to live. We don't have a deadline as to when a woman has to graduate from the center. Some women need a month, and others need a year. We don't kick anyone out on the street.

We also support women for three months after they graduate. For example, if they rent, we pay for their rent for three months so they can save up, accumulate resources, and get into a new life.

We have several women whom we have been supporting for two years now. They still call our psychologist. These women are already married and have children, but they still come and write to us. Every June 1, Children's Day, we hold a reunion for our graduates.

Children from the shelter go to public school. A bus takes the children to and from school. Some children study online in the schools they went to before the invasion. We also have our own kindergarten and sports clubs. We try to give these kids the best childhood we can.

"We need everything"

We need everything we can eat. We need everything people buy for their homes: dishes, linens, towels, etc.

We need people, especially men, who can carry heavy things, repair knobs, tighten nuts, and fix electricity.

Almost all men are now fighting to protect us. We get help from teenagers. They are our pillar of support.

As soon as the Russians invaded, I posted on Facebook that evacuated children were being brought to our shelter, and we only had part of the building done and lacked utilities. The following morning, I was shocked to see over 40 men come and start plastering, installing electrical equipment, and doing plumbing work.

A week and a half later, we finished the construction and did an interior renovation.

We are experiencing difficulties with the third building because even those who helped us before are now defending our country. If there are men who want to help us, we would be truly grateful to them.

We also need teachers, particularly in English and Mathematics. We need volunteers. You can even teach kids online. Some children have missed a lot of curricula, and others need help catching up with some subjects.

We need artists to teach kids drawing, dance teachers, and vocal teachers. We need musicians, too. Mike Kaufman-Portnikov came to our *City of Goodness*, lived with us for half a year, and taught the children music. So if there are musicians willing to help, they would be welcome.

We even need a veterinarian for our dogs and cats. So we'll find a place for all the talent.

"We're trying to live for the moment"

I have no post-victory plans. I believe that every day I live is a small victory. We have to hold on and live for the moment. I know we will continue building and developing and will open centers in Odesa, Lviv, and other cities. Every city must have its own *City of Good-*

ness. I know we will finalize legislation to recognize women as victims of violence when a child witnesses their father beating their mother. We have to address many issues. I know what we have to do to protect children even better. These are not just our personal plans; these are plans for the country. We want our work to make a real difference.

It comes at a price, so it has to make sense. Ukraine must be a better place. I want mother-and-child centers to be built in liberated areas, not child barracks. I want children growing up without parents to be protected by the state.

We must demand psychological rehabilitation for people who come back from war to keep them and their families from suffering.

I once said that I would sit in a rocking chair and write a book of people's stories when I reached old age. You live each story and don't understand how that could ever happen. For example, when a child grows up in a basement, tied with a rope, and eats worms to survive. All of it happens in the village right in front of the neighbors! Then this child grows up a bit, breaks out, looking for protection and love, and meets a guy who humiliates her. And she already finds it quite normal to get beaten... And then her son is growing, knowing that beating his mom is okay. And society tolerates that. In particular, the priest, who instructed her to be patient, just like Christ, who also suffered a lot. You hear such stories and wonder how that can happen in the 21st century in the first place. I am sure that after the war, Ukraine will be nothing like that. Our country will be different.

I have a lot of such horror stories. But working with literally hundreds of children, it's important to see each of them individually. You should see a living person behind all those documents and certificates. Recognize their voice, know about their talents, and understand their fears. When helping a child, it's essential to know that you have a unique chance to make a difference in the future of your country by putting your heart into someone's story. Knowing that you can change somebody's life for the better is honorable and inspiring yet very scary and exhausting.

"Being able to do what I enjoy is a gift of fate"

I don't ever feel blue. Why would a person feel blue when they're doing something they enjoy? When you see a bedridden child walking; a woman who couldn't write is working as a secretary; a girl who had her first coffee at the *City of Goodness* has become a professional barista. That's what gives you strength and support. When you see that it's real to build a 2,000-square-meter building for affected people, bring them together, and change their destinies. All you have to do is care and join in. That's what gives you resources.

My plans are to hold our front. It is my personal responsibility to every child we could not save and every child who died in this war. Our goal is to make sure that our country develops.

I used to worry about having something to eat in the *City of Goodness*, about mothers to be happy, and their destinies would change for the better. And now, I want things to get better not only in the *City of Goodness* but in the whole country. After the victory, we have just as much work ahead. We will build a country where human rights are respected, animals are cared for, and happy children grow up. Sometimes people ask me why I do what the state should do. We should understand that we are the state. Each of us lives in our own city and our own backyard and can change the color of our entryway, our own street, and the life of people around us.

We should make our country shine, and we should shine bright ourselves. We should love each other.

2022.09.29.

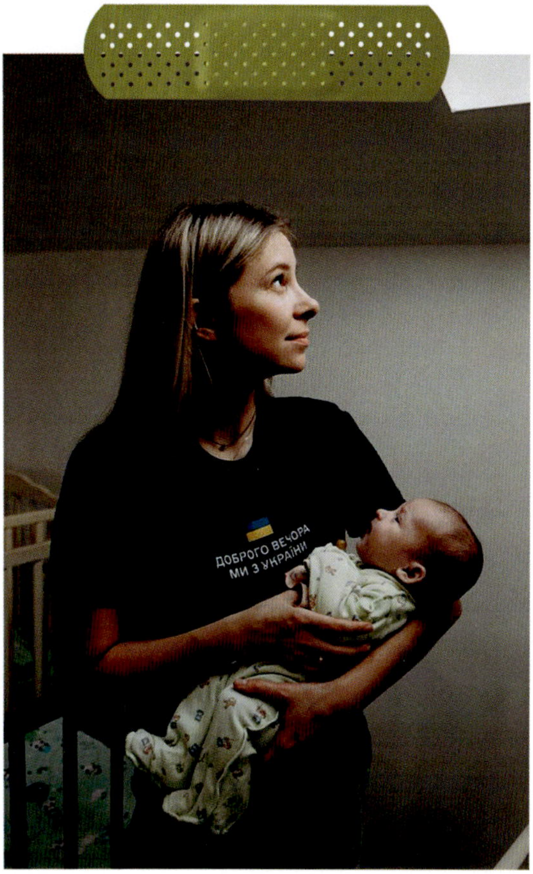
ДОБРОГО ВЕЧОРА
МИ З УКРАЇНИ

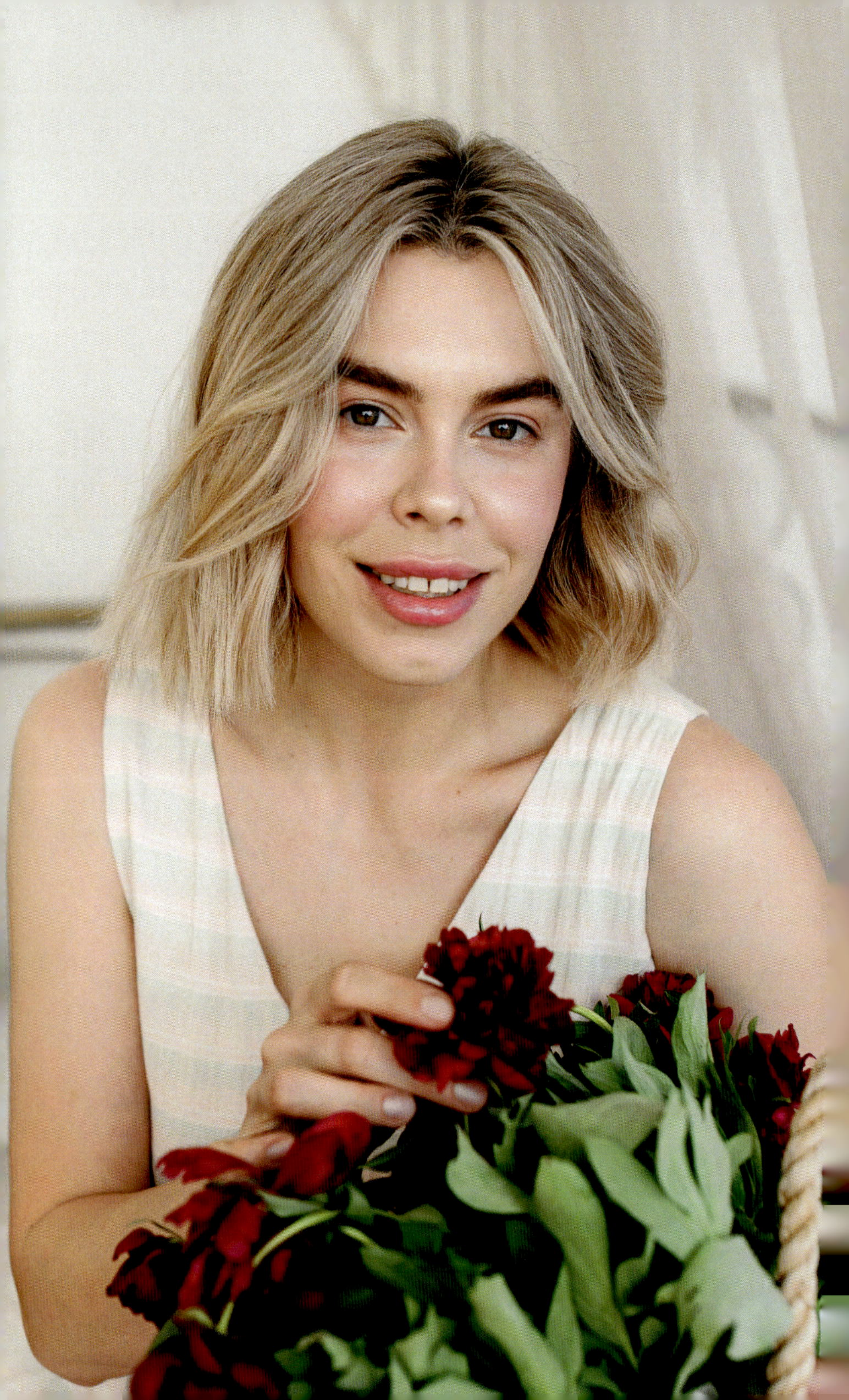

Olha Belytska

*Founder of the Beauty
Volunteers initiative*

Olha Belytska is a makeup artist and representative of a French brand. After the outbreak of full-scale war, she founded the *Beauty Volunteers* initiative to provide free services to the inhabitants of communities that survived the Russian occupation. Olha manages to combine taking care of her little son, her job, and volunteer work.

Remote liberated cities need more than just humanitarian aid

How the war has slowed down plans but not canceled them

I was on maternity leave with my little son when the warfare started. But I also gave makeup lessons to aspiring artists at the *MakeUpMe* Academy and took clients who would come to me for eyebrow shaping and tinting or pre-event makeup. I planned to go on vacation with my family, but the full-scale invasion changed our plans.

I used to have thoughts of going to live abroad, but when the invasion started, and I got the chance, I did not take it. My home is in Ukraine, and I cannot just leave everything.

The war did not cancel my plans. I am always looking for an opportunity, not an excuse. Nothing has changed much. It only takes longer to fulfill my plans. If I have the opportunity to do something, I do it. The war has taught me that the next day may not come, so putting life on hold and waiting for other conditions is not worth it. While we are alive and not being bombed, we should do something.

The invasion caught us at home in sleep. My husband and I woke up to loud explosions, just as the rest of Ukraine probably did. Of course, we heard about a possible full-scale invasion, but we didn't believe it until the last minute. When we heard the explosions, we started looking for the news on Telegram channels. We stayed at home for the first day. But the next morning, we took our child and went to the shelter. After half a day there, we decided to go to my parent's summer house near Kaharlyk because it was quiet there. My child and I stayed there for a few weeks. My husband returned to Kyiv to join the Territorial Defense Forces, but they did not take him because of the large number of volunteers. So he started supplying body armor to the military and came to see us once every few days.

My child and I returned to Kyiv in March. My friends did not understand my decision, but something told me it was safer at home than anywhere else. Besides, my friends, who were in the army, confirmed it.

In April, I started volunteering. I went to *Ohmatdyt* Children Hospital, where the doctors lived back then, to help all the wounded. The *Tabletochki* Foundation arranged so-called beauty days at the hospitals. Makeup artists who were in Kyiv would come to the hospital once every one or two weeks. They beautified the doctors, patients, and residents sheltered there. Then doctors went home, and beauty days became out of line.

One day, I went into the ward with a wounded family from Chernihiv. There was a girl with her legs broken because of a cluster bomb explosion. "Oh, I'm not wearing makeup, and I don't have my hair done," she said when she woke up. "That's a real Ukrainian woman!", I though then. This girl was very inspired and positive, and this meeting is photographed in my memory. A little later, I was at home watching TV news about occupied areas. And it occurred to me we should organize such beauty days in the liberated territories.

In early May, I decided I would do what I could best, so I posted a few stories on Instagram that I was looking for specialists who would go with me to the liberated areas to support people. Both acquaintances and strangers. My *Instagram* was literally bursting with private messages from people wanting to join in. I created a Telegram group for those who wrote to me. In a week or two, there were about 60 specialists. Gradually, I formed a team of 12 people. I knew only a few of them, but it felt like we all knew each other for a hundred years. Our first trip was to the Dubky sanatorium in Irpin on May 24. People who had lost their homes were placed there. I had little idea how we would work. I decided that we would sort it out when we got there. It was a nice warm day. We put our tables and chairs outside and worked using an extension cord to connect to the power grid.

Salon services in extreme conditions

After that successful trip, I started looking for where to go next. At first, we did everything at our own expense, but friends who saw my posts asked for a card number and transferred money.

Now we have a permanent team of about 20–22 specialists: 7 hairdressers, two masseurs, two nail artists, an eyebrow master, and beauticians. People still text me wanting to join our team, but I am scrupulous about it because we have a well-established reputation and social responsibility. I have confidence in my team because I know that these people can give a good haircut or manicure and know how to communicate with people who have survived the occupation. You should understand who you're going to and what's waiting for you there. If we come to a place with running water and a toilet, it's luck. Usually, we have to fill bottles with water, and the toilet is outside. For example, once we came to one village just when the lights went out. The local administration brought us a generator, and specialists took turns using a hairdryer so that the electricity didn't go out.

The team's phenomenon is that all its members have a strong level of empathy. They go to places with no working conditions but try to do their job as well as they always do. They are experienced specialists who know how to work with people, how to communicate, and what to ask. We did not take beginners who wanted to practice because we were afraid they could ask an inappropriate question that might make a person feel bad because many of our visitors have lost their homes and loved ones.

We did not buy equipment. Each specialist has their own. We have a separate bank account for donations that we spend on fuel and consumables, like wipes, cotton swabs and sticks, solvents, and dye for eyebrow artists and hairdressers.

People we visit are very grateful and often help us. For example, if there is no place to wash off hair dye, they bring a bowl or put on a hat or handkerchief and say they will wash their hair at home.

Cosmetic procedures and more

When I decided to go to the liberated territories with a specific mission, I thought it was worthwhile not only to provide hairdressing services but also to morally support people who sometimes sat in basements for 40 days, enduring interrogations by the occupiers, unable even to wash, let alone get a haircut. People told us a lot of terrible stories. At first, it was hard to listen to. We always went back in silence because we couldn't even talk with each other.

We don't just come and provide a service. We listen to everyone and support them as best we can. It is more about psychological support. I used to think of involving a psychologist, but I understand that people won't come to them. It's easier for them to tell a story to the beauty specialist, who works with their hair or nails. But I want to find a volunteer psychologist for our team because it is hard to see destroyed houses and places where peaceful people were killed and listen to the stories of the victims. We hear these stories, discuss them, and try to leave them there. If we allow it all to pass through ourselves, it will affect our work.

Stories related to children are extremely touching. Once, people told me that when they came back home after the occupation, they found the child's bed mined.

I try not to take all these stories to heart because they can drive me crazy. There were some funny stories, though. For example, residents of Zdvyzhivka village told us that when Russian troops were retreating on April 1, some soldiers were running through the streets looking for their APC because others left them behind. A resident of another village told that an APC drove into her yard and broke the fence. She demanded that a Russian soldier called the commander to repair the fence.

These trips are actually very inspiring because the gratitude we get from people is encouraging. We try to work with the population and explain that not everything is done for money. People are often embarrassed to come, thinking they must pay for it. We explain that our services are free because we want to help and support them. Eventually, people grow bolder, and we make friends with them.

Some team members also have their own stories: a lot of their loved ones are in the AFU. So these trips help us take our minds off depressing thoughts.

About humanitarian aid and future plans

Our mission has expanded a little. We took under our wing some villages that we had visited several times. When serving people, we ask them what they need. At first, we asked for the necessary things on social networks. People brought us everything we needed, and we took it to a certain place. Sometimes, we got so much humanitarian aid that we had to leave one of the specialists behind because the vehicle was overloaded. So now we deliver less humanitarian aid because that's what other volunteers do. But our stylist, Kyrylo, still orders soap, laundry detergent, toothpaste, and other hygiene products weekly for us to deliver to people. It is a minimum set of products, but at least we give people a chance to save some money.

We plan to buy our own bus to go around the villages because now we have problems with logistics. Every time, you plan whom to pick up first and where. The Dymer village community provides a school bus that picks us up near the subway. It helps a lot. We plan to continue our trips after the victory because the victims will still need our help.

We buy fuel and humanitarian aid at our own expense and with donations sent to our account. There are 3–4 cars and a bus on each trip. We allocate about 500 hryvnias per trip, although it always comes out more expensive.

We also have PayPal for foreigners to transfer money, but we do not take this money. We save it for a rainy day. Our specialists do not have a lot of paid work, so they also need support.

A day at a location

Every Monday, we go to a location at 10 a. m. Thanks to word of mouth, we now have many options. Previously, we used to look for a place to go ourselves. We asked for contacts of local councilors on Facebook groups or from our friends. Now, village heads tell each other about us.

We work at the location until 4 p. m. But now we will go out earlier because the daylight hours are getting shorter, and we do not have enough time to work. We traveled over Dymer and Bucha communities. Recently, we went to Demydiv, where the dam had been blown up, and the village survived the flood. Due to communication difficulties, we haven't been to Brovary area, Hostomel, and Horenka yet.

It is often hard to make an agreement with councilors because they readdress the request to each other. Eventually, it ends up in nothing because they have more important things to do. It is a mystery to me why they sometimes leave what we propose unattended. But those who know us help.

As for Bucha community, we are in direct contact with its head. We met by chance in the town during one of our trips, and I offered that we visit villages around Bucha area. We also cooperate with the administration of Dymer community. Every week, we make a poster and send it to them to put in local chats and let people know we are coming. We have exact dates and premises. Usually, it is a school or town hall. Now we get ready for winter because there is going to be no heating there. We are not afraid of it. We decided to buy heaters and thermal socks.

Usually, we serve up to 60 clients, although we had about a hundred in Bucha. We have a receptionist who makes lists and signs people in. We determine who gives haircuts to children only and who gives haircuts to men. This way, other specialists are free for women as it takes longer to cut their hair. We will involve more hairdressers from now on because haircuts are in demand.

Before going to some settlement, I check the information about the occupation. Once, a resident of a village in Chernihiv Region wrote to us that they were under occupation. Although another person who was there assured us that everything was quiet and calm in that village. I asked the village head about the occupation as it was not our goal to go to a village, residents of which just saw military equipment passing by. If we had the chance, we would have gone everywhere. But some settlements need our help more. Many villages in Kyiv Region were also badly affected, but the media mostly spoke about Bucha, Irpin, and Borodianka. Until we got to Blystavytsia village together with journalists, we had not even heard about the events there.

This village is located just next to Hostomel airport. One of the streets is completely destroyed, and 22 houses are ruined to the ground. And there are many such places. Enemy sabotage and reconnaissance groups are still detained near some villages.

We should talk about these villages for they receive little humanitarian aid because of not being mentioned in the media.

About believing in victory

I am an optimist by nature. I always tune in positively and believe that victory will come soon. I dream of visiting liberated settlements in Kharkiv and Kherson Regions with my team, although it will be logistically challenging for us to do.

If the AFU gives you a chance to live, you should take it: plant flowers, eat, work, walk, and seize the moment.

Our front is volunteering. We have a chance to live. If you sink yourself into depression, it won't make anyone feel better. I believe we should engage in volunteering in peacetime, too. Doing something for free once or twice a week doesn't hurt your job, but you can help people. If you bring good into the world, it will return it.

I'm on maternity leave now, but I work in an international company as a chief makeup artist for a French brand, serve clients, and take care of my little son. I hope I will resume my work and sales shortly. After the victory, I would like to go to the sea abroad or to Crimea with my family because we did not have time to do that before invasion.

The war taught me to enjoy basic things like walks, flowers, and working out outside because the gym I attended before the full-fledged warfare was hit by a rocket. It really angered me because it was my safe place. The gym had already been repaired, and I resumed training, but at the time, it was a disaster. I started working out in the park by my house. I woke up every morning and thanked the AFU that I could go out and see the birds, the sky, and the trees. These are things you never paid attention to before. Now it's easier to filter out people. I used to feel uncomfortable saying something to toxic people, but now I can tell them everything I think. I realize I only live once. And there is no telling what's going to happen tomorrow.

My belief in victory helps me. I can't wait any longer to hear that we have won. I'd probably cry first and then go hug the people I'd meet in the streets.

2022.09.15.

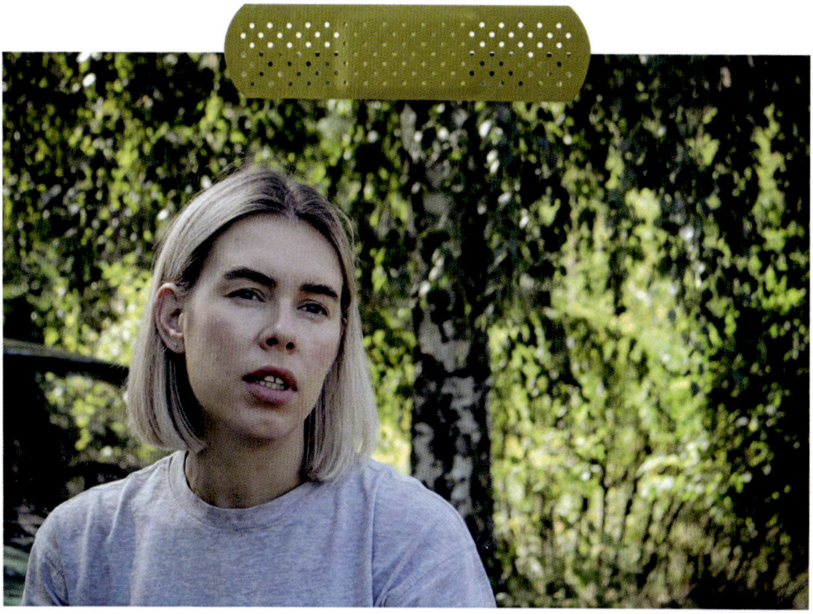

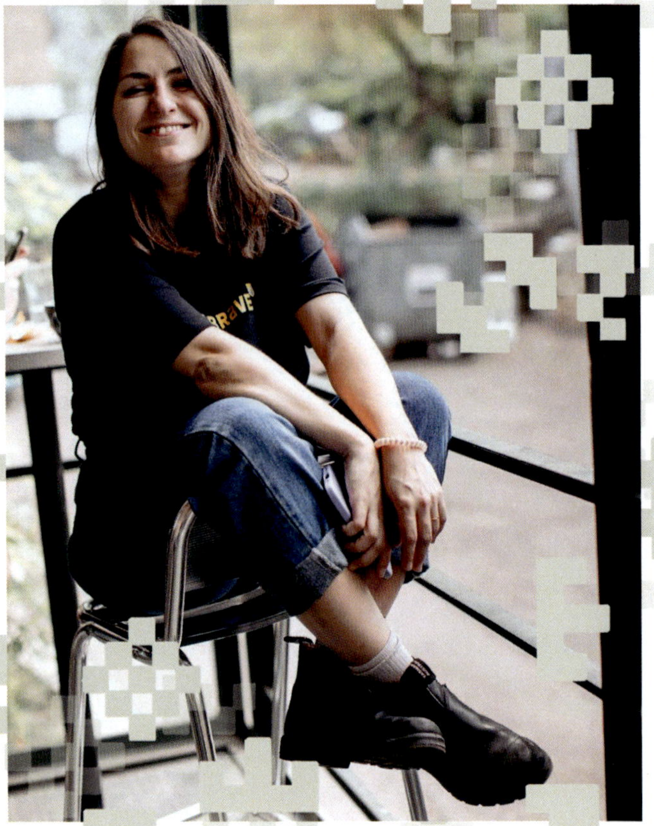

Leila Tuvakliieva

*Co-founder of the Kyiv Volunteer
Charitable Foundation*

Leila Tuvakliieva has worked in the restaurant business for many years. She was a corporate sales manager at *GoodWine*. She had no idea that one day she would cook for the AFU soldiers and people in the liberated territories near Kyiv.

How to feed 10 thousand people every day in an occupied city

Volunteering as a way to overcome stress

On February 24, I woke up and realized that a full-scale war had begun. Explosions were heard in Kyiv, and panic-stricken people were leaving in droves for other cities. On the third day of the full-scale invasion, I had a kind of emotional exhaustion. Every five minutes, I hesitated about whether to go or stay. When I put my younger sister on the train to Chernivtsi, I realized I wasn't leaving Kyiv. I made a final decision to stay with my friends and colleagues under those difficult circumstances.

Days passed. My friend Sasha Borovskyi, who runs the *Dyletant* and *Dubler* restaurants, co-owned by the well-known architect Slava Balbek, said they wanted to feed people. I asked to join this initiative because I felt I had to do something. Scrolling through the newsfeed means prolonging the uncertainty and sinking deeper into depression. For me, *Kyiv Volunteer* became a way to overcome stress and do good, which gives instant results: you cook, you take food to people (for example, to a retirement home), and you immediately get gratitude and motivation to work further.

Feeding people during the war

On February 28, we cooked the first thousand servings. Due to word of mouth, we gathered the team of people who stayed in Kyiv: some were *Dubler* employees, and others were just our friends. On the very first day, our phones started ringing off the hook: we got requests for food and requests to find some things and deliver them where needed. We realized we wouldn't be able to handle all of these requests the next day. Besides, we got another problem: we couldn't find bread anywhere. We figured we needed to team up with other restaurateurs. We have a pretty large social circle, so we spread the word on social networks, and 14 restaurants joined us by the end of the week. We cooked an average of 10,000 servings a day. During the peak period in March, the number reached 15,000.

At first, it was a so-called endorphin period when we completed different tasks, like the "we-need-buckwheat" quest. For example, we needed about 100,000 disposable sets of dishes a week to deliver food to checkpoints or subway stations. Many manufacturers opened their warehouses and let us take whatever we needed. People who had little to do with logistics (for instance, restaurant managers and directors) helped us cook and deliver the food. Everything hinges on volunteers now. Even the military say so. The war revealed all the old problems. Before the full-scale invasion, we ignored how much people really needed help. There were pensioners living alone in Kyiv, people with disabilities or other health problems, people with children who needed help, and many internally displaced people. And we had to feed all of them. Luckily, we have the proper expertise when it comes to nutrition.

We know that the maternity hospital needs dietary meals, and the military needs calorie-rich food. We often work with the Territorial Defense Forces. Young guys do not know how to cook meat so that it does not spoil quickly in above-zero temperatures, and sometimes do not even know how to cook eggs and just stew instant noodles. So we help them with simple tips and process flow charts and teach them how to cook food in the field.

How we established the charity organization

When the battles were on the outskirts of Kyiv, we had no way to buy or bring in what we needed. International funding was only supposed to be available for registered companies, and the Ministry of Justice offices were not working. We made phone calls to whomever we could to register the organization and managed to do it on March 23.

We established a pretty large community with a specific structure. We worked with various international foundations. Three hundred forty volunteers worked in our kitchens alone, and the project had about 500 people in total. We had a back office of 30 people that included a fundraising team, a PR department, and a separate medical department. The wounded got the necessary care at the hospital, after which they needed outpatient care. If there were no places or medications available, we took that over. In April, we received our first grant of 1 million hryvnias for tactical medicine. The need for first-aid kits and tourniquets was and still is great because, before the full-scale war, none of us believed that all of this would be needed in such large quantities.

When we started our volunteer activity, Sasha took care of transportation issues: supplying fuel, looking for drivers and trucks, including to carry food to restaurants. Slava Balbek and his colleagues created a system that made everything work smoothly: we registered a request, a manager assigned it a sequential number and sent it to the drivers' chat room, and the latter took the order and delivered it to the necessary location. At first, we had 120 orders a day. And all these orders were processed by Mariia Pidvysotska and me alone. We prepared a table every evening indicating what we would need, and how much, and where to take it. It was the same with restaurants and customers. When we got orders from the Territorial Defense or the Armed Forces, it was critical to retain confidentiality. We could not divulge their location, so we used highly protected *Signal* messenger, and then used geolocation software, so that the military would meet us halfway to take their order.

We almost always took urgent orders, but each restaurant had its own capacity and couldn't always do everything in full. So we had to distribute orders so that they would be prepared on time and conveniently delivered. We built a whole system of communication between the restaurant and the drivers. I remember we needed 20 tons of potatoes urgently. Slava just put a word out, and we found it. We formed a sort of volunteer corporation: coordinators for drivers and customers, volunteer chefs, bakers, packers, loaders, drivers, and a procurement department, which searched for the best prices for food since funding was limited. Although, we got a lot for free, too.

We became an alliance of institutions that responded to challenges promptly and effectively carried out the tasks at hand.

How war changed us all

I am like a firefighter. I always know what to do. That's my forte, which helps me. What I have had to learn is to distance myself emotionally. I have an emotional reaction to everything. But I realized that all those emotions around what was happening in the country began to destroy me from the inside, and I could not work as fruitfully as before. Bad news came every day. So I somehow managed to get a grip on myself and move on.

We arrived in Bucha the second day it was liberated. We brought food to the military and residents of the city. People started crying when they saw the bread they hadn't had in a month and a half. I just kept poker-faced. It was my way of coping with all the horror around me.

I have never asked myself what I am doing this for. The answer is obvious: I am where I am supposed to be. We helped many people, but we also helped ourselves. We created a new sense for 500 people who could be helpful here and now, without preparatory courses or degrees. We are creating a new society and new Ukraine. Values are changing. Many people identified themselves as Ukrainians for the first time. They are no longer indifferent to problems and want to help each other. Everyone has understood the value of human life. Ukrainians have become united as never before.

I'm sure that *Kyiv Volunteer* will operate for the next five years.

When Kyiv residents started returning home, many found themselves jobless. And some even worked without pay. Luckily, our organization was able to pay people working in the kitchen after the first two months of work because we got funding. But the problem of the lack of jobs is considerable. Our people are really hardworking, but they have nowhere to work. A lot of jobs have been destroyed, and the newly opened companies in Kyiv do not work at full capacity. That is why we are planning to organize a training center. We are specialists and can teach people to be cooks, waiters, bartenders, and managers. You can master these professions in a few weeks and get a job. I think our work will become even more relevant after we win. We delivered food to villages of Kyiv Region. There are places 70 kilometers from the capital where there has never been electricity, and the war made life even more difficult for people living there.

We also help those who have had their homes or households damaged. For example, one older woman's

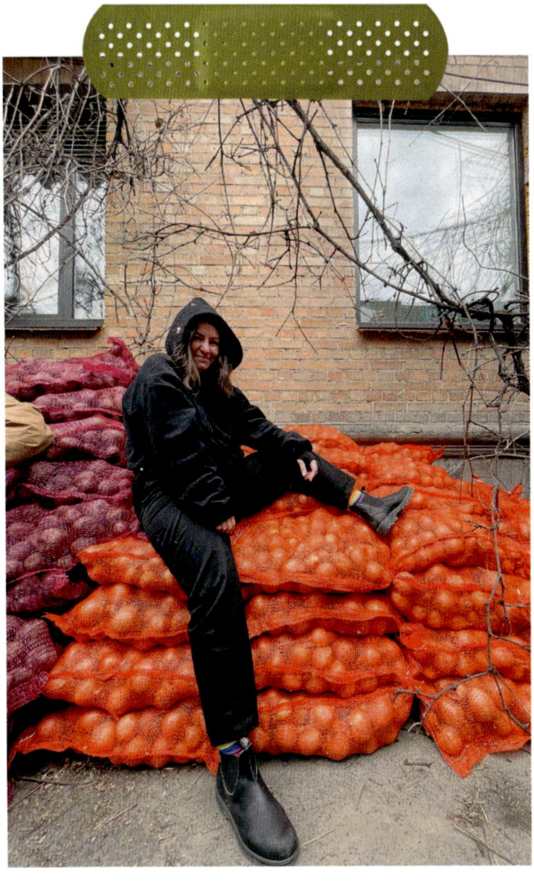

backyard was hit by a shell that damaged her chicken coop. We helped her restore it. And now Slava will build the first new houses in Bucha.

Now the *Kyiv Volunteer* Charitable Foundation continues humanitarian missions to troubled places (liberated territories, front-line areas, settlements exposed to missile attacks), develops a medical line of work, provides the AFU with warm uniforms and appliances, and implements long-term initiatives aimed at improving the quality of social life.

I'm lucky to work with people who implement inspiring scale projects. I am sure we can do incredible things together.

2022.06.28.

Acknowledgments

Usually, when I read books up to this point, I wondered why there was only one author and dozens of people whom they thanked for helping the book come out. Being at the stage of putting the book layout into print, I realize what a big and time-consuming process it is. It can take a year or ten years since an idea commences until the book is published. And it's so important to have support along the way from someone who first says, "Cool, you must publish it," and from your own team who takes the risk of doing it with you, and from partners at the second stage, and from friends when you have no energy to move on, and from publishers who will persist in working on the book and improving it. So now I can thank all those who took part in the birth of this book, especially at a difficult time like that when we are still at war and patiently approaching victory.

First, I want to thank my team, my co-author, journalist Yaroslava Zhukovska, and Yuliia Kovalenko, who started the project with me in March, searching for contacts, transcribing, coordinating texts, looking for partners, and writing all the stories with me.

I thank our partners: the Director of the French-Ukrainian Chamber of Commerce and Industry Maud Joseph; the Swedish Ambassador to Ukraine Tobias Thyberg; and the head of *Friedrich Naumann Foundation For Freedom in Ukraine* Anna Kravchenko, for supporting the project so that we could write the book even during the most difficult months of the war since April till the end of summer.

I thank my *ekonomika+* team! Thank you to Illia Chudnovskyi for being the first to say that the book was a great idea, for supporting me all the way through, and for repeating it even when it seemed all was lost! I also thank Serhii Dodi and Tetiana Kravchenko for their creativity and the cover idea. Thank you to Artem Serodoiv and Oleksandr Klimashevskyi for showing it to everyone.

Vast gratitude to my Communications Director, Tetiana Kharcheva, and her *Direct Communication on Impact* agency team for sharing with us all the adventures that happened along the way, for helping us 24/7, and above all, for the powerful communication strategy.

Thank you to Olia Rondiak, an American artist of Ukrainian heritage, who reflected on the war through her art, drew the world's attention to the incredible courage of Ukrainian women through her art and provided her picture as the cover of our book.

Thank you to *Yakaboo* Publishing for appreciating and immediately getting down to the idea! Especially to Yuliia Laktionova for the first "yes" and to the entire editorial team for their responsibility and persistent work and for the illustrations and design of the book.

Profound gratitude to our partners who supported the publishing of the book.

And finally, I thank each of our heroines for their resilience, for the example of struggle and not giving up during the war, and for the inspiration to write stories and not fall into despair. Thank you to each Ukrainian woman for contributing to the fight and our victory. And for the fact that both our country and our book will have a future!

Book Reviews

The French-Ukrainian Chamber of Commerce and Industry has always stood with women and supported them in their professional careers and entrepreneurship. We witnessed the incredible strength of Ukrainian women, and today we are astonished by their courage. Congratulations to Viktoriia Pokatis, Editor-in-Chief of *WoMo*, on her book, *Invincible*

> **Maud Joseph,**
> **Director of the French-Ukrainian Chamber**
> **of Commerce and Industry**

Women are important agents and leaders of change. Since the beginning of the war, they have not stopped their work and changed their activities according to urgent needs. Women must participate in decision-making on all fronts because we know from experience that women's participation makes decisions more inclusive and better meets the needs of all, including vulnerable groups. This book is an opportunity to hear women's stories and show their work.

> **Tobias Thyberg,**
> **Swedish Ambassador to Ukraine**

As an American and an artist who has lived in Ukraine for 25 years, I am very passionate about preserving Ukrainian culture and history. My ancestors taught me to respect freedom and how hard it is to fight for it. The next generation must recognize, remember, and respect the heroines on the front line of defending freedom in Ukraine.

Olia Rodniak,
American artist
of Ukrainian heritage

Sociopolitical publication

POKATIS Viktoriia

INVINCIBLE

a book about the resistance of Ukrainian women
in the war against Russian invaders

Literary Editor *Yevhen Miroshnychenko*
Layout Editor *Nataliia Koval*
Desktop Publisher *Serhii Zadvornyi*
Art editor *Anna Havryliuk*
Cover Designer *Tetiana Kravchenko*
Responsible Editor *Svitlana Andriushchenko*

Authorized for printing: December 27, 2022
Format 60x90/16
Digital font: Source Serif Pro
Offset printing
Printed copies: 1,100
Order No. ZK-005700

Publisher: Yakaboo Publishing LTD
Publisher certificate: DK No. 5243 of November 8, 2016
160U Kyrylivska Str.,
Kyiv 04037 Mailing address:
P.O.B. 88 Kyiv 04070
publishing@yakaboo.ua
www.yakaboo.ua

Printed by: Kharkiv Globus Book Factory
JSC 11 Rizdviana Str., Kharkiv 61011, Ukraine
Publisher certificate: DK No. 7032 of December 27, 2019
www.globus-book.com